1969

# MEDIEVAL
# RHETORIC AND POETIC

# MEDIEVAL
# RHETORIC AND POETIC

(to 1400)

## INTERPRETED FROM REPRESENTATIVE WORKS

BY

### CHARLES SEARS BALDWIN

PROFESSOR OF RHETORIC IN COLUMBIA UNIVERSITY

Gloucester, Mass.
PETER SMITH
1959

SANCTO THOMÆ AQVINATI
PHILOSOPHO POETÆ
ARTEM ILLIVS SÆCVLI
RHETORICAM ATQVE POETICAM
REDINTEGRATAM
COMMENDAT INTERPRES

# PREFACE

The rhetoric and the poetic of any age, as the complementary theories of composition, are indicative of its habits in education and in literature. Thus their medieval history concerns all students of the middle age. For consecutive interpretation in this single aspect both supplements the more comprehensive surveys and adds significance to many special studies. Whether for initiation, for review, or for suggestions of further inquiry, medieval rhetoric and poetic offer a directly literary guide.

As in my preceding volume, *Ancient rhetoric and poetic*, conciseness has been sought by proportion. Space is given to those salient tendencies which mark the literary course. Minor relations and collateral studies, indicated no less carefully, are relegated to the notes, but included in the index. Detailing the actual theory and the actual practise of composition, often for the first time, I have tried no less to show their bearing, to make medieval rhetoric and poetic available by interpreting them in historical sequence. Thus are interpreted the tasks of the schools, the poetic developments of and from the hymns, the habits of prose rhythm, the encroachment of logic upon rhetoric and of rhetoric upon poetic, the progress of verse narrative.

Ancient theory being eminent in a few cardinal texts long recognized as representative, the former volume subordinates history to exposition. Medieval theory, on the other hand, being best grasped as development from an inheritance, the plan of the present volume is historical.

vii

Though each aims at sufficiency within itself, the second refers again and again to the first, and the two volumes together offer a history down to 1400. Throughout this history rhetoric and poetic are seen to be indeed complementary. Where they were distinguished, as where they were confused, they are most fruitfully studied side by side. Each illuminates the other because their relations are always significant historically.

Their medieval history must begin with those particular influences from antiquity which were transmitted through the last schools of the Roman Empire, especially through the schools of Gaul. It is a Latin history; for contact with Greek was soon lost and was not widely reëstablished till the Renaissance. But in the imperial centuries before the separation East and West, Greek and Latin, agreed so far in literary ideals and practise that the whole Mediterranean basin had a substantially common system of education through rhetoric. An inert survival of what is known historically as the second sophistic, this was sharply challenged by St Augustine's reversion through Cicero to the elder tradition for authority to direct the real oratory of preaching. Nevertheless the schools of Gaul continued the sophistic tradition beyond the fall of Rome.

Nor were the large philosophy of rhetoric in Cicero's *De oratore*, the great survey of Quintilian, the later medieval guides. The prevalent textbooks were Cicero's youthful digest *De inventione* and a second book universally attributed to him, the *Rhetorica ad Herennium*. Though the survival of these minor works may be due partly to the accidents of manuscripts, their persistence has other causes. *De inventione* reduces to summary what the middle age taught least, those counsels of prepa-

ration and ordering which ancient teaching had progressively adjusted to oral discourse, and for which the earlier
middle age had less opportunity. The *Rhetorica ad Herennium*, comparatively summary also as to analysis and sequence, is devoted largely to style, and reduces stylistic
ornament to a list so conveniently specific that medieval
schools made it a ritual. Though the greater Cicero and
Quintilian were known to such original minds as Gerbert
in the tenth century and John of Salisbury in the twelfth,
they were hardly available for the usual course of teaching.
Medieval rhetoric was generally a lore of style. Here
*rhetorica* tended to coincide with that school study of
Latin poetry which was a recognized function of *grammatica*. The constant quotation of Horace's "Ars poetica"
is one of the signs of the merging of poetic with rhetoric.
The conventional doctrine from both was largely of
descriptive dilation. Among the effects of this teaching
which outlast schooling and reach beyond Latin are certain conventions of vernacular poetry. Conversely,
poetic advance in the vernaculars is seen in breaking away
not only from school rhetoric, but from rhetoric altogether.

The main medieval fields proper to rhetoric were sermons and letters. The former, exploring their rhetoric
in the earlier centuries, continued to feel the example,
perhaps more than the precept, of St Augustine. Even
the Dominicans had no need to seek a new lore of oral
composition. What is distinctive in sermon composition
of the twelfth century is oftener poetic than rhetoric.
Letters, on the other hand, are at once a legitimate application of ancient rhetoric and a distinctively medieval
development. They practically comprehend the medieval
rhetoric of written prose. Though ordinary routine was
largely content, as in any other time, with correctness,

and therefore with recipe and formulary, serious study of both composition and style is evident in the better manuals, and conspicuous in those achievements which are part of medieval literature.

The teaching of *poetica*, from of old a part of *grammatica*, included extensive practise in Latin verse. This had early to take account of that dominance of stress which had gradually supplanted the ancient control by time. The characteristic medieval achievements in Latin lyric are the hymns. Radiating into other songs, even into humorous and satirical verse, the hymns were the common lyric fund of medieval Latin. As early as St Ambrose they had created a new Latin poetry; and the beauty of their various art was not exhausted with Adam of St Victor. Meantime they opened to the vernaculars those poetic possibilities of stanza which arise from the development of rime. Medieval poetic theory, on the contrary, went but a little way. Mainly pedagogical formulation, it lagged far behind the most characteristic medieval poetic advance, which was in verse narrative. Here is a sharp contrast with the Renaissance. The fifteenth century opens a long series of critical inquiries into poetic. The middle age, merging poetic with rhetoric in the schoolroom, was little concerned to make it tally with vernacular achievement. With the death in 1400 of Chaucer, whose criticism exposed this lack, the poetic of medieval narrative reaches its term.

I owe to the unstinted courtesy and scholarly interest of a trustee of Barnard College, Mr. George A. Plimpton, the privilege of studying at leisure his manuscript of one of the most important Bolognese *dictamina*, the thirteenth-century *Candelabrum*. Far better than Boncompagno or Thomas of Capua, better even than Conrad, this unprinted manual exhibits *dictamen* in both scope and method. My other debts are too manifold to rehearse. The bibliographical notes, if they recorded the reading of years, would defeat their proper object of serving further study. Therefore they have been made, as in the former volume, at once specific and strictly selective, applied to each chapter separately, and further indicated both in the index and on a page of recurring abbreviations after the table of contents.

As I record gratefully my obligation for generous help with the proofs to my colleagues Professors Ayres, Clark, Krapp, McCrea, Moore, Perry, and Van Hook, and to my old friend, the Jesuit scholar Dr. Donnelly, I see further in such coöperation great promise for the progress of medieval studies.

C. S. B.

BARNARD COLLEGE
COLUMBIA UNIVERSITY
JANUARY, 1928.

# CONTENTS

CONTENTS

# ABBREVIATIONS RECURRING IN THE NOTES

[The abbreviations used in each chapter will be found with the list of references below the chapter heading.]

AH      Dreves and Blume, *Analecta hymnica medii aevi*, Leipzig, 1886–1911 (cited by volume and page).

ARP      Baldwin (C. S.), *Ancient rhetoric and poetic*, New York, 1924.

Clerval      Clerval (l'Abbé A.), *Les écoles de Chartres au moyen âge, du Ve au XVIe siècle*, Chartres, 1895.

CSE      *Corpus scriptorum ecclesiasticorum latinorum*, Vienna.

F      Faral (E.), *Les arts poétiques du XIIe et du XIIIe siècle*, recherches et documents sur la technique littéraire du moyen âge, Paris, 1924.

Halm      Halm (K.), *Rhetores latini minores*, Leipzig, 1863.

Keil      Keil (H.), *Grammatici latini*, Leipzig, 1870–1880 (cited by volume and page).

Manacorda      Manacorda (G.), *Storia della scuola in Italia*, volume I, *Il medio evo*, Milan, 1913 (2 parts in separate volumes).

Manitius      Manitius (M.), *Geschichte der lateinischen Literatur des Mittelalters*, Munich, 1911, 2 vols. (in Von Mueller's Handbuch der klassischen Alterthums-Wissenschaft, IX, ii).

Mearns      Mearns (J.), *Early Latin hymnaries*, an index of hymns in hymnaries before 1100, Cambridge (University Press), 1913.

MGH      *Monumenta Germaniæ historica* (cited by page of the appropriate volume).

NE      *Notices et extraits des manuscrits de la Bibliothèque Nationale* . . . (cited by volume, part, and page).

PL      *Patrologia latina* (Migne, cited by volume and column).

# MEDIEVAL
# RHETORIC AND POETIC

# MEDIEVAL RHETORIC AND POETIC

## CHAPTER I

## THE SOPHISTIC TREND IN ANCIENT RHETORIC

### REFERENCES AND ABBREVIATIONS

Ameringer  Ameringer (T. E.), *The stylistic influence of the second sophistic on the panegyrical sermons of St. John Chrysostom*, Washington, 1921 (Catholic University of America Patristic Studies).

ARP  Baldwin (C. S.), *Ancient rhetoric and poetic*, New York, 1924.

Boulanger  Boulanger (A.), *Ælius Aristide et la sophistique dans la province d'Asie au ii siècle de notre ère*, Paris, 1923.

Burgess  Burgess (T. C.), *Epideictic literature*, University of Chicago Studies in Classical Philology III (1902), 89–251.

Campbell  Campbell (J. M.), *The influence of the second sophistic on the style of the sermons of St. Basil the Great*, Washington, 1922.

Guignet  Guignet (M.), *St. Grégoire de Nazianze, orateur et épistolier*, Paris, 1911.

Hubbell  Hubbell (H. M.), *The influence of Isocrates on Cicero, Dionysius, and Aristides*, New Haven (Yale dissertation), 1914.

Méridier  Méridier (L.), *L'influence de la seconde sophistique sur l'œuvre de Grégoire de Nysse*, Paris, 1906.

Wright  Wright (W. C.), *Philostratus and Eunapius, the lives of the sophists*, with an English translation, London and New York, Loeb Library, 1922.

1

## A. The Two Historic Conceptions of Rhetoric

Plato's distrust of rhetoric is a permanent reminder. It is so significantly typical that it recurs throughout the history of education, and must recur. Again and again educational practise has found that it cannot do without rhetoric; again and again educational theory has grudgingly inquired what to do with it. For distrust of rhetoric may be more than the impatience of the philosopher with the orator, of speculation with ordered presentation, of the quest for truth with persuasion. This is involved too; for philosophers have often been impatient of presentation. They have wished to think aloud, or to question and answer, or merely to analyze for themselves, without being held to consecutive explanation. Plato himself falls short of discerning the importance of making truth available and effective for the mass of men incapable of scientific analysis; and this is the ground of Cicero's rejoinder.[1] But Plato's distrust is more deeply of rhetoric as he heard it taught. Even in his day Greek rhetoric was largely sophistic, the rhetoric of personal display and triumph. In the *Gorgias*[2] Socrates admits the function of a nobler rhetoric, but cannot find it in use. In the *Protagoras*[3] he asks the vital question, "*About what* does the sophist make a man more eloquent?" In the *Phædrus*, which discusses rhetoric more specifically, his satire is most evidently of sophistic. To this the ultimate objection is moral. A man should train himself "not with a view to speaking and acting before the world, but for the sake of making himself able . . . to please the gods."[4] Plato challenges not merely the method of the sophists,

[1] *De orat.* I. xiii.    [2] 503.    [3] 312.    [4] 273-4.

but their ideal. Since rhetoric has almost always had some part in education, and since it always ultimately involves morality, Plato raises a leading question.

The ultimate, the only final answer to Plato's challenge is the *Rhetoric* of Aristotle. This proceeds from a conception not only larger than the sophistic of Gorgias and Protagoras, but also significantly divergent in aim. The true theory of rhetoric as the energizing of knowledge, the bringing of truth to bear upon men, [5] is there established for all time. Aristotle amply vindicated rhetoric by defining its place among studies, its necessary correlation with inquiry and with policy, its permanent function. He settled the question of rhetoric philosophically. He established its theory. But this theory was oftener accepted than followed. The sophists had, indeed, been put in their place more surely by Aristotle than by Plato; but they continued to thrive, until ancient rhetoric became more and more sophistic.

The conception animating the practise and the teaching of sophistic, far from being limited to antiquity, is medieval as well, and modern. Apparently it is permanent. Rhetoric is conceived by Aristotle as the art of giving effectiveness to truth; it is conceived alike by the earlier and the later sophists and by their successors as the art of giving effectiveness to the speaker. The conceptions are not contradictory. The second may be theoretically included within the first; and actually Demosthenes may learn something from Isocrates. But to embody them in educational procedure, to carry out either as the controlling idea of a course of study, is to discover that sooner or later they become practically incompatible. Ingenuous youth will be devoted either to energizing truth or to

[5] ARP Chapter II, especially pages 9–11.

exploiting itself. There will come a parting of the ways; for the two conceptions are divergent. What Aristotle discerned as differentiating is differentiating still. The flaw in sophistic is moral. It may not impair technical training; but by deviating motive it tends to impair education.

For Aristotle's theory is a touchstone. To recall rhetoric to the true function discerned by him has repeatedly been the object of reform in teaching. What has intervened to deviate rhetoric and frustrate its best use has again and again been the preoccupation with giving effectiveness not to the message, but to the speaker. Ancient sophistic is thus typical. It is not merely historical; it is historic. The false conception divined by Plato, and exposed finally by Aristotle's demonstration of the true conception, led ancient rhetoric through empty personal triumphs into an elaborate art of display, devoid, at its worst, of other motive. As sophistic spread, as its idea of rhetoric became dominant, ancient education was narrowed;[6] and ancient oratory eddied in shallows until it found a new course with the new motive of Christian preaching.

In exorcising the false conception Aristotle removed the false sophistic emphasis from style. He does not despise, nor even slight, technic. He finds analysis of sentence rhythms necessary. But his goal in this, as in his analysis of figures, is beyond the technical means of securing particular effects. He does not classify figures for reference; he seeks in both phrase and cadence the function; and he discusses neither until he has spent some two-thirds of his treatise on the function of rhetoric as a whole course of study. This he finds philosophically necessary. Other-

[6] Cf. Tacitus, *Dialogus*, in ARP 88.

wise rhetoric cannot be justified; otherwise, he clearly implies, it is narrowed and degraded. For him rhetoric is so inextricably moral that it should never be divorced from subject matter of real significance.

But what subject matter of real significance has oratory when it is barred from discussion of present policy? Here appears a strong external cause of the spread of sophistic. The sophistical trend, already marked, was furthered by the narrowing of public discussion. Of the three fields [7] of oratory distinguished by Aristotle, deliberative, forensic, and occasional, the first was restricted by political changes. It faded with democracy. So later it faded at Rome, and still later in other realms. Deliberative oratory presupposes free discussion and audiences that vote. The steady increase of government from above administered by an appointed official class hastened also the tendency of the second kind of oratory, forensic, to become technical, the special art of legal pleading. Thus the only field left free was the third, occasional oratory, encomium, or panegyric, the commemoration of persons and days, the address of welcome, the public lecture. A favorite field even in Plato's time, it is in any time the freest field for imaginative and emotional appeal and for personal triumphs. Thus it was early and assiduously cultivated by the sophists. Though it opens, on the other hand, the highest reaches of eloquence, though Isocrates is more than a sophist and Lincoln's Gettysburg address is as far from sophistic as possible, still its becoming the main field of Greek oratory gave the lead to sophistic. In such conditions sophistic could control education; and its control of education reacted upon the conditions to make a vicious circle. Oratory and the training for it

[7] ARP    14–17.

became preponderantly an art of display; and the rhetoric finally bequeathed by the ancient schools was sophistic.

In sum, the sophistic tendency, which may be found in any highly developed literature, was confirmed in Greek by causes both intrinsic and extrinsic. Becoming a habit, it became a scheme of education. Against this Plato represents Socrates in fundamental opposition. Aristotle does more than oppose it; he establishes constructively a rhetoric whose persuasion shall be more than personal appeal and personal triumph. But the rhetoric nobly and philosophically conceived by him did not succeed in supplanting the tendency seen at its best in Isocrates. The conception of Isocrates in Philostratus, though inadequate, is not wrong essentially.

> The siren which stands on the tomb of Isocrates the sophist—its pose is that of one singing—testifies to the man's persuasive charm, which he combined with the laws and habits of rhetoric. Balances, antitheses, rimes, though he was not their discoverer but only the skilful user of what had been discovered already, he put his mind to, and also to amplitude, rhythm, sentence-movement, beat. These things prepared the diction of Demosthenes, who was a pupil, indeed, of Isæus, but a disciple of Isocrates.
>
> Philostratus, *Lives of the Sophists*, I.17 (Wright's translation, page 50, modified).

The Isocratean ideal of eloquence, influential even upon its critic Dionysius of Halicarnassus, even upon so great an orator as Cicero,[8] became more sophistic in the practise of the schools. In the first century of our era sophistic had won its place, by the second century an eminence undisputed till Christian preaching returned to the sound ancient tradition.

[8] See Hubbell.

For sophistic is the historic demonstration of what oratory becomes when it is removed from urgency of subject matter. Seeking some inspiration for public occasions, it revives over and over again a dead past. Thus becoming conventionalized in method, it turns from cogency of movement to the cultivation of style. Cogency presupposes a message. It is intellectual ordering for persuasion, the means toward making men believe and act. Style, no longer controlled by such urgencies of subject, tends toward decoration and virtuosity. A necessary study in any rhetoric, it had been highly cultivated during Greek democracy; but under monarchy and Empire it became a preoccupation, almost a monopoly. Sophistic practically reduces rhetoric to style. The old lore of investigation (*inventio*), paralyzed by the compression of its trunk nerve, has little scope beyond ingenuity. Organized movement [9] (*dispositio*), similarly impaired at the source, tends to be reduced to salience and variety, or to be supplanted by pattern. Memory becomes verbal. But style and delivery, becoming the main reliance, are elaborated into a systematic technic to a degree almost incredible to-day. In sheer virtuosity the second sophistic has hardly a parallel in earlier or later centuries. It is more like the art of Paderewski or Bernhardt than like that of Demosthenes.

[9] This defect is discerned as early as the *Phædrus* (264, seq.); but Socrates does not carry the remedy beyond logical analysis into cogency of sequence.

## B. The Second Sophistic [10]

### 1. Philostratus, *The Lives of the Sophists* [11]

*The Lives of the Sophists* by Philostratus derives the "new" sophistic of his day from the old. New, says he, it is not. We may call it a second sophistic; but it keeps an old tradition. Far from apologizing for sophistic, old or new, Philostratus is proud of it. He sets out to celebrate it as a great tradition. Gorgias is not defended from Socratic exposure; he is claimed as a distinguished ancestor.[12] That rhetoric is not what Aristotle urged, that it is after all sophistic, Philostratus assumes. Nor is the assumption merely provincial vanity; it was widespread and secure. There was no need to vindicate what was generally accepted. Moreover the facts justify not only the assumption of Philostratus, but his history. Though he is not historical in method, his assertion of continuity from Gorgias down to the platform artists of his day has been approved by studies really historical, and affirmed for the fourth century as well. *The Lives of the*

[10] The term *second sophistic* is generally applied to the Greek rhetoric and oratory of the second, third, and fourth Christian centuries, and is also applicable to the Latin. Already defined as a tendency in the first century (ARP IV. ii), it is reviewed at that point by H. von Arnim in the introduction to *Leben und Werke des Dio von Prusa*, Berlin, 1898. The second century is reviewed more specifically by Boulanger. Wright's introduction provides the best summary guide and bibliography for English readers. The studies of the influence of the second sophistic on the Christian orators of this period (see the list at the head of this chapter) review and define sophistic more precisely and more significantly than the general works cited in their bibliographies. But E. Norden's *Die antike Kunstprosa* and E. Rohde's *Der griechische Roman* are still suggestive.

[11] Written between 230 and 238. For the dates of the orators celebrated by Philostratus see Wright, xxii–xl.

[12] I. 9 (30). Substantially the same things, including the public honors, are recorded of Scopelian, I. 21 (84), and of Polemo, I. 25 (112).

*Sophists*, therefore, exhibit the second sophistic as the fixing of an old tendency in habitual practise and teaching.

During the second, third, and fourth centuries, and throughout the Roman world, rhetoric meant a sophistic generally constant. The leanings of particular schools, such as Stoic Pergamum, were not wide enough to bring new departures. They were merely shifts of emphasis within a common doctrine and practise. The cult of "Atticism" was too artificial to check the general tendency to "Asianism." [13] What was learned at Athens could be practised at Rome; and neither Athens nor Rome dimmed the glory of Smyrna and Antioch. [14] The schools of Bordeaux were to become essentially like those of Gaza and Carthage. The same "Gorgian figures" were learned by St Augustine in Latin Africa, by St Gregory Nazianzen in the Greek East, and by the pagan Libanius. Greco-Roman rhetoric was as pervasive as Roman law and almost as constant.

## 2. The Character of Sophistic

### a. VIRTUOSITY

In estimating this rhetoric, then, little allowance need be made for place or date. [15] Its main characteristics were so constant as to stand out clearly. The most ob-

[13] See the general histories, Guignet, 85, and Campbell's summary, pages 7–10.

[14] Boulanger, 16, 57; Méridier, 46–47. "By the middle of the first century A. D., Ephesus, Smyrna, Miletus, and Mytilene were become world centers for the instruction of rhetoric." Campbell, 10.

[15] "L'abandon du point de vue historique, qui serait condamnable ailleurs, devient légitime pour la sophistique, puisque toute évolution y est rendue impossible par l'existence d'un canon oratoire réligieusement observé. Libanios s'applique à copier Aristide, qui croit être un imitateur fidèle de Démosthène." Méridier, page vi.

vious arise from the general aim of virtuosity. This is
the constant assumption of Philostratus. Individual
triumphs were not so much triumphs of individuality as
outstanding exhibitions of skill in working out a pattern.
In method, in composition, there was little difference between a teacher's assignments to his amateur pupils and
his own professional orations.[16] Sophistic is largely an
oratory of themes.

## (1) *Declamatio* [17] (μελέτη)

### THEMES OF THE SOPHISTS CELEBRATED BY PHILOSTRATUS

#### HISTORICAL OR SEMI-HISTORICAL THEMES

The Lacedemonians deliberate concerning a wall.  I. 20 (70).[18]
(Isæus; so Aristides, II. 9 (220) .)

Demosthenes swears that he did not take the bribe.

Should the trophies erected by the Greeks be taken down?

The Athenians should return to their demes after Ægos-
potami.

Xenophon refuses to survive Socrates.

Solon demands that his laws be rescinded after Pisistratus has
obtained a bodyguard.  I. 25 (122–132).  (Polemo.)

The Cretans maintain that they have the tomb of Zeus.  II. 4
(188).  (Antiochus.)

Scythians, return to your nomadic life.  II. 5 (194).  (Alexander of Seleucia; so Hippodromus, II. 27 (296). )

The wounded in Sicily implore the Athenians who are re-
treating thence to put them to death with their own hands.

Pericles urges them to keep up the war even after the oracle
declares Apollo's support of the Lacedemonians.  (II, 5;
both also of Alexander.)

---

[16] "Un public qui ne se lasse pas de faire éternellement sa classe de
rhétorique."  Boulanger, 271.

[17] See προγυμνάσματα under section c below, and, in the index to
ARP, *declamatio.*

[18] The references are to sections and, in parenthesis, to Wright's pages.

Isocrates tries to wean the Athenians from their empire of the sea.

Callixenus is upbraided for not having granted burial to the Ten.

Deliberation on affairs in Sicily.[19]

Æschines, when the grain had not come.

Those whose children have been murdered reject a treaty of alliance.  II. 9 (220, seq).  (Aristides.)

Hyperides, when Philip is at Elatea, heeds only the counsels of Demosthenes.  II. 10 (230).  (Hadrian of Tyre.)

Islanders sell their children to pay taxes. II. 12 (238). (Pollux.)

The Thebans accuse the Messenians of ingratitude.  II. 15 (244).  (Ptolemy.)

Callias tries to dissuade the Athenians from burning the dead. II. 20 (256).  (Apollonius of Athens.)

The citizens of Catana.

Demades against revolting from Alexander while he is in India. II. 27 (296).  (Hippodromus.)

### FICTITIOUS THEMES

The adulterer unmasked.  I. 25 (132).  (Polemo.)

The instigator of a revolt suppresses it.  I. 26 (136).  (Secundus.)

The ravished chooses that her ravisher be put to death.  II. 4 (188).  (Antiochus.)

A tyrant abdicates on condition of immunity.  (*Ibid.*)

The man who fell in love with a statue.  II. 18 (250).  (Onomarchus.)

The magician who wished to die because he was unable to kill another magician, an adulterer.  II. 27 (292).  (Hippodromus.)

Evidently the themes were generally the same as those of the *declamationes* celebrated by Seneca.[20]  Some of them were identical.  Such subjects give the oratory of the imperial centuries, both Greek and Latin, the air of ath-

---

[19] Cf. Ælius Aristides XXIX and XXX D, summarized by Boulanger, 275.          [20] ARP Chapter IV. ii. 90–93.

letics, and make its teaching seem largely gymnastic. Gregory Nazianzen, indeed, calls the sophists "oratorical acrobats." [21] But instead of dismissing sophistic with so obvious a sarcasm, we may learn something from its delight in verbal artistry.

For what, then, ultimately do we blame them? For their absolute emptiness of thought? But who shall say that they were trying to think, or that they were asked to think? . . . a kind of eloquence, and also a system of education, of which we have not any longer even the notion; for it rested on a sentiment which has disappeared, *the absolute and disinterested love of speaking well*—disinterested not always, indeed, as to personal advantage, but always as to thought. Who knows whether thought was for them anything else or anything more than a simple *motif*, a theme to be developed, something which sustained the discourse without imparting to it any value, something like the libretto of an opera? [22]

Since the oratory of display is still with us, the second sophistic should be taken to heart as a complete historic demonstration of what must become of rhetoric without the urgencies of matter and motive.

Philostratus has no qualms. For him *declamatio* (μελέτη), far from being merely a school exercise, is a form of public speaking on a par with any other. It is

[21] xxvii, page 12. A; quoted by Guignet, 46.
[22] Petit de Julleville, *L'école d'Athènes au quatrième siècle*, 105. Méridier arrives at the same estimate: "Or, dans aucun de ces exercices oratoires, le sophiste n'a à compter avec la réalité. . . . La question de fond importe peu; elle sert simplement de thème, de point de départ, pour ne pas dire de prétexte. . . . La grande affaire, c'est de donner au public l'impression d'un tour de force surprenant exécuté sans difficulté apparente. Le sophiste est proprement un virtuose qui est capable de jouer, sur n'importe quel thème, des variations brillantes. Indifférent aux sujets qu'il traite, il s'applique à multiplier les difficultés de la forme." 9. Pliny's account of Isæus Rhetor (ARP 95) gives substantially the same impression.

even *the* form of his sophists. He pays little attention
to any other except encomium, which is also a school
exercise. Reading the past with the eyes of the present,
he finds it in Gorgias,[23] who elaborated "encomia of the
Medic trophies." "Medics" (Μηδικά), dilations on the
old glories of the Persian wars, were the favorite subjects
of *declamatio*. This is evident both from their frequent
recurrence and from Lucian's satire.[24] Scopelian, Philostratus thinks, was best

> in Medics, in the Darius and Xerxes things, I mean; for, to me
> at least, he of all the sophists seems to render these best and
> to set a tradition of rendering for his successors. I. 21 (84).

Ptolemy of Naucratis, however, was nicknamed Mara-
thon.[25] The wonder is that the nickname was sufficiently
distinctive.[26]

### (2) Improvisation and Memory

The vogue of such subjects does much to explain the
otherwise incredible accounts of improvisation. "Propose
a theme," the sophist's challenge which Philostratus
traces back to Gorgias,[27] becomes less startling when we
find that the theme, as well as the treatment, might come
from stock. Even so the readiness and fluency seem
phenomenal and were the great boast. See Mark of
Byzantium recognized by pupils in the school of Polemo.

[23] I. 9 (32).
[24] E. g., *Demonax*, 33, 36; *Rhetorum præceptor*, 17.
[25] II. 15 (244).
[26] "Troics" (Τρωικά), which Philostratus traces back to Hippias of
Elis (I. 11 (36)), seem more like ἠθοποιίαι (ARP 68, 71, 187, and see
Hermogenes below, section c. The Τρωικά of Dio Chrysostom are an
exercise of another sort, the refutation of a classic (Boulanger, 249).
It is discussed by Von Arnim, 166.
Further on μελέτη see Boulanger, Chapter ii, section v; Méridier,
Chapter i.               [27] Introduction (8).

Accordingly when Polemo asked for themes to be proposed, they all turned towards Mark. . . . Mark, lifting up his voice and tossing his head, said: "I will both propose and execute." Thereupon Polemo . . . discoursed at him long and wonderfully on the spur of the moment; and when he had declaimed and heard Mark declaim, he was both admired and admiring. I. 24 (104).

Aristides was exceptional in declining to speak thus; and Philostratus thinks the less of him.[28]   Generally improvisation was expected as a mark of virtuosity.[29]   The *locus classicus*, perhaps, of improvisation, the most daring and phenomenal virtuosity, is ascribed by Eunapius to Prohæresius.

Then from his chair the sophist first delivered a graceful prelude . . . then with the fullest confidence he rose for his formal discussion. The proconsul was ready to propose a definition for the theme, but Prohæresius threw back his head and gazed all round the theater . . . and beheld in the farthest row of the audience, hiding themselves in their cloaks, two men, veterans in the service of rhetoric, at whose hands he had received the worst treatment of all, and he cried out: "Ye gods! There are those honourable and wise men! Proconsul, order them to propose a theme for me. Then perhaps they will be convinced that they have behaved impiously." . . . Whereupon, after considering for a short time and consulting together, they produced the hardest and most disagreeable theme that they knew of, a vulgar one, moreover, that gave no opening for the display of fine rhetoric. Prohæresius glared at them fiercely, and said to the proconsul: "I implore you to grant me . . . to have shorthand writers assigned to me." . . . Then he said: "I shall ask for something even

[28] II. 9 (222).
[29] I. 24 (102); II. 15 (244). Several of the sophists celebrated by Philostratus withdrew for a brief meditation after receiving the theme: Scopelian, I. 21 (82); Dionysius of Miletus and Isæus, I. 22 (90); Polemo. I. 25 (120). Apollonius of Naucratis, he complains, took too long. II, 19 (254).

more difficult to grant . . . there must be no applause whatever." When the proconsul had given all present an order to
this effect . . . Prohæresius began his speech with a flood of
eloquence, rounding every period with a sonorous phrase. . . .
As the speech grew more vehement and the orator soared to
heights which the mind of man could not describe or conceive
of, he passed on to the second part of the speech and completed
the exposition of the theme. But then, suddenly leaping in
the air like one inspired, he abandoned the remaining part,
left it undefended, and turned the flood of his eloquence to
defend the contrary hypothesis. The scribes could hardly
keep pace with him, the audience could hardly endure to remain silent, while the mighty stream of words flowed on.
Then, turning his face towards the scribes, he said: "Observe
carefully whether I remember all the arguments that I used
earlier." And without faltering over a single word, he began
to declaim the same speech for the second time. (Wright's
translation, 493.)

This performance is extraordinary only in degree.
That of Isæus, as reported by Pliny,[30] seems the same in
kind; and so, apparently, are many other recorded triumphs. Taken together, they reveal strict limits. The
improvisation was mainly of style. It consisted in fluency
of rehandling, of variations upon themes, and in patterns,
so common as to constitute a stock in trade. It permitted
the use over and over again not only of stock examples
and illustrations, but of successful phrases, modulated
periods, even whole descriptions. It was the art of a
technician, not of a composer.[31] Memory, too, thus
trained, was no longer the orator's command of his material;[32] it was the actor's command of words. Though a

[30] ARP 95.
[31] The sound ancient doctrine of *facilitas* is most definitely formulated
by Quintilian in his tenth book (see ARP 79). It is different not only
in detail, but in its conception and method.
[32] See *memoria* in the index to ARP.

sophist might, indeed, be a thinker, he hardly needed to be for the purposes of his oratory. His fluency was typically not in seizing and carrying forward ideas and images, but in readiness to draw upon a store.

### (3) Delivery

The character of this oratory is further expressed in the records of its delivery. Even more than modulation Philostratus exhibits sonority and force. Polemo's delivery was thrilling as an Olympian trumpet.[33] Scopelian imitated the volume of Nicetes and had the sonority of Gorgias.[34] Favorinus fascinated even those who did not understand Greek.[35] The carrying voice spoke in marked rhythms. Gesture, pushed sometimes to the extent of acting, was habitually demonstrative. Sitting at first, the orator might then leap to his feet, smite his thigh, walk, stamp, sway as a Bacchante. If such theatrical delivery seems to moderns of the West more violent than it seemed to its own audiences, it has never been extinct; and any one familiar with the oratory of display in any time will recognize the sophist's heavy frown, his mien of deep thought, his air of authority.[36] Chaucer's Pardoner speaks for the whole sophist line:

I peyne me to han an hauteyn speche. *Canterbury Tales*, C. 330

Such weight and vehemence of delivery, sometimes conceding a benignant smile, oftener relying on arrogance,[37] was the bodily expression of the impressiveness ($\delta\epsilon\iota\nu\delta\tau\eta s$) cultivated no less assiduously in style. The sophist was

[33] I. 25 (130).          [34] I. 21 (80–82).          [35] I. 8 (28).
[36] II. 8 (212), 10 (226).
[37] "Polemo was so arrogant that he conversed with cities as his inferiors, emperors as not his superiors, and the gods as his equals." I. 25 (114).

over-expressive lest for a moment he should cease to be impressive. The audience need not be held to any course of thought; it must not be held too long by any one device of style; but it must unflaggingly admire. It must be spellbound. The constant implication of Philostratus probably echoes the ideal of orator and audience alike: behold a great speaker!

## b. DILATION

Such oratory must be dilated, even inflated. That it was so in fact any one may satisfy himself who has the patience. The amplification [38] practised by Cicero and taught by Quintilian, though in print it may seem over-anxious, is an oratorical necessity. It is not merely Greek expansiveness; for it moves also the more stinted Latin. In any language it must almost always be practised as a means to oral clearness.[39] But sophistic amplification has no such warrant. It is often purely decorative. Instead of marking a stage of progress, it often merely dwells on a picture, or elaborates a truism, or acts out a mood. It is there for itself, expecting its own applause. Many of the figures of speech are devices of dilation; for sophistic is an art not only of elaboration, but of elaborateness.

### (1) *Ecphrasis*

Without enumerating devices that constitute a large part of sophistic, we may see the characteristic dilation at the full in the single form known as ἔκφρασις.[40] An

[38] See *amplification* in the index to ARP.

[39] E. g., see *chria* in the index to ARP and in section c below.

[40] Méridier, 41–44, and Chapter ix; Guignet, Chapter ix; Burgess, 201; Ameringer, 72, 78, 87; and the "Tempe" and "Memnon" of Dio Chrysostom. For restraint of this form of dilation by Augustine

ecphrasis is a separable decorative description, usually of a stock subject. "I will draw this for you in words," says Himerius,[41] using the formula of introduction, "and will make your ears serve for eyes." The natural beauty of a prospect or of the human body is detailed for admiration, even oftener the artistic beauty of statue or temple. The orator turns on, as it were, a storm, a feast, the prospect of a city. The essentially artificial character of the ecphrasis is obvious in the favorite exercise of word-painting a peacock.[42] Apparently a boy could carry this peacock from school to the platform and continue to use it with merely verbal variations.

Of course the ecphrasis might rise to a higher level. So it did often. An accomplished orator might make it splendid, even really moving. Oratory cannot afford to neglect the appeal of oral description. None the less the ecphrasis had two essential vices. First it was extraneous, separable, detachable, a clear sign that sequence did not count. Secondly, instead of following the Aristotelian

see Barry, 246; by Basil, Campbell, 128. For ἔκφρασις in the προγυμνάσματα see below, section c.

Among his many sallies Lucian has inserted a sober warning: "Restraint in description of mountains, walls, rivers, and the like is very important; you must not give the impression that you are making a tasteless display of word-painting, and expatiating independently while the history takes care of itself. . . . . You have the mighty Homer's example in such a case. . . . If Parthenius, Euphorion, or Callimachus had been in his place, how many lines do you suppose it would have taken to get the water to Tantalus' lips; how many more to set Ixion spinning?" *Quomodo historia*, 57; Fowler's translation, II. 134.

[41] Orat. x, quoted by Guignet, 188. Hermogenes uses much the same words. See below, section c.

[42] E. g., [Hippodromus] "recited an encomium on fair-speaking, beginning with the peacock and showing how admiration makes him spread his plumage aloft." II. 27 (288). For this peacock see also Méridier, 144.

counsels of specific concrete imagery, it habitually generalized and rapidly became conventional.

Ecphrasis is no less significant for poetic. A form of
Alexandrianism [43] avoided by Vergil and adopted with
enthusiasm by Ovid, it perverts description because it
frustrates narrative movement. The habit of decorative
dilation in oratory confirmed a decadent habit of literature.[44] That the habit is decadent even when indulged
with more taste is suggested by certain passages in De
Quincey, in Pater, most clearly perhaps in that English
sophist Laurence Sterne. Among the ecphrases of the
*Sentimental Journey* is one that he executed upon a theme
taken from the most expert mocker of the sophists,
Lucian,[45] and has made quite typical of the soothing
rhythms and the elegant dilation of sophistic eloquence.

The town of Abdera, notwithstanding Democritus lived
there, trying all the powers of irony and laughter to reclaim
it, was the vilest and most profligate town in all Thrace.
What for poisons, conspiracies, and assassinations, libels,
pasquinades and tumults, there was no going there by day;
'twas worse by night. Now when things were at their worst,
it came to pass that the Andromeda of Euripides being represented at Abdera, the whole orchestra was delighted with it.
But of all the passages which delighted them, nothing operated
more upon their imaginations than the tender strokes of
nature which the poet had wrought up in that pathetic speech
of Perseus, "O Cupid! prince of gods and men." Every man,
almost, spoke pure iambics the next day, and talked of nothing
but Perseus' pathetic address—"O Cupid! prince of gods and
men!" In every street of Abdera, in every house—"O Cupid!
Cupid!" in every mouth, like the natural notes of some sweet
melody, which drop from it whether it will or no, nothing but

[43] ARP 168, 203, 218.                    [44] ARP 100.
[45] The theme, which Lucian handles with biting conciseness, is at
the opening of *Quomodo historia*.

"Cupid! Cupid! prince of gods and men!" The fire caught; and the whole city, like the heart of one man, opened itself to love. No pharmacopolist could sell one grain of hellebore; not a single armorer had a heart to forge one instrument of death. Friendship and Virtue met together and kissed each other in the street. The golden age returned and hung over the town of Abdera. Every Abderite took his oaten pipe, and every Abderitish woman left her purple web, and chastely sat her down, and listened to the song. "'Twas only in the power," says the fragment, "of the god whose empire extended from heaven to earth, and even to the depths of the sea, to have done this."

### C. PATTERN

For the composition of the whole speech sophistic generally had little care. That planned sequence, that leading on of the mind from point to point, which is the habit of great orators and the chief means of cogency, presupposes urgency toward a goal. Sophistic often had no goal. The audience need be won only to admiration, not to decision. Easily, therefore, rhetoric came to pay no more attention to logical movement than poetic to movement in narrative. Like Alexandrian narrative, sophistic oratory cares little for onwardness; and its lore is reduced to prescription for detail.

If Philostratus seems occasionally aware of the value of planned movement, scrutiny will reveal that he is thinking not of the order of the whole, but only of sentences. For instance, the passage praising Isocrates for his "brilliant composition" [46] specifies his handling of

---

[46] ἡ συνθήκη λαμπρά I. 17 (50) (54). Συνθήκη here seems to be used for σύνθεσις, and νόημα in the context to be equivalent to *sententia*, as in I. 22 (90) of Dionysius of Miletus. If so, τάξις also, which in the older rhetoric means *dispositio*, is restricted by Philostratus to *compositio*. The latter, at any rate, is all that he ever discusses specifically.

rhythms; "for thought after thought concludes upon a balanced period."

This lack of plan may seem paradoxical in the works of writers as artistic as the Greek men of letters. So, indeed, it is; but it is explained by the quite different conception that the Greeks—at least those of the decadence—have of the beauty of a discourse. For them the whole value is in the detail. The perfecting of the whole is secondary; they have no taste for it. By a sort of deliberate intellectual myopia they restrict their field of vision to the analysis of a paragraph, a period, a phrase, even a word. Their esthetic sense, so to speak, is fragmentary.[47]

As if to mark the lack of individual planning for cogency, sophistic is commonly compcsed upon set patterns. No other body of oratory has so uniformly resigned itself to forms. The orator could devote his whole attention to each separate development because its place was predetermined in a traditional series of topics. The encomium [48] of a country was expected to deal with its situation, climate, products, its race, founders, government, its advancement in learning and literature, its festivals and its buildings, unless indeed the whole encomium were based on one of these topics. Similar topics controlled the praise of a city, a harbor, a bay, an acropolis. The classification of these as separate forms goes on to enumerate the speech at an embarkation, a marriage, a birthday, a festival, etc., as in a complete letter-writer.[49] Similarly prescribed was the encomium of a person. So pervasive

[47] Guignet, 214.

[48] Menander Rhetor, περὶ ἐπιδεικτικῶν, analyzed by Burgess, 110 seq. Cf. Boulanger, 342, 363. See below, pages 30, 31.

[49] The same topics, indeed, are found in letters, anticipating the medieval *dictamen*. See Guignet, *Les procédés épistolaires de St. Grégoire de Nazianzen*, Paris, 1911 (added to the work previously cited).

were its topics that they invaded even written biography.[50]
Philostratus follows them in his account of Herodes At-
ticus.[51]   Basil, on the other hand, explicitly rejects them
as inept for encomia of Christian martyrs; and his protest
shows at once their prevalence and their typical vice.

> The school of God does not recognize the laws of the en-
> comium, but holds that a mere telling of the martyr's deeds
> is a sufficient praise for the saints and sufficient inspiration
> for those who are struggling towards virtue.  For it is the
> fixed habit of encomia to search out the history of the native
> city, to find out the family exploits, and to relate the educa-
> tion of the subject of the encomium, but it is our custom to
> pass over in silence such  details and to compose the en-
> comium of each martyr from those facts which have a bearing
> on his martyrdom.  How could I be an object of more rever-
> ence or be more illustrious from the fact that my native city
> once upon a time endured great and heavy battles and after
> routing her enemies erected famous trophies?  What if she
> is so happily located that in summer and winter her climate
> is pleasant?  If she is the mother of heroes and is capable
> of supporting cattle, what gain are these to me?  In her herds
> of horses she surpasses all lands under the sun.  How may
> these facts improve us in manly virtue?  If we talk about the
> peaks of mountains near, how they out-top the clouds and
> reach the farthest stretches of the air, shall we deceive our-
> selves into thinking that drawing praise from these facts we
> give praise to men?  Of all things it is most absurd that when
> the just despise the whole world, we celebrate their praises from
> those things which they contemned.[52]

Such composing upon a pattern is legitimately a school
exercise.  Its use in elementary education is not confined

[50] Miss Kennedy shows that the cramping of biography by encomiastic pattern hampers Ammianus in imitating Tacitus, whose method
is narrative (*The Literary Work of Ammianus*, Chicago, 1912, pages
11–14).

[51] II., opening.

[52] Basil, *In Gordium*, 142 D–143 A, as translated by Campbell, 147.

to sophistic. What is sophistic is its extent and its pre-
scriptiveness, still more its extension from school into
adult and professional practise. How far the oratory of
the imperial centuries was controlled by fixed topics becomes startingly evident in its conformity to the rules
set forth by the manuals of elementary exercises.[53] Theon's
of uncertain date may have been superseded [54] by that
of Aphthonius in the fourth century, which at any rate
had a long life.[55] But the pattern is most concisely shown
in the second century by Hermogenes,[56] whose work is
typical of them all. There some of the most characteristic
habits of form in sophistic oratory are seen as prolonga-
tions of school exercises.

## THE ELEMENTARY EXERCISES (ΠΡΟΓΥΜΝΑΣΜΑΤΑ) OF HERMOGENES [57]

### MYTH (FABLE)

Myth is the approved thing to set first before the young,
because it can lead their minds into better measures.

Myths appear to have been used also by the ancients, Hesiod
telling that of the nightingale, Archilochus that of the fox.

From their inventors myths are named Cyprian or Libyan
or Sybaritic; but all alike are called Æsopic, because Æsop
used myths for his dialogues.

[53] For προγυμνάσματα in a general sense see ARP 249.

[54] Sandys, *History of Classical Scholarship*, I. 311. Theon is quoted
by Walden, *The Universities of Ancient Greece*, 200–1, 205–10.

[55] E. g., there is a commentary on Aphthonius by the Byzantine John
Doxopater in the twelfth century, and an Amsterdam edition as late
as 1665.

[56] "The most famous technical writer on rhetoric in the second century . . . categories quoted by all the technical rhetoricians who suc-
ceeded him." Wright, xxxvi. See also Boulanger, 241; and Radermacher in Pauly-Wissowa.

[57] My translation is from the Teubner text of Rabe, Leipzig, 1913,
pages 1–27.

The description of a myth is traditionally something like
this. It may, they say, be fictitious, but thoroughly practical
for some contingency of actual life. Moreover it should be
plausible. How may it be plausible? By our assigning to
the characters actions that befit them. For example, if the
contention be about beauty, let this be posed as a peacock;
if some one is to be represented as wise, there let us pose a
fox; if imitators of the actions of men, monkeys.

Myths are sometimes to be expanded, sometimes to be told
concisely. How? By now telling in bare narrative, and now
feigning the words of the given characters. For example,
"the monkeys in council deliberated on the necessity of
settling in houses. When they had made up their minds to
this end and were about to set to work, an old monkey restrained them, saying that they would more easily be captured
if they were caught within enclosures." Thus if you are concise; but if you wish to expand, proceed in this way. "The
monkeys in council deliberated on the founding of a city;
and one coming forward made a speech to the effect that
they too must have a city. 'For see,' said he, 'how fortunate
in this regard are men. Not only does each of them have a
house, but all going up together to public meeting or theater
delight their souls with all manner of things to see and hear.''
Go on thus, dwelling on the incidents and saying that the
decree was formally passed; and devise a speech for the old
monkey. So much for this.

The style of recital, they say, should be far from periods and
near to pleasantness. The moral to be derived from the myth
is sometimes put first, sometimes last. Orators [58] too appear
to have used myth instead of example.

[58] This section and the following remind both of the traditional importance of narrative and description in oratory and of the general confusion of poetic with rhetoric.

### TALE

A tale, they say, is the setting forth of something that has happened or of something as if it had happened. Sometimes, however, authorities set the chria instead of this.

A tale differs from a story as a poem from an extended poetical work. For a poem or a tale is about one thing, a poetical work or a story about several. Thus a poetical work is the *Iliad*, for example, or the *Odyssey;* but a poem is (one of the component parts, such as) the making of the shield, the visit to the shades, or the slaying of the suitors. And again, a story is the history of Herodotus or the composition of Thucydides; a tale is the incident of Arion or that of Alcmæon.

The forms of the tale are said to be four: the mythical; the fictitious, which is also called the dramatic, as those of the tragic poets; the historical; and the political or personal. But for the present we consider the last.

The modes of tales are five: direct declarative, indirect declarative, interrogative, enumerative, comparative. Direct declarative is as follows: "Medea was the daughter of Æetes. She betrayed the golden fleece"; and it is called direct because the whole discourse, or the greater part, keeps the nominative case. Indirect declarative is as follows: "The story runs that Medea, daughter of Æetes, was enamored of Jason," and so on; and it is called indirect because it uses the other cases. The interrogative is this mode: "What terrible thing did not Medea do? Was she not enamored of Jason, and did she not betray the golden fleece and kill her brother Absyrtus?" and so on. The enumerative mode is as follows: "Medea, daughter of Æetes, was enamored of Jason, betrayed the golden fleece, slew her brother Absyrtus," and so on. The comparative is as follows: "Medea, daughter of Æetes, instead of ruling her spirit, was enamored; instead of guarding the golden fleece, betrayed it; instead of saving her brother Absyrtus, slew him." The direct mode is suited to stories, as being clearer; the indirect, rather to trials; the interrogative to cross-questioning; the enumerative, to perorations, as rousing emotion.

## CHRIA

A chria [59] is a concise exposition of some memorable saying or deed, generally for good counsel.

Some chriæ are of words, others of deeds, still others of both: of words, i. e., essentially sayings, as "Plato said that the Muses dwell in the souls of the fit"; of deeds, i. e., essentially doings, as "Diogenes, seeing an ill-bred youth, smote his tutor, saying 'why did you teach him thus?'"

A chria differs from a memoir mainly in scope; for some memoirs may run to considerable length, but a chria must be concise. It differs from a proverb in that the latter is a bald declaration, whereas a chria is often (developed) by question and answer; and again in that a chria may be based upon deeds, whereas a proverb is based only upon words; and again in that a chria introduces the person who did or said, whereas the proverb has no reference to a person.

Chriæ have been distinguished, mainly by the ancients, as declarative, interrogative, and investigative.

But now let us come to the point, that is the actual working out. Let this working out be as follows: first, brief encomium of the sayer or doer; then paraphrase of the chria itself; then proof or explanation. For example, Isocrates said that the root of education is bitter, but its fruit sweet: (1) encomium, "Isocrates was wise," and you will slightly develop this topic; (2) chria, "said, etc.," and you will not leave this bare, but develop the significance; (3) proof, (a) direct, "the greatest affairs are usually established through toil, and, once established, bring happiness"; (b) by contrast, "those affairs which succeed by chance require no toil and their conclusion brings no happiness; quite the contrary with things that demand our

[59] The exercise is still included in the Jesuit Latin manual of rhetoric, Kleutgen's *Ars dicendi* (1898), but is relegated to an appendix.

zeal"; (c) by illustration, "as the farmers who toil ought to reap the fruit, so with speeches"; (d) by example, "Demosthenes, who shut himself up in his room and labored much, finally reaped his fruit, crowns and public proclamations." (e) You may also cite authority, as "Hesiod says, 'Before virtue the gods have put sweat'; and another poet says, 'The gods sell all good things for labor.'" (4) Last you will put an exhortation to follow what was said or done.

So much for now; fuller instructions you will learn later.

## PROVERB

A proverb is a summary saying, in a statement of general application, dissuading from something or persuading toward something, or showing what is the nature of each: dissuading, as in that line "a counsellor should not sleep all night"; persuading, as in the lines "he who flees poverty, Cyrnus, must cast himself upon the monster-haunted deep and down steep crags." Or it does neither of these, but makes a declaration concerning the nature of the thing: "Faring well undeservedly is for the unintelligent the beginning of thinking ill."

Again, some proverbs are true, others plausible; some simple, others compound, others hyperbolic:

(1) true, such as "no one can find a life without pain";
(2) plausible, such as "never have I asked what manner of man takes pleasure in bad company, knowing that birds of a feather flock together";
(3) simple, such as "wealth may make men even benevolent";
(4) compound, such as "no good comes of many rulers; let there be one";
(5) hyperbolic, such as "earth breeds nothing feebler than man."

The working out is similar to that of the chria; for it proceeds by (1) brief encomium of him who made the saying, as in the chria; (2) direct exposition; (3) proof; (4) contrast; (5) enthymeme; (6) illustration; (7) example; (8) authority. Let the proverb be, for example, "*a counsellor should not sleep all night*." (1) You will briefly praise the speaker. Then to (2) direct exposition, i. e., to paraphrase of the proverb, as "it befits not a man proved in counsels to sleep through the whole night"; (3) proof, "always through pondering is one a leader, but sleep takes away counsel"; (4) contrast, "as a private citizen differs from a king, so sleep from wakefulness"; (5) "how, then, might it be taken? if there is nothing startling in a private citizen's sleeping all night, plainly it befits a king to ponder wakefully"; (6) illustration, "as helmsmen are incessantly wakeful for the common safety, so should chieftains be"; (7) example, "Hector, not sleeping at night, but pondering, sent Dolon to the ships to reconnoiter." (8) The last topic is the one from authority. Let the conclusion be hortatory.

### Refutation and Confirmation

Destructive analysis is the overturning of the thing cited; constructive analysis, on the contrary, its confirmation.

Things fictitious, such as myths, are open to neither destruction nor construction; destruction and construction apply only to things that offer argument on either side.

Destructive analysis proceeds by alleging that the thing is (1) obscure, (2) incredible, (3) impossible, (4) inconsistent or, as it is called, contrary, (5) unfitting, (6) inexpedient: (1) obscure, as "in the case of Narcissus the time is obscure; (2) incredible, as "it is incredible that Arion in the midst of his ills was willing to sing"; (3) impossible, "it is impossible that Arion was saved on a dolphin"; (4) inconsistent or contrary, "quite opposite to preserving popular government is wishing to destroy it"; (5) unfitting, "it was unfitting for Apollo, being a god, to love a mortal woman"; (6) inexpedient, when we say that it is of no use to hear this.

Confirmation proceeds by the opposites of these.

### Commonplace

The so-called commonplace is the amplification of a thing admitted, of demonstrations already made. For in this we are no longer investigating whether so-and-so was a robber of temples, whether such-another was a chieftain, but how we shall amplify the demonstrated fact. It is called commonplace because it is applicable to every temple-robber and to every chieftain. The procedure must be as follows: (1) analysis of the contrary, (2) the deed itself, (3) comparison, (4) proverb, (5) defamatory surmise of the past life (of the accused) from the present, (6) repudiation of pity by the so-called final considerations and by a sketch of the deed itself.

Introductions will not be merely within the commonplace, but will be maintained up to it. For instance, if the commonplace be about a temple-robber, the introduction, not in sense but in type, may be as follows: "All evil-doers, honorable judges, should be hated, but especially those whose audacity is directed toward the gods"; or again, "If you wish to deprave other men, let this one go; if not, punish him"; or again, "To outward seeming the only one on trial here is the accused, but in truth you judges, too; for to be false to one's oath of office may be more criminal than transgression."

Then, before proceeding to the deed itself, (1) discuss its contrary; e. g., "Our laws have provided for the worship of the gods, have reared altars and adorned them with votive offerings, have honored the gods with sacrifices, festal assemblies, processions." Then the application to the indictment. "Naturally, for the favor of the gods preserves cities; and without this they must be destroyed." (2) Now proceed to the case in hand. "These things being so, what has this man dared?" and tell what he has done, not as explaining it, but as heightening. "He has defiled the whole city, both its public interests and its private; and we must fear lest our crops fail; we must fear lest we be worsted by our enemies," etc. (3) Next go on to comparison. "He is more dangerous than murderers; for the difference is in the object of attack. They have presumed against human life; he has outraged the gods. He is like despots, not like them all, but like the most dangerous. For in them it appears most shocking that they lay hands on what has been dedicated to the gods." And you will bring into the denunciation comparisons with the lesser, since they are destructive. "Is it not shocking to punish the thief, but not the temple-robber?" (4, 5 above.) You may draw defamation of the rest of his life from his present crime. "Beginning with small offenses, he went on to this one last, so that you have before you in the same person a thief, a housebreaker, and an adulterer" (5, 4 above). You may cite the proverb in accordance with which he came to this pass, "Unwilling to work in the fields, he wished to get money by such means"; and, if you are denouncing a homicide, (you may tell) also the consequences, "a wife made widow, children orphans." (6) Use also the repudiation of pity. Now you will repudiate pity by the so-called final considerations of equity, justice, expediency, possibility, and propriety, and by description of the crime. "Look not on him as he weeps now, but on him as he despises the gods, as he approaches the shrine, as he forces the doors, as he lays hands on the votive offerings." And conclude upon exhortation. "What are you about to do? what to decide concerning that which has been already judged?" So much for the present; the ampler method you will know later.

## ENCOMIUM

Encomium is the setting forth of the good qualities that belong to some one in general or in particular: in general, as encomium of man; in particular, as encomium of Socrates. We make encomia also of things, such as justice; and of animals without reason, such as the horse; and even of plants, mountains, and rivers. It has been called encomium, they say, from poets' singing the hymns of the gods in villages long ago; and passes also used to be called villages.

Encomium differs from praise (in general) in that the latter may be brief, as "Socrates was wise," whereas encomium is developed at some length. Observe too that censure is classified with encomia, either because the latter may be euphemistic or because both are developed by the same commonplaces. In what, then, does the encomium differ from the commonplace? For in some cases the two seem very much alike. The difference, they say, appears in the end, in the issue. For whereas in the commonplace the aim is to receive a reward, encomium has no other (end) than the witness to virtue.

Subjects for encomia are: a race, as the Greek; a city, as Athens; a family, as the Alcmæonidæ. You will say [60] what marvelous things befell at the birth, as dreams or signs or the like. Next, the nurture, as, in the case of Achilles, that he was reared on lions' marrow and by Chiron. Then the train-

---

[60] The topics for encomium of a person are analyzed by Burgess (120) from Aphthonius, and by Méridier (15, 44, 226) and Burgess (120 seq.) from Menander Rhetor. Menander distinguishes four kinds: simple encomium (of one dead some time), funeral oration, monody, speech of consolation. The topic *achievements* might also be divided as of war and of peace, or by virtues. That the topic *comparison* (σύγκρισις) might be distributed, as in Menander, Hermogenes admits below.

| | APHTHONIUS | | | MENANDER |
|---|---|---|---|---|
| I. | prologue | | | |
| II. | race | 1. nationality | | native country |
| | | 2. native city | | race |
| | | 3. ancestors | | birth |
| | | 4. parents | | nature |
| III. | education | 1. pursuits | | education |
| | | 2. art | | pursuits |
| | | 3. laws | | |
| IV. | achievements (the main topic) | 1. of soul | (a) manliness | |
| | | | (b) judgment | |
| | | 2. of body | (a) beauty | |
| | | | (b) speed | achievements |
| | | | (c) strength | |
| | | 3. of fortune | (a) power | |
| | | | (b) wealth | |
| | | | (c) friends | |
| V. | comparison | | | comparison with each of the foregoing |
| VI. | epilogue | | | |

ing, how he was trained and how educated. Not only so, but the nature of soul and body will be set forth, and of each under heads: for the body, beauty, stature, agility, might; for the soul, justice, self-control, wisdom, manliness. Next his pursuits, what sort of life he pursued, that of philosopher, orator, or soldier, and most properly his deeds, for deeds come under the head of pursuits. For example, if he chose the life of a soldier, what in this did he achieve? Then external resources, such as kin, friends, possessions, household, fortune, etc. Then from the (topic) time, how long he lived, much or little; for either gives rise to encomia. A long-lived man you will praise on this score; a short-lived, on the score of his not sharing those diseases which come from age. Then, too, from the manner of his end, as that he died fighting for his fatherland, and, if there were anything extraordinary under that head, as in the case of Callimachus that even in death he stood. You will draw praise also from the one who slew him, as that Achilles died at the hands of the god Apollo. You will describe also what was done after his end, whether funeral games were ordained in his honor, as in the case of Patroclus, whether there was an oracle concerning his bones, as in the case of Orestes, whether his children were famous, as Neoptolemus. But the greatest opportunity in encomia is through comparisons, which you will draw as the occasion may suggest.

Similarly also living things without speech, so far as they permit. You will draw your encomia from the place in which the thing lives; and in addition to the country of its birth you will tell to which of the gods it is dedicated, as the owl to Athena, the horse to Poseidon. In like manner also you will tell its nurture, the nature of soul and body, its deeds and their use, the length of its life; and you will use throughout such comparisons as fall in with these topics.

Encomia of things done you will draw from their inventors, as the things of the chase from Artemis and Apollo; from those who practised them, as heroes. But the best procedure for such encomia is to consider those who pursue them, of what sort these are in soul and body, e. g., hunters as manly, courageous, more alert in intelligence, physically vigorous. Finally you will observe that we must make encomia of the gods; and it is to be borne in mind that such encomia must be called hymns.[61]

Furthermore plants similarly, each from the topics of its habitat, of the god to which it is dedicated, as the olive to Athena, of its nurture, as how it is grown. If it needs much care, you will marvel at this; if little, at that. You will tell concerning its body its rapid growth, its beauty, and whether it is ever-blooming, as the olive. Then its usefulness, on which you will dwell most. Comparisons you will lay hold of everywhere.

Furthermore encomium of a city you may undertake from these topics without difficulty. For you will tell of its race that its citizens were autochthonous, and concerning its nurture that they were nourished by the gods, and concerning its education that they were educated by the gods. And you will expound, as in the case of a man, of what sort the city is in its manners and institutions, and what its pursuits and accomplishments.

## COMPARISON

Comparison has been included both under *commonplace* as a means of our amplifying misdeeds, and also under *encomium* as a means of amplifying good deeds, and finally has been included as having the same force in censure. But since some (authors) of no small reputation have made it an exercise by itself, we must speak of it briefly. It proceeds, then, by the encomiastic topics; for we compare city with city as to the men who came from them, race with race, nurture with nurture, pursuits, affairs, external relations, and the manner of death and what follows. Likewise if you compare plants, you will set over against one another the gods who give them, the places in which they grow, the cultivation, the use

[61] For the relation of encomium to poetry, see Burgess, 130.

of their fruits, etc.  Likewise also if you compare things done, you will tell who first undertook them, and will compare with one another those who pursued them as to qualities of soul and body.  Let the same principle be accepted for all.

Now sometimes we draw our comparisons by equality, showing the things which we compare as equal either in all respects or in several; sometimes we put the one ahead, praising also the other to which we prefer it; sometimes we blame the one utterly and praise the other, as in a comparison of justice and wealth.  There is even comparison with the better, where the task is to show the less equal to the greater, as in a comparison of Heracles with Odysseus.  But such comparison demands a powerful orator and a vivid style; and the working out always needs vivacity because of the need of making the transitions swift.

### Characterization (ΗΘΟΠΟΙΙΑ) [62]

Characterization is imitation of the character of a person assigned, e. g., what words Andromache might say to Hector.  (The exercise is called) *prosopopœia* when we put the person into the scene, as Elenchus in Menander, and as in Aristides the sea is imagined to be addressing the Athenians.  The difference is plain; for in the one case we invent words for a person really there, and in the other we invent also a person who was not there.  They call it image-making (εἰδωλοποιία) when we suit words to the dead, as Aristides in the speech against Plato in behalf of the Four; for he suited words to the companions of Themistocles.

Characterizations are of definite persons and of indefinite; of indefinite, e. g., what words a man might say to his family when he was about to go away; of definite, e. g., what words Achilles might say to Deidamia when he was about to go forth to war.  Characterizations are single when a man is supposed to be making a speech by himself, double when he has an

[62] For ἠθοποιία and προσωποποιία see the index to ARP.

interlocutor: by himself, e. g., what a general might say on re-
turning from a victory; to others, e. g., what a general might
say to his army after a victory.

Always keep the distinctive traits proper to the assigned
persons and occasions; for the speech of youth is not that of
age, nor the speech of joy that of grief.  Some characterizations
are of the habit of mind, others of the mood, others a combination of the two: (1) of the habit, in which the dominant
throughout is this habit, e. g., what a farmer would say on
first seeing a ship; (2) of the mood, in which the dominant
throughout is the feeling, e. g., what Andromache might say
to Hector; (3) combined, in which character and emotion
meet, e. g., what Achilles might say to Patroclus—emotion
at the slaughter of Patroclus, character in his plan for the
war.

The working out proceeds according to the three times.
Begin with the present because it is hard; then revert to the
past because it has had much happiness; then make your
transition to the future because what is to happen is much
more impressive.  Let the figures and the diction conform to
the persons assigned.

## ECPHRASIS [63]

An ecphrasis is an account in detail, visible, as they say,
bringing before one's eyes what is to be shown.  Ecphrases
are of persons, actions, times, places, seasons, and many other
things: of persons, e. g., Homer's "crooked was he and halt of
one foot"; of actions, e. g., a description of a battle by land
or sea; of times, e. g., of peace or of war; of places, e. g., of
harbors, sea-shores, cities; of seasons, e. g., of spring or sum-
mer, or of a festal occasion.  And ecphrasis may combine
these, as in Thucydides the battle by night; for night is a
time and battle is an action.

Ecphrasis of actions will proceed from what went before,
from what happened at the time, and from what followed.

[63] See above, page 17.

Thus if we make an ecphrasis on war, first we shall tell what happened before the war, the levy, the expenditures, the fears; then the engagements, the slaughter, the deaths; then the monument of victory; then the pæans of the victors and, of the others, the tears, the slavery. Ecphrases of places, seasons, or persons will draw also from narrative and from the beautiful, the useful, or their contraries. The virtues of the ecphrasis are clearness and visibility; for the style must through hearing operate to bring about seeing. But it is no less important that the expression correspond to the thing. If the thing be fresh, let the style be so too; if it be dry, let the style be similar.

Note that some precisians do not make ecphrasis a (separate) exercise on the ground that it has been anticipated both in fable and in tale, in commonplace and in encomium; for in these too, they say, we expatiate descriptively on places, rivers, deeds, and persons. Nevertheless, since some (authors) of no small account have numbered this also among their exercises, we too have followed them, lest we be accused of negligence.

## THESIS

The limits of the thesis are traditionally that the thesis is a discussion of a matter considered apart from every particular circumstance. For the thesis usually occupies the field of general debate, not referring to any assigned person, but simply taking a typical course of exposition, as of any person whatsoever, by consideration of such things only as are inherent in the subject matter. Thus when we analyze the advisability of marriage, we speak not with reference to such and such an one, as Pericles or Alcibiades, nor to one in such and such circumstances, time of life, or fortune; but subtracting all these, we shall consider simply the subject in itself, making our analysis of what is inherent in that, i. e., whether this should be done by anybody whatsoever because such and such are the results for those who do so; whereas if we take a definite person and circumstances, and thus make our exposition of reasons, it will be not a thesis, but an hypothesis.

Some theses are political, some not.  Political are such as fall within common considerations, e. g., the advisability of studying oratory, etc.; unpolitical are such as are peculiar to a certain field of knowledge and proper to those versed in it, e. g., whether the heavens are spherical, whether there are many worlds, whether the sun is a fire.  These suit the philosophers; the others are the exercises of the rhetors.  Some have called the latter practical, the former theoretical; for action underlies the former, whereas the goal of the latter is theory.

The thesis differs from the commonplace in that the commonplace is the amplification of a subject matter admitted, whereas the thesis is an inquiry into a matter still in doubt.  Some theses are simple, others relative, others twofold: if we discuss the advisability of marriage, simple; if the advisability of marriage for a king, relative; if we discuss whether it is better to contend in games than to farm, twofold, for we must dissuade from the one and persuade to the other.

Theses are determined by the so-called final headings: justice, expediency, possibility, propriety; e. g., that it is just to marry and make to life the contribution of life itself; that it is expedient, as bringing many consolations; that it is possible by analogy; that it is fitting, as showing a disposition not savage.  Thus for your constructive argument; your destructive will be from the opposites.  You will refute also whatever theses may have been found on the other side.  At the end, exhortations and the common moral habits of mankind.

## INTRODUCING A BILL

Some include in their exercises the introduction of a bill.  And since in practise lawmaking and the categories falling within it constitute a (separate) study, they make this distinction.  In practise there is a (particular) circumstance; in an exercise there is not; e. g., if "in dearth of necessaries it is

proposed that governmental positions be put on sale," you
have an occasion in the dearth; in an exercise there is none,
but simply a proposal to put governmental positions on sale,
without occasion or other circumstance.

It is determined as evident, just, legal, expedient, possible,
proper; evident, as in Demosthenes "but that this is just is
simple and evident for all to know and learn"; legal, as when
we say "it is contrary to the ancient laws"; just, as when we
say "it is contrary to nature and morals"; expedient, as when
we say "nor can it be done"; proper, as when we say "it hurts
our reputation."

Arid, impersonal as arithmetic, pedantically over-
classified, sometimes inconsistent, these rules [64] are nevertheless illuminating. They expose sophistic oratory. The
patterns set forth for boys are recognizably the patterns
of the public oratory of men. Such higher attainment as
might come with experience was not in composition. In
composition adult oratory too, as well as these elementary
exercises, was feeble at the source. For lack of animating
conception and advancing urgency of thought, it eddied
in forms. It is the historic demonstration of the doom
of an oratory of themes. The resounding reputations so
expertly cultivated for themselves time has reduced to
absurdity. Hippodromus, Mark, Polemo, Scopelian—
which of the beadroll of Philostratus is even the echo of
an echo?

[64] The other works of Hermogenes deal with *status* (Περὶ στάσεων),
with *inventio* (Περὶ εὑρέσεως), with the rationale of impressiveness
(Περὶ μεθόδου δεινότητος), with types of style (Περὶ ἰδεῶν). They
show him to be not altogether a pedant, nor incapable of style.
He was frequently commented, especially by the Byzantines. For
modern comment see, besides Radermacher in Pauly-Wissowa, Jæneke,
*De statuum doctrina ab Hermogene tradita*, Leipzig, 1904; Becker, *Hermogenes de rhythmo oratorio*, Münster, 1896.

### d. ELABORATION OF STYLE

The long reign of sophistic reduced rhetoric to style.[65]
That this was the preoccupation even of the earlier sophistic we may guess from the derision of the *Phædrus* and
from other references.[66]

> And there is also Polus, who has schools of diplasiology and
> gnomology and eikonology, and who teaches in them the
> words of which Licymnius made him a present; they were to
> give a polish.
>
> *Phædrus*, 267, Jowett's translation.

The wider scope demanded by Aristotle's different conception is recognized in the traditional fivefold division [67]
found in Cicero and Quintilian.    This division, which
has such validity as to be essential for securing the educational values proposed by the ancients, seems to have
been inactive from Quintilian on to the fall of Rome.[68]
That the limitation to style impoverishes rhetoric and
impairs even the study of style itself is evident in the
sophistic period and is confirmed in the medieval.

Incidentally, the focus on style contributed to the
confusion of rhetoric with poetic.[69]    Neither being conceived often in its larger aspects of movement, both being
studied habitually for words and sentences, the distinction
between the two was the more easily blurred.    Here poetry
had the more to lose.    The use of poetic diction to decorate

---

[65] See above, section A.

[66] See O. Navarre, *La rhétorique grecque avant Aristote.*

[67] ARP 21, 42, 64.

[68] Hermogenes, though he has a treatise on *inventio* (εὕρεσις), and
a separate one on *status* (στάσις), deviates the former into the formal
parts of *dispositio* and still more widely into *elocutio*.

[69] ARP, 125–6, 229; Burgess, 166.

oratory must have confirmed the tendency to conceive poetic itself as an art of decoration.

But the main results of giving to style a monopoly are the cultivation of literary flavor, with conformity to past usage, and the forcing of figure and rhythm. The style inevitably acquired by those who seek style is decorative and elaborate. In order to sound literary, the orator is impelled both to depart from common speech and to force his note. Devices valuable in revision, to clarify and impress a message, become artificial in practise and unduly elaborated in theory by being pursued for themselves.

### (1) Literary Allusion and Archaism

The preoccupation that seized any opportunity for "Medics" [70] led to frequent literary allusions. Allusion is a legitimate, sometimes an important, means of heightening eloquence. Reviving old associations by familiar words and rhythms, it helps to suggest a mood or intensify an appeal.

> Who is this that cometh from Domrémy? Who is she in bloody coronation robes from Rheims? Who is she that cometh with blackened flesh from walking the furnaces of Rouen?
>
> De Quincey, *Joan of Arc*, last paragraph.

But the sophists used this form of suggestion so incontinently, and often so conventionally,[71] as to betray an anxiety to sound literary.

The same anxiety led to their frequent use of obsolescent words. Archaism became an habitual form of decoration. They borrowed the language of Demosthenes to welcome a proconsul and win from him some otiose appointment,

[70] See above, page 13.    [71] See the store classified by Burgess, 150.

or played upon an audience to capture its applause for
literary tone. "Atticism" was often little more than pride
in a highly sanctioned diction. The aim of the sophists
was not to model their composition on Demosthenes,
still less on the restrained habit of Lysias, but to borrow
from them words enough to give antique flavor. Pre-
suming to be apostles of Hellenism, they were anxious to
sound traditional. That they often thereby became
stilted is early evidence that this conception of elegance
is false.[72]

### (2) Decorative Imagery

Metaphor, which is a reliance of all popular oratory,
seldom has in sophistic the suggestiveness of fresh observation. Rather the sophist relied on far-fetching or
on the abundance of his literary stock.[73] "Living tombs,"
said of vultures, is ascribed to Gorgias by the treatise
*On the Sublime*,[74] and passed on through the schools. If
Athens was "the eye of Greece," another city might be
"the eye of Asia." Sophistic metaphor generally lacks
vitality. That it should achieve so little imaginative
suggestion is a clear sign of artificiality. No less conventional and decorative are the frequent similes. They
are more sophistic only in being more elaborate. In both
cases it is not the imagery that is sophistic; it is the strain-
ing, or the conventional decoration, or the dilation. For
all its store of tropes, for all its lavish use of them, sophistic is poor in active imagery. Quintilian's eighth book

[72] See Boulanger, 57; Méridier, 17; and St. Augustine on *integritas*,
below, page 65.

[73] "En principe, il fallait 'bourrer' sa matière du plus grand nombre
d'images possible, même quand rien n'y obligeait. En fait, on ne devait
donner asile dans ses écrits qu'à certaines images . . . dont la nature
et le nombre étaient rigoureusement fixés." Guignet, 132.

[74] iii.

analyzes the heightening of diction which comes from
concreteness [75] (iii), amplification (iv), epigram (*sententia*,
v), and tropes (vi). Of these the second and third were
the reliance of the sophists. The first they neglected;
the fourth they had conventionalized.

## (3) Balance

Imagery, what the ancients called trope, covers all that
is usually meant by the term *figure* in modern use. Ancient
manuals and their medieval derivatives generally use
*figures* to mean typical adaptations of sentence movement.
These are minutely classified even in the older rhetoric.
The treatise *Ad Herennium*,[76] which does not distinguish
them from tropes, enumerates sixty-one and groups them
by the traditional twofold division followed by Quintilian:
*figuræ sententiarum* (σχήματα διανοίας), and *figuræ verborum* (σχήματα λέξεως). Quintilian (IX), distinguishing
them from tropes, both reduces the number of figures
and by grouping simplifies the analysis. Of *figuræ sententiarum* he enumerates twelve.[77] *Figuræ verborum* he

[75] Quintilian's use of the terms ἐνάργεια and φαντασία are among
the evidences that he remembered the vital counsels of Aristotle (see
ARP 23, 127), though his own treatment of metaphor (VIII. vi. 4) is
hardly vital.

[76] Long thought to be Cicero's. The list of figures is given, pages
62–64, in Wilkins's digest, section 5 of his introduction to Cicero's
*De Oratore*.

[77] Interrogatio (rhetorical question), præsumptio (πρόληψις), dubitatio
(ἀπορία, with several modifications), simulatio (including παρρησία
and prosopopœia), apostrophe, sub oculos subjectio (ὑποτύπωσις, corresponding to the trope evidentia), dissimulatio (εἰρωνεία, distinguished
from the trope ironia, and appearing also as ἀντίφρασις, confessio,
concessio, consensio), reticentia (ἀποσιώπησις, with interruptio and
digressio), imitatio (ἠθοποιία), pœnitentia, emphasis (also a trope),
and finally various forms of insinuation by hint and double meaning.
Other figures, as included by Rutilius Lupus and Celsus, Quintilian
lists (IX. ii. 102), but does not describe.

groups as: (1) variations of syntax, (2) modes of iteration, (3) word-play, (4) balance and antithesis. The sophists especially cultivated these figures, most of all the last, those forms of balance which were traditionally called the figures of Gorgias (Γοργίεια σχήματα).[78]

Balance, as an obvious way of marking a comparison or a contrast, is so familiar in every language and in every period as hardly to be thought of as a figure. It becomes a figure by becoming a preoccupation; and the preoccupation, evident in certain modern literary periods, has never been stronger than in sophistic. The sophists pursued balance with such zeal as to display its typical faults of padding and superficiality. A habit of balance tends to slip in here and there a makeweight of mere words, or

[78] For convenience of reference Quintilian's grouping of *figuræ verborum* in IX. iii. may be tabulated as follows:—

Group 1, variations of syntax (3–27), such as hyperbaton.

Group 2, modes of iteration (28–65), figuræ per adjectionem; e. g., ἐπάνοδος (regressio), πολύπτωτον, μεταβολή, πλοκή, συνωνυμία, πλεονασμός, διαλλαγή (with the accompanying syntactical variations, βραχυλογία, ἀσύνδετον, πολυσύνδετον), and, most important, climax (κλῖμαξ, gradatio), a term applied consistently to progressive iteration; related figuræ per detractionem, συνεζευγμένον, παραδιαστολή (distinctio).

Group 3, word-play, paronomasia, annominatio (66–73), e. g., ἀντανάκλασις.

Group 4, balance and antithesis (74–86). Quintilian introduces these Gorgian figures by saying: "Magnæ veteribus curæ fuit gratiam dicendi paribus et contrariis acquirere. Gorgias in hoc immodicus, copiosus ætate prima utique Isocrates fuit. Delectatus est his etiam M. Tullius" (74), and proceeds (75) to divide balance into: πάρισον, ὁμοιοτέλευτον, ὁμοιόπτωτον, ἰσόκωλον.

The Gorgian figures are analyzed and exemplified by Méridier, 33. 162; Guignet, 106. Campbell includes them in a different classification, more distinctive for his analysis, and is generally followed by Sr M. Inviolata Barry, *St Augustine the orator, a study of the rhetorical qualities of St Augustine's Sermones ad Populum*, Washington, 1924 (Catholic University of America Patristic Studies, VI). Sr Barrys' table, pages 18–19, is useful for reference.

to force the sense into the form. Over-balancing, sophistic shows abundantly, invites false balance. It is the way not to precision, but to epigram.

Description of the several forms of balance distinguished by sophistic cannot go far without examples. The only sufficient examples must be sought in Greek and Latin; for the sophistic refinements often depend upon the recurrence of inflections or upon transpositions possible only in a language that is highly inflected. Modern languages depend so much less on inflection that they chime less readily and can transpose for symmetry sometimes only by more conspicuous violation of normal sentence order. Nevertheless some of the sophistic forms of balance, with other figures of words, can be exhibited accurately, and the character and effect of them all can be generally suggested, by English examples. Both the charm and the danger of the ancient figures are exemplified by De Quincey in what he called "impassioned prose."

De Quincey's encomium *Joan of Arc*, insistent in apostrophe, has one hyperbole that might have been uttered by Polemo or Scopelian. "The graves that had closed sixty years ago seemed to fly open in sympathy with a sorrow that echoed their own." His alliteration, too, often suggests the same anxiety to enhance. In the ecphrasis on the forest and fountain of Domrémy (paragraph 12), and again in the corresponding one toward the close, he is more delicate. On the other hand he uses with sophistic fondness the device of a carrying iteration. The encomium opens:

What is to be thought of *her?* What is to be thought of the poor shepherd girl from the hills and forests of Lorraine, that—like the Hebrew shepherd boy from the hills and forests of Judea—rose suddenly out of the quiet, out of the safety, out of the religious inspiration rooted deep in pastoral solitudes, to a station in the van of armies, and to the more perilous station at the right hand of kings? [79]

An even more marked example is the paragraph next to the last. Its opening and its close are as follows:

> The shepherd girl that had delivered France—she, from her dungeon, she, from her baiting at the stake, she, from her duel with fire, as she entered her last dream—saw Domrémy, saw the fountain of Domrémy, saw the pomp of forests in which her childhood had wandered. . . . For all, except this comfort from her farewell dream, she had died—died amidst the tears of ten thousand enemies—died amidst the drums and trumpets of armies—died amidst peals redoubling upon peals, volleys upon volleys, from the saluting clarions of martyrs.

There are few more striking examples of a value in iteration much sought by the sophists, its carrying on to a climax. Refrain carrying to climax is used at greater length, and with finer balances and allusions, in the twenty-eighth paragraph of *The English Mail-Coach*.

> The situation here contemplated exposes a dreadful ulcer, lurking far down in the depths of human nature. It is not that men generally are summoned to face such awful trials; but potentially, and in shadowy outline, such a trial is moving subterraneously in perhaps all men's natures. Upon the secret mirror of our dreams such a trial is darkly projected, perhaps, to every one of us. That dream so familiar to childhood, of meeting a lion, and, through languishing prostration in hope and the energies of hope, that constant sequel of lying down before the lion, publishes the secret frailty of human nature, reveals its deep-seated falsehood to itself, records its abysmal treachery. Perhaps not one of us escapes that dream; perhaps, as by some sorrowful doom of man, that dream repeats for every one of us, through every generation, the orig-

[79] Incidentally the comparison and contrast with David is carried out much in the manner of a σύγκρισις.

inal temptation in Eden.  Every one of us, in this dream, has a bait offered to the infirm places of his own individual will; once again a snare is presented for tempting him into captivity to a luxury of ruin; once again, as in aboriginal Paradise, the man falls by his own choice; again, by infinite iteration, the ancient earth groans to heaven, through her secret caves, over the weakness of her child: "Nature, from her seat, sighing through all her works," again "gives signs of woe that all is lost"; and again the counter sigh is repeated to the sorrowing heavens for the endless rebellion against God. It is not without probability that in the world of dreams every one of us ratifies for himself the original transgression. In dreams, perhaps under some secret conflict of the midnight sleeper, lighted up to the consciousness at the time, but darkened to the memory as soon as all is finished, each several child of our mysterious race completes for himself the treason of the aboriginal fall.

Whether De Quincey's reading of Greek may have dwelt too long on Isocrates is less important than that his devices of style spring from similar preoccupations.  The balances of Sir Thomas Browne, whose style he tells us that he studied, have none of this sophistic chiming and oral dilation.  De Quincey reminds us of the sophists because he is a sophist.  Sophistic was not extinguished with the Roman Empire; and De Quincey's style has marked family traits.  Thus it is easy to detach many suggestive examples of the Gorgian figures, balances used not for clearness, but generally for emotional emphasis and sometimes for emotional expansiveness.

No! for her voice was then silent;
no! for her feet were dust. *Joan of Arc*, 1.

The moments were numbered;
the strife was finished;
the vision was closed. *The English Mail-Coach*, last paragraph.

These are simple balances. "Which was heaven's vice-gerent, and which the creature of hell" marks the antithesis by reverse balance (*chiasmus*). The following are enhanced by alliteration:

> Flower nor bud, bell nor blossom, would ever bloom for her.
> *Joan of Arc*, 2.

> It was not wonderful that in such a haunted solitude, with such a haunted heart, Joanna should see angelic visions, and hear angelic voices. *Ibid.*, 10.

Nor does De Quincey's refinement stop there. The following balances have antithesis, alliteration, chiasmus, hyperbaton. The first varies its contrasting rhythms; the second leads up to the climax quoted above ("For all, except this comfort").

> Bishop of Beauvais! thy victim died in fire upon a scaffold—thou upon a down bed. But, for the departing minutes of life, both are oftentimes alike. At the farewell crisis, when the gates of death are opening, and flesh is resting from its struggles, oftentimes the tortured and the torturer have the same truce from carnal torment; both sink together into sleep; together both sometimes kindle into dreams.
> *Joan of Arc*, 30.

> The storm was weathered; the skirts even of that mighty storm were drawing off. The blood that she was to reckon for had been exacted; the tears that she was to shed in secret had been paid to the last. The hatred to herself in all eyes had been faced steadily, had been suffered, had been survived. And in her last fight upon the scaffold she had triumphed gloriously; victoriously she had tasted the stings of death.
> *Ibid.*, 31.

The sophistic marking of balance by rime (*homœoteleuton*), easy in Greek or Latin through the recurrence of inflectional endings, is so forced in English as to be very rare and in very bad taste.  Word-play, on the other hand, has always been one of the commonest devices for enhancing balance into epigram.  "Figures do not lie. The trouble with statistics is not that figures lie, but that liars figure."  Paronomasia is not sophistic; but, like other jingles, it attracted the sophists too much, as to-day it attracts Mr. Chesterton and Mr. Bernard Shaw.

### (4) *Clausula*

Balance is only one mode of rhythm.  The sophists were so preoccupied with it as often to risk monotony. For though they boasted of variety, they were too fond of certain rhythms, and too anxious to mark them, to achieve much flexibility.  Their idea of aptness as con- formity to an assumed character or occasion led them rather to cast a whole passage in one stylistic pattern.

Next to the perfecting of balances, they studied most attentively sentence cadences.[80]  Of *clausulæ*, as of other effects of style, they had a classified store for selection. Though we find it hard to follow them here, and impossible to translate their *clausulæ* in terms of English stress rhythms, we are not warranted in dismissing their studies of rhythm as idle.  True, they often overdid rhythm as they overdid technic in general; but English prose has rarely been in danger of this excess, and in particular it has been surest with those who have controlled cadence. Sentence emphasis is the clue to mastery of sentence movement.  Its greater masters, modern as well as ancient, have grasped this not only as logic, but as cadence.  The flaw in sophistic rhythms is their emptiness, the pursuit of them for themselves.  The difference between the

[80] For Aristotle, Cicero, and Quintilian on sentence rhythm, see ARP 27, 28, 59–61, 79.

sounding *clausula* of dilation and the solving *clausula* of
mounting emotion can be heard in the same English
sophist. All the following sentences conclude well for
the ear; but whereas the first two are prolonged by decorative additions, the last is an ascending period.

The boy rose to a splendour and a noonday prosperity, both
personal and public, that rang through the records of his
people, and became a by-word amongst his posterity for a
thousand years, until the sceptre was departing from Judah.
*Joan of Arc*, 1.

How if it should be some Marie Antoinette, the widowed
queen, coming forward on the scaffold, and presenting to the
morning air her head, turned grey by sorrow, daughter of
Cæsars kneeling down humbly to kiss the guillotine, as one
that worships death? *Ibid.*, 26.

Still in the confidence of children that tread without fear
every chamber in their father's house, and to whom no door
is closed, we, in that Sabbatic vision which sometimes is revealed for an hour upon nights like this, ascend with easy
steps from the sorrow-stricken fields of earth upwards to the
sandals of God. *The English Mail-Coach*, 32.

## (5) Vehemence

"Scopelian, when one of Polemo's pupils said that his
instrument was the drum, picked up the sneer with 'the
drum, indeed; but it is the shield of Ajax.'" [81] The passage is characteristic not only in allusion, figure, and
ingenuity, but in grandiloquence. It is itself a drum-beat;
and the sophistic harmony was fond of drums. The
stylistic effects most sought are those most marked.[82]
Scott's deprecatory "The big bow-wow strain I can do

[81] Philostratus, I. 21 (84).
[82] See Méridier's analysis (20) of the distinction made by Hermogenes
between true and false δεινότης.

myself" [83] has neither this aim nor this attitude.   He is
generously wishing that he could control the quiet sure-
ness of Jane Austen.   A sophist was complacent in his
own style.   He was anxious only that his bow-wow should
always be big, or, to return to Scopelian's more precise
figure, that the audience should always hear the drum.
It is the drum that marks sophistic.   Few of the devices
of style so carefully cultivated are sophistic in themselves.
What is sophistic is the use of them all, as from a classified
store, in excess and with insistent emphasis.   The sophistic style cannot be escaped.   It is always saying, Here is
style.

Such rhetoric is not worthless.   Some of its technical
skill is available for better ends.   But as other arts, to
survive and progress, must be more than technics, so
especially the art of words cannot go far without being
animated by power of conception.[84]   Technic is promotive
and educative only as it gives free course to motive and
vision.   As a system of education, therefore, sophistic
was hollow.   This is the issue raised by Plato; and he
is justified by history.   Sophistic could use its many devices only to exhibit skill, not to guide either the state or
the individual.   The only force that could revive rhetoric
with the lore older than this spent tradition was a new
motive.

[83] Diary, March 14, 1826.
[84] The classic formulation of this is the treatise *On the Sublime*, viii.

# CHAPTER II [1]

## ST AUGUSTINE ON PREACHING

### (*DE DOCTRINA CHRISTIANA*, IV)

With this elaborate pedagogical tradition a clean break is made by St Augustine. The fourth book of his *De doctrina christiana* [2] has historical significance in the early years of the fifth century out of all proportion to its size; for it begins rhetoric anew. It not only ignores sophistic; it goes back over centuries of the lore of personal triumph to the ancient idea of moving men to truth; and it gives to the vital counsels of Cicero a new emphasis for the urgent tasks of preaching the word of God.

Abstractly and in retrospect the very character of Christian preaching seems necessarily to reject sophistic. But at the time this seemed anything but inevitable.

---

[1] Reprinted by courteous permission from vol. XXII (April, 1925) of Proceedings of the (British) Classical Association, to which it was presented under the title *St Augustine and the rhetoric of Cicero*.

[2] In *Patrologia latina* and in the Vienna *Corpus scriptorum ecclesiasticorum latinorum;* reprinted, Missouri Lutheran Synod, St. Louis, 1882; translated (1) by Dods (M.), Edinburgh, 1872–1875 (reprinted in Schaff's Nicene and post-Nicene Fathers), (2) by Baker (W. J. V.) and Bickersteth (C.) in *Preaching and teaching according to St Augustine* (Book IV only, with *De catechizandis rudibus*), London, 1907, (3) by Sister Thérèse, S.N.D. (IV, with text and commentary), Washington, 1928.

To the references and abbreviations at the head of Chapter I add: Barry (Sister Inviolata), *St. Augustine the orator*, Washington, 1924 (in the Catholic University of America Patristic Studies, VI); and Christopher (J. P.), *S. Aureli Augustini . . . de catechizandis rudibus* translated with an introduction and commentary, Washington, 1926 (in the same series, VIII).

Sophistic was almost the only lore of public speaking then active. It dominated criticism and education. The Greek fathers Gregory of Nyssa and Gregory Nazianzen might expose its falsity of conception; but they could not escape it. It had brought them up. Its stylistic habits were ingrained in their expression. Augustine too had been brought up on sophistic. Nor could he escape it. Again and again his style rings with its tradition.[3] Not only had he learned it for good; he had taught it. He had been himself, in Plutarch's sense and Strabo's, a sophist. We must hasten to add that the great Christians of the fourth century, if they could not escape sophistic, at least redeemed it by curbing its extravagance and turning it to nobler uses. But Augustine did much more. He set about recovering for the new generation of Christian orators the true ancient rhetoric. He saw that for Christian preaching sophistic must not only be curbed; it must be supplanted. Against the background of his day his quiet, simple book, renouncing the balances and figures of his other works without renouncing their fervor, is seen to be a startling innovation.

Not the least striking trait of the innovation is its reserve. Augustine does not attack sophistic as the Gregorys do; he ignores it. In Chapter xxxi of Book II he had, indeed, mentioned it. Discussing there not style, but matter, he had contrasted the necessary training in argument with sophistic quibbling, and had then added, forecasting Book IV, that superfluous stylistic ornament also is sophistic.

> But training in argument on questions of all such kinds as are to be investigated and resolved in sacred literature is of the highest value; only we must beware of the lust for

[3] For detailed analysis, see Barry.

quarrelling, and of the puerile display of skill in disappointing
an opponent. . . . This sort of quibbling conclusion Scripture execrates, I think, in the text *Qui sophistice* [4] *loquitur
odibilis est.* Even though not quibbling, a speech seeking
verbal ornament beyond the bounds of responsibility to subject matter (*gravitas*) is called sophistic. II. xxxi.

But an uninformed modern reader of Book IV would
hardly be aware that sophistic existed. No denunciation
could be more scathing than this silence. In Augustine's
view of Christian preaching sophistic simply has no place.
A good debater, instead of parrying he counters. He
spends his time on his own case. A good teacher, he tells
his neophytes not what to avoid, but what to do. He
has so far renounced sophistic that he has no concern to
triumph. He wishes simply to teach sound rhetorical
doctrine. He achieves an extraordinary conciseness not
so much by compression as by undeviating straightfor-
wardness.

A reader familiar with the times, however, will be reminded of sophistic by many allusions. Single phrases
or sentences some of them, a few more extended, they all
serve to illuminate by contrast the true rhetoric.

All these things, when they are taught by rhetors, are
thought great, bought at a great price, sold with great boasting. Such boasting, I fear, I may suggest myself in speaking
so; but I had to answer those ill-educated men who think
that our authors are to be despised, not because they lack the
eloquence which such critics love too much, but because they
do not use it for display. vii.

[But an audience of Christian sobriety] will not be pleased
with that suave style in which though no wrong things are

[4] Even though the application of the text from *Ecclus.* xxxvii. 20
be questioned, the rebuke of sophistic display, whether in dialectic or
in style, is none the less clear.

said, right things slight and frail are adorned with foamy
circumlocution. xiv.

I think I have accomplished something not when I hear
them applauding, but when I see them weeping. xxiv.[5]

Display, inflation, thirst for applause—every reader of
Augustine's time would recognize in these allusions a
repudiation of sophistic.

For Augustine thinks that Christian preaching is to be
learned best from Christian preachers. As if in reply to
Julian's scornful "Let them elucidate their Matthew and
Luke," [6] he recommends not only for doctrine, but for
rhetoric, the Epistles, the Prophets, and the Fathers, and
proceeds to analyze their style. The analysis, though
based on the current Latin version, is generally transferable
to the Greek, since it is much simpler than the classification
set forth by sophistic. It exhibits sentence movement
simply in climax, period, balance—those devices which
are most easily appropriated and most useful. The general ancient counsels of aptness and variety are applied
specifically to preaching. As to cadence (*clausula*), Augustine dispenses with all subdivisions, and even makes
bold to assert that it must sometimes be sacrificed. Similarly omitting all classification of figures, he manages to
suggest in a few words what figures are for. In a word,
he shows how to learn from the Canon and the Fathers
the rhetoric that is vital to homiletic.

This rhetoric, not only simpler than sophistic, but quite
different in emphasis, is set forth in the terms of Cicero.
Augustine has gone back four and a half centuries to the
days before *declamatio*. The instruction that he draws

---

[5] Other allusions may be found in the passages quoted below from vi,
from xiv, and from xxv.

[6] βαδιζόντων εἰς τὰς τῶν Γαλιλαίων ἐκκλησίας ἐξηγησόμενοι Ματθαῖον καὶ
Λουκᾶν. Julian, *Epist.* 42, cited in Gibbon's twenty-third chapter.

from his analysis of Christian literature is planned upon the "instruct, win, move" (*docere, delectare, movere*) of *De oratore* and upon the corresponding three typical styles (*genus tenue—medium—grande*) of *Orator*.[7] Evidently Augustine had the greater Cicero, not the lesser that sufficed for the Middle Age. He neither quotes nor cites any other rhetorician; and though his doctrine of aptness and of variety is common throughout the older rhetoric, for this too he had no need to go beyond the master's two great works. Nor have any others been more persuasive as to imitation,[8] which is Augustine's controlling idea. This first Ciceronianism, too immediately aware of the perverted imitation of style taught by sophists to fall into the archaism and redundancy of later worship of Cicero, is a penetrative recovery of Cicero's larger meaning. Augustine's application of the three typical styles is more just and more practically distinct than Cicero's own. Would that all Ciceronians had been equally discerning!

TABULAR VIEW OF ST. AUGUSTINE'S *DE DOCTRINA CHRISTIANA* IV

A. For learning to preach, models are more fruitful
than rules   .   .   .   .   .   .          i–v
B. Eminent models are offered by the literature of
Christian eloquence   .   .   .   .   .          vi–viii
  1. Christian eloquence not merely comparable with pagan, but distinctive.
  2. Analysis of *Romans* v. especially of climax, period, clauses, etc.
  3. Analysis of *2 Corinth*. xi. 16, especially of variety.
  4. Analysis of *Amos* vi. especially of figures.

[7] ARP 51, 56. The reminiscences of Cicero are so numerous as to show a pervasive preoccupation. See J. B. Eskredge, *The influence of Cicero upon Augustine*, etc. (Chicago dissertation), 1912.

[8] E. g., *De oratore*, II. xxi. 88.

The fourth book of the *De doctrina christiana* is specifically linked by its proem to the preceding three as setting forth presentation (*modus proferendi*). Books I–III have dealt with study of the subject matter (*inventio*); Book IV is to deal with expression. Augustine thus makes the traditional fivefold division twofold. *Inventio*, which under sophistic had lapsed, he restores to its rightful place and gives it a new application to the exegesis of Scripture. Of the remaining four left to his second heading he discusses only style (*elocutio*). Delivery and memory are mentioned incidentally; plan is omitted. The omission is not negligent. The first chapter warns us not to expect a manual of rhetoric. Nevertheless a modern student cannot help wishing that so suggestive a treatise had both applied to preaching the ancient counsels as to plan and exhibited the New Testament in this aspect. Thus to analyze for imitation not only the style of the Pauline epistles, but their cogency of order, would doubtless have made the work unduly extensive. One hopes that seminarians of the fifth century were stimulated, and that seminarians of the twentieth century will be stimulated, by the example of the treatise itself to study *Romans* not only for appeal, but for cogency. Meantime Augustine's fourth book remains one of the most fruitful of all discussions of style in preaching.

Who dare say that the defenders of truth should be unarmed against falsehood? While the proponents of error know the art of winning an audience to good will, attention, and open mind,[9] shall the proponents of truth remain ignorant? While the [sophist] states facts concisely, clearly, plausibly,[10] shall the preacher state them so that they are tedious to hear, hard to understand, hard to believe? While the one attacks truth and insinuates falsehood by fallacious argument, shall the other have too little skill either to defend the true or to refute the false? Shall the one, stirring his hearers to error, urging them by the force of oratory, move

---

[9] The traditional maxim for the *exordium*, *reddere auditores benevolos, attentos, dociles*, as again in iv.

[10] The traditional maxim for the *narratio*.

them by terror, by pity, by joy, by encouragement, and the other slowly and coldly drowse for truth?   ii.

But to learn such skill from rules, he goes on, is the way rather for boys than for men who have immediately before them the urgent tasks of preaching.

> For eloquence will stick to such men, if they have the talent of keenness and ardor, more easily through their reading and hearing of the eloquent than through their following of the rules of eloquence.   Nor does the Church lack literature, even outside the Canon established in the citadel of authority, to imbue a capable man with its eloquence, even though his mind be not on the manner but on the matter, provided he add practise in writing, in dictating, finally also in composing orally [11] what he feels according to the rule of piety and faith. Besides, if such talent be lacking, either the rules of rhetoric will not be grasped, or if by great labor some few of them are partially grasped, they will be of no avail. . . . [Young preachers] must beware of letting slip what they have to say while they attend to saying it in good form.   iii.

They must, indeed, know the principles of adaptation (iv), and develop their expression as far as they can; but they will do so best by imitation.

> Whoever wishes to speak not only with wisdom, but with eloquence. . . .   I rather direct to read or hear the eloquent and to imitate them by practise than advise to spend his time on teachers of the art of rhetoric.   v.

Expressed in modern terms, Augustine's position is that rhetoric as a classified body of doctrine is properly an undergraduate study.   It is not the best approach for seminarians because its method is analytical.   The young preacher, needing rather promotion than revision, will advance more rapidly by imitation.

[11] Exercitatione sive scribendi, sive dictandi, postremo etiam dicendi. Cf. the close of xxi.

Starting from this principle, that the more fruitful study for learning to preach is imitation of Christian eloquence, Augustine proceeds to show (vi–viii) how distinctive is the eminence of such models and how repaying to analysis. His vindication should be pondered by those who still permit themselves to disparage without distinction the literary value of the New Testament, and by those who, granting poetic to Ambrose, remain unaware of his rhetoric.

At this point the question, perhaps, arises whether our authors, whose divinely inspired writings constitute for us a canon of most salutary authority, are to be called philosophers [12] only, or also orators. To me and to those who agree with what I am saying, the question is very easily answered. For where I comprehend them, nothing can seem to me either more philosophical or more eloquent. And all, I venture to say, who rightly comprehend what they speak, comprehend at the same time that they could not have spoken otherwise. For as there is an eloquence becoming to youth, another to age, nor can that be called eloquence which does not befit the character of the speaker, so there is an eloquence becoming to men most worthy of the highest authority and evidently inspired. Our authors have spoken with such eloquence. No other is becoming to them, nor theirs to others. For it is like themselves; and, the more it rejects display, the more it ranges above others not by inflation, but by cogency. Where on the other hand I do not comprehend them, though their eloquence is less apparent to me, I have no doubt that it is such as I find it where I do comprehend. The very obscurity of inspired and salutary utterances has been tinged with such eloquence that our minds should be stimulated not only in study [of their meaning], but in practise [of their art]. Indeed, if there were leisure, all the virtues and graces of eloquence with which those are inflated who put their style ahead of the style of our authors not by greatness, but by distension, could be exhibited in the sacred literature of those whom

[12] Thus I venture to translate *sapientes*, remembering the connotation of the word both for Augustine and for his master Cicero.

divine Providence has sent to instruct us and to draw us from this corrupt world to the world of happiness. But what delights me more than I can say in their eloquence is not what it has in common with pagan orators and poets. What I rather admire, what fills me with amazement, is that the eloquence which we hear around us has so been used, as it were through another eloquence of their own, as to be neither deficient nor conspicuous. For it should be neither condemned nor displayed; and they would have seemed to do the one if they shunned it, the other if it became noticeable. Even in those places where perhaps it is noticeable to experts, such is the message that the words in which it is expressed seem not to be sought by the speaker, but to subserve that message naturally, as if one saw philosophy issuing from her own home in the heart of the philosopher, and eloquence following as an inseparable servant even when not called.[13]  vi.

The vindication of an eloquence distinctly Christian has the more weight because its doctrine of form and substance echoes from Cicero the best ancient tradition. The older tradition had in Augustine's time been so overlaid that he could do no better service to rhetoric than to recall it. In fact, Christian eloquence redeemed public speaking by reviving the true persuasion.

The insistence on the Ciceronian doctrine that style is not separable has a bearing more than historical. Not only for Augustine's time, but for any time, the truism must be reasserted. His iteration is more than preoccupation with Cicero, more than repudiation of sophistic. It springs from the cardinal importance of the truism for homiletic. In the pulpit the sophistic heresy of art for art's sake becomes intolerable.

[13] So toward the close "The Christian preacher prefers to appeal rather with matter than with manner, and thinks neither that anything is said better which is not said more truly, nor that the teacher must serve words, but words the teacher." xxviii.

Augustine's next step (vii) is to support his general claims for Christian eloquence, and to show how it may be studied, by analyzing briefly three typical passages. In the first, *Romans* v. 3–5, he analyzes prose rhythm under the familiar heads of classical sentence movement (*compositio*): phrases and subordinate clauses (*cæsa*), co-ordinate clauses (*membra*), period (*circuitus*), climax (*gradatio*), adding the equivalent Greek terms.[14]

### RHYTHMICAL ANALYSIS OF *ROMANS* V. 3, 4, 5

(1) καυχώμεθα ἐν ταῖς θλίψεσιν,  (1) Gloriamur in tribulationibus,

(2) εἰδότες ὅτι ἡ θλῖψις ὑπομονὴν κατεργάζεται,  (2) scientes quod tribulatio patientiam operatur,

(3) ἡ δὲ ὑπομονὴ δοκιμήν,  (3) patientiam autem probationem,

(4) ἡ δὲ δοκιμὴ ἐλπίδα,  (4) probatio vero spem,

(5) ἡ δὲ ἐλπὶς οὐ καταισχύνει,  (5) spes autem non confundit,

(6) ὅτι ἡ ἀγάπη τοῦ θεοῦ ἐκκέχυται ἐν ταῖς καρδίαις ἡμῶν  (6) quia caritas Dei diffusa est in cordibus nostris,

(7) διὰ πνεύματος ἁγίου τοῦ δοθέντος ἡμῖν  (7) per Spiritum sanctum qui datus est nobis.

The passage is short enough, and the sentence movement simple enough, to be grasped readily. Its balance is striking without being monotonous, and is reinforced by a linking iteration that leads to a climax.[15] He is a wise teacher who begins with an instance so memorable. It must have seized even more quickly a generation familiar with both the terms and the method.

[14] For this sort of analysis see ARP, Chapter v, and the terms in the index. For the more elaborate sophistical analysis see Méridier, Guignet, and the other studies of Greek fathers cited above. To suggest such further study, the Greek of the first example and the King James English of the third have been set beside. St Augustine not only confines himself to the Latin version, but disclaims competence in Greek style.

[15] The linking iteration is characteristic of climax as practised by sophistic.

The next example, 2 *Corinthians* xi. 16–31, shows the same sentence devices carried through a much longer reach, and is therefore used both to reinforce the first and to add the importance of rhythmical variety. The counsel of variety, though a commonplace of the older rhetoric, had especial point by contrast with the sophistic fondness for trimming and prolonging balances. Incidental to the exhibition of variety is a reminder of aptness; and the analysis concludes:

> Finally all this breathless passage is closed with a period of two members. . . . But how after this impetus the brief statement interposed comes to rest, and rests the reader, how apt it is and how charming, can hardly be said.  vii.

The analysis of the third example, *Amos* vi. 1–6, leads the study to longer and more sustained rhythmical reaches. Lest it seem the more difficult in the more figurative version of the Septuagint, Augustine quotes it "as translated from the Hebrew into Latin style through the interpretation of the priest Jerome, expert in both languages."

### ANALYSIS OF *AMOS* VI. 1–6

(1) Woe to them that are at ease in Zion and trust in the mountains of Samaria, which are named chief of the nations, to whom the house of Israel came!

(2) Pass ye unto Calneh, and see; and from thence go ye to Hamath the great: then go down to Gath of the Philistines: be they better than these kingdoms? or their border greater than your border?

(1) Væ qui opulenti estis in Sion et confiditis in monte Samariæ, optimates, capita populorum, ingredientes pompatice domum Israel;

(2) transite in Chalanne et videte, et ite inde in Emath magnam, et descendite in Geth Palæstinorum, et ad optima quæque regna horum, si latior terminus eorum termino vestro est:

(3) Ye that put away the evil day, and cause the seat of violence to come near;

(4) That lie upon beds of ivory, and stretch themselves upon their couches, and eat the lambs out of the flock, and the calves out of the midst of the stall;

(5) That chant to the sound of the viol,

(6) and invent to themselves instruments of musick, like David; that drink wine in bowls, and anoint themselves with the chief ointments:

(7) but they are not grieved for the affliction of Joseph.

(3) qui separati estis in diem malum, et adpropinquatis solio iniquitatis;

(4) qui dormitis in lectis eburneis, et lascivitis in stratis vestris; qui comeditis agnum de grege, et vitulos de medio armenti;

(5) qui canitis ad vocem psalterii:

(6) sicut David putaverunt se habere vasa cantici, bibentes in phialis vinum, et optimo unguento delibuti;

(7) et nihil patiebantur super contritione Joseph.

Much more urgent, leaping to attack, rising, prolonging, varying, subsiding to a pregnant close, the prophecy widens the conception of rhythmical range. Marking the rhythms briefly, Augustine uses it also to show the oratorical force of figures.[16] Thus a few pages of analysis are made to yield wide and definite suggestion. This, perhaps, is their outstanding merit; while they show the student what to look for, they invite him to go on for himself. But the pedagogical achievement does not stop there. The professor of rhetoric has seen that rhetorical analysis must be simplified, and that it must be made progressive. Where else shall we find so much drawn from three analyses? The first reduces the complicated lore of rhythm

[16] Chapter xxix of Book III relegates the study of figures to *grammatica;* but there also Augustine reminds his readers that figures, without regard to books or teaching, are a natural expression of the imaginative impulse.

to its essentials. The second, reinforcing and extending these, dwells upon aptness as a corrective of rhetorical zeal, and as a constructive principle. The third, quoting rhythms still more urgent with emotion, passes to the emotional value of concrete words. To bring the over-classified lore of sophistic back to the simplicity of Aristotle was a service not only to homiletic, but to all rhetoric. A greater service was to substitute for the static and formalized pedagogy of the day a vital order. Augustine had been doubtless a popular professor; Christianity made him a great teacher.

Pedagogically, therefore, even his incidental definitions are worth noticing. That the function of grammar is traditionally to impart correctness of speech (iii) is used to support the contention that even this elementary skill comes best in fact from imitation. The period (vii) is defined so as to throw the emphasis on delivery. Its "clauses are suspended by the speaker's voice until it is concluded at the end." Therefore it "cannot have fewer than two clauses." So he points out in the passage above from *Amos* that the rhythm is available for delivery (*in potestate pronuntiantis*) either as a series of six or as three pairs, and that the latter is more beautiful. So he suggests limiting analysis to give room for oral interpretation.

> This same passage which we have set as an example can be used to show other things relevant to the rules of eloquence. But a good hearer is not so much instructed by discussion in detail as he is kindled by ardent delivery. vii.

The next and longest section (ix–xix) is based on Cicero's "inform, please, move" (*docere, delectare, movere*). Distinguishing each of these tasks clearly, Augustine is at the same time careful to unite them, by progressively iterative transitions, in the single and constant task of persuasion. In exposition (*docere*) clearness may demand the use of popular expressions. What avails correctness in a diction that is not understood?

> He who teaches will rather avoid all words that do not teach. If he can find correct words that are understood, he will choose those; if he cannot, whether because they do not exist or because they do not occur to him at the time, he will use even words that are less correct, provided only the thing itself be taught and learned correctly. ix.

The correctness (*integritas*) of diction boasted by the sophists, and carried by them even to the pedantry of archaism, is here faced squarely. The assertion that it must sometimes be sacrificed, the making of clearness absolutely paramount, is the bolder at a time when Christian preaching was not yet recognized as having secure command of elegance. Unmistakable clearness, Augustine goes on, is so much more important in preaching than in discussions permitting question and answer that the speaker must be quick to help unspoken difficulties.

> For a crowd eager to grasp will show by its movement whether it has understood; and until it has given this signal the subject must be turned over and over by various ways of expressing it—a resource beyond the power of those who deliver speeches written out and memorized.[17] x.

No warrant here, he adds (xi), for dilation beyond the demands of clearness, but good warrant for making instruction pleasant and appealing in order to hold attention. Passing thus to the two other tasks of oratory, he quotes (xii) Cicero's "to instruct is of necessity, to please

[17] As to this form of *memoria* see also Chapter xxix.

is for interest, to move is for victory." [18]   The three
are then both carefully distinguished and shown to be a
sort of geometrical progression.  The first is first of necessity.  It must be mastered; but it is rarely sufficient.
To supply the lack, the second demands more rhetoric by
demanding further adaptation to the audience; but it
too must remain insufficient.  So the third task, to move,
is not merely the third item in a classification; it is the
final stage in a progress.  That progress is increasingly
emotional.  The last stage demands not only all the
rhetoric of the preceding, but also the art of vivid imagery [19]
and of urgent application.  So Augustine arrives at one
of those linking summaries which constitute almost a
refrain.

> Therefore the eloquence of the Church, when it seeks to
> have something done, must not only explain to instruct and
> please to hold, but also move to win.  xiii.

The next chapter (xiv) warns against resting in the
second stage. [20]   To make the pleasing of the audience an
end in itself is the typical vice of sophistic.  If preaching
tolerates it, "the time will come when they will not endure
sound doctrine; but after their own lusts shall they heap
to themselves teachers, having itching ears."  Augustine

[18] Docere necessitatis est, delectare suavitatis, flectere victoriæ.
*Or.* xxi. 69, with *docere* for the original *probare.*

[19] Ante oculos dicendo constituis (xii) recalls the *De sublimitate*, and
behind that the *Rhetoric* of Aristotle.  Its immediate source is doubtless
Cicero.

[20] The warning is repeated where Augustine is gathering the three
tasks into the final and constant idea of persuasion: "But that which
is handled in the way of charm . . . is not to be made an end in itself
(xxv) . . . nor does it seek merely to please."  Nothing is more admirable in Augustine's exposition than this expert linking of his chain
of progress.

quotes, not these words of St. Paul, but Jeremiah, and rises to denunciation of mere pleasing. "Far from us be that madness." One of Cyprian's rare descriptive passages is adduced to show how "the wholesomeness of Christian preaching has recalled his diction from [sophistic] redundancy and held it to a graver eloquence of less display." As the ultimate objection to the sophistic ideal is moral, so is the preacher's ultimate resource. Since his strength is derived from a source deeper than human skill, his best preparation is prayer. Augustine is not above enforcing this reminder by playing upon the words *orare*, *orator, oratio*. Nevertheless human skill is to be cultivated. Prayer itself proves the folly (xvi) of making no other preparation. He who abjures human lore of preaching because God gives us our messages might equally well abjure prayer because God knows us and our needs. The Pauline counsels specify how Timothy should preach. As God heals through doctors and medicines, so he gives the gospel to men by men and through man.

The transition (xvii) to the final task of moving men to action is another full and explicit iteration of all three, and at the same time a preparation for the next section on the corresponding three typical styles. Since the subject matter of preaching is always great, at least in implication (xviii), does it not always demand a great style? No; for a great matter (xix) may at the time rather demand exposition; and this in turn demands a restrained style. Again, a great matter may at the time rather demand praise or blame; and here enters the second task of so adapting the style as to win sympathy.

But when something ought to be done, and we are talking to those who ought to do it and will not, then the great subject is to be expressed greatly and in such wise as to bend

their minds. . . . What subject is greater than God? Is
it therefore not a subject for instruction? Or how can any
one expounding the unity of the Trinity do it except by con-
fining himself to exposition, that so difficult a distinction may
as far as is possible be understood? Is ornament demanded
here, and not rather argument? [21] Is there here something that
the audience is to be moved to do, and not rather something
that it is to be taught to learn? Again, when God is praised
in himself or in his works, what a vision of beautiful and
splendid diction rises before any one praising as well as he
can him whom no one praises aright and no one fails to praise
in some way or other! But if God be not worshipped, or if
idols be worshipped with him or even in his stead, whether
dæmons or any other created being, then to meet so great an
evil, and from this evil to save men, the preaching too must
be great. xix.


Augustine has passed (xvii–xix) from Cicero's three
tasks of oratory to his three typical styles by applying to
the preacher Cicero's definition of the orator: "He, then,
shall be called eloquent who can speak small things quietly,
larger things proportionally, great things greatly." [22]
Thus the three styles are *genus submissum* (or *tenue*), *genus
temperatum* (or *medium*), and *genus grande*. As in Cicero,
these correspond to *docere*, *delectare*, *movere*, and the second is connected with panegyric.

Augustine now proceeds to exemplify the first style (xx)
from *Galatians* as calling for skill in reasoning and for a
memory trained to bring in objections and difficulties
where they can best be met. This debater's memory is
precisely the ancient *memoria*, the fifth of the traditional
parts of rhetoric. It seems to have fallen into abeyance
under sophistic. What the sophists boasted was verbal

[21] Numquid hic ornamenta et non documenta quæruntur?
[22] *Orator*, xxix. 101.

memory, which Augustine merely mentions in his appendix as something quite different.[23]

The same chapter (xx) exemplifies the second, or median style from *Timothy* and *Romans* as having the charm of aptness. Here Augustine confronts squarely the sophistic habit of making rhythmical beauty paramount and the pagan disparagement of Christian style. Some one may find the cadence of *Romans* xiii. 14 defective. Certainly it would soothe the ear more rhythmically if the verb came last.

But a graver translator has preferred to keep the usual word-order [and, he might have added, the logical emphasis]. How this sounds in the Greek used by the apostle they may see whose expertness in that language goes so far. To me at least, the word-order, which is the same as in our version, does not seem there either to run rhythmically. Indeed, the stylistic beauty (*ornatum*) which consists of rhythmical cadences is defective, we must confess, in our authors. Whether this is due to our versions, or whether, as I incline to think, the authors deliberately avoided these occasions for applause, I do not venture to affirm, since I confess that I do not know. But this I know, that anyone who shall make their cadences regular in the same rhythms—and this is done very easily by shifting certain words that have equal force of meaning in the new order—will recognize that these inspired men lacked none of those things which he learned as great matters in the schools of the grammarians or rhetors. Moreover, he will discover many sorts of diction of so great beauty as to be beautiful even in our customary language, much more in theirs, and never found in the literature with which [the sophists] are inflated. But we must beware lest the addition of rhythm detract from the weight of inspired and grave sentences. Most learned Jerome does not carry over into his translation the musical skill in which rhythm is learned most

[23] Cf. xxix with the quotation from x above; and see *memoria* in the index to ARP.

fully, though our prophets did not lack even that, as he shows in the Hebrew meters of some of them; [and he gave this up] in order to keep truth to their words. . . . As in my own style, so far as I think I may do so modestly, I do not neglect rhythmical cadences,[24] so in our authors they please me the more because I find them there so rarely.  xx.

The third, or great style, whether it be elegant or not, has for its distinguishing quality the force of emotional appeal.  The instances are from 2 *Corinthians* vi and *Romans* viii.  *Romans* is a long epistle, not a sermon. Though it was read aloud, of course, it is essentially a treatise, a philosophy of history.  It is largely expository and argumentative.  Since it is addressed primarily to reflection and reason, its main artistic reliance is on cogency of order.  But even here presentation does not remain purely logical.  For persuasion it must rise also emotionally.  As we read in *Acts* xvii the outline of the apostle's Areopagus speech, we discern beyond the logical chain of propositions an expanding conception of the Lifegiver.  Who can doubt that the style too, as in *Romans*, rose to *grande?*  The traditional doctrine of the peroration, easily as it may be abused, is only the expression in rhetoric of the audience's final demand and the speaker's final answer.  That demand and that answer are emotional.

Adding *Galatians* iv, Augustine says of it:

Although the whole epistle, except in the elegant last part, is written in the plain style, nevertheless the apostle inserts a certain passage of such moving force that it must be called great even though it has no such embellishments as those just cited. . . .  Is there here either antithesis, or subordination for climax, or rhythm in phrase, clause, or period?  None the less for that there is no cooling of the great emotion with which we feel the style to glow.  xx.

[24] For his cadences, see Barry.

After quoting without further comment examples from Cyprian and Ambrose, Augustine shows (xxii, xxiii) the need of variety. More even than other forms of oratory, preaching seems to suffer from a stylistic level. No one of the three styles, least of all the third, can effectively be prolonged; the change from style to style gives relief; and subordination of what might be heightened may enhance the emotion of what must be. What must be heightened is what is to rouse the audience to action. So the test of achievement in the third style is not applause, but tears and change of life (xxiv). So also the end of all eloquence, in whatever style, is persuasion (xxv).

> In the restrained style the orator persuades of truth. In the great style he persuades to action. In the elegant style is he to persuade himself that he is speaking beautifully? With such an end what have we to do? Let them seek it who glory in language, who display themselves in panegyrics and such exercises, in which the hearer is neither to be instructed nor to be moved to any action, but merely to be pleased. But let us judge this end by another end. xxv.

Thus Augustine is more explicit than Cicero in showing that the three typical styles are but three ways (xxvi) of achieving a single end, even as the three corresponding tasks, though one of them absorbs attention at a time, are but three aspects of the single task. Nor can persuasion dispense with a means beyond art, the appeal of the speaker's life [25] (xxvii). Though the Church speaks not merely through a man, but through his office, persuasion needs for full effect his whole influence. Because his life is without shame, the preacher speaks not shamelessly (xxviii), not only with restraint and charm, but with power, to win obedience to the truth.

[25] Aristotle, *Rhetoric* I. ii.

The historical significance of the *De doctrina christiana*, important as it is, should not obscure its value as a contribution to homiletic. The first homiletic, though one of the briefest, remains one of the most suggestive. It omits no essential; while it reminds us of the general principles of rhetoric, it emphasizes those applications to preaching which are distinctive; and it proceeds pedagogically. Though the *doctrina* of the title refers strictly to exposition, and this is amplified and iterated as a constant necessity, Augustine includes specifically and from the start both charm and appeal, and concludes by showing emotional appeal to be the final stage of the comprehensive task of persuasion. Homiletic is an application of rhetoric long established as permanent, consistent, and in both materials and conditions fairly constant. That it is also comprehensive, demanding all three typical styles, including argument in its exposition, winning sympathy in order to urge action, varying its art [26] while holding to its single aim, is most suggestively established here in its first great monument.

Not only does Augustine forbid the arid and the tedious, not only does he insist on emotional appeal; he also vindicates for Christian eloquence the importance of charm. This was the more delicate because charm was both abused by contemporary sophists and still suspected by contemporary preachers. Augustine presents it at once frankly and with just discrimination. To make it an

[26] That the Scriptures enter all the three fields of oratory indicated by Aristotle in *Rhetoric* I. iii, is suggested by the language of a passage in Augustine's third book: *Non autem adserit* [*scriptura*] *nisi catholicam fidem rebus præteritis et futuris et præsentibus. Præteritorum narratio est, futurorum prænuntiatio, præsentium demonstratio*, III. x. For the last two words suggest in the context ἐπιδεικτικός, and hence δικανικός for the first phrase of the sentence and συμβουλευτικός for the second, according to the Aristotelian division. If so, Augustine has not followed Cicero's reducing of the fields to two (ARP 47, 53).

end in itself, he is careful to show, is indeed sophistic; but to ignore it is to forget that preaching is a form of the oratory of occasion.[27]  The Areopagus speech of St. Paul,[28] though it is only summarized in *Acts* xvii, is evidently occasional, and has clear indications of that adaptation to win sympathy which is Augustine's interpretation of Cicero's *delectare*.  The speech on occasion, favorite form of oratory in Augustine's time, had been conventionalized to the point of recipe.  The recipes, though he knew them all, Augustine simply ignores; the field he redeems.  He shows Christian preaching how to cultivate it for real harvest.  History has shown no other direction of rhetoric to be so peculiarly homiletic.

Already Christian eloquence had reached conspicuous achievement in panegyric and more widely in the field of occasional oratory.  The pagan sophist must look to his laurels.  But these very triumphs had brought the danger of lapsing into too familiar conventions.  What in pagan oratory might be no worse than pretty or merely exciting, in Christian oratory would be meretricious.  To hold his difficult course, the preacher, as Augustine reminds him again and again, must at every moment steer for his message.  He must never deviate.  Though sophistic lost its dominance centuries ago, it has never been quite dead, and it always besets preaching.  Therefore a constant concern of homiletic is to exorcise it by a valid rhetoric; and no book has ever revealed this more succintly, more practically, or more suggestively than the *De doctrina christiana*.

[27] In the passage quoted above from Chapter xix, and in other places there are clear references to occasional oratory.

[28] See Norden, *Agnostos Theos, Untersuchungen zur Formengeschichte religiöser Rede*, Leipzig, 1913.  But this speech, to judge from the indications of *Acts* xvii, was as original in plan as in idea.

# CHAPTER III

## THE LAST ROMAN SCHOOLS AND THE COMPENDS (FIFTH TO SEVENTH CENTURIES)

### REFERENCES AND ABBREVIATIONS

ARP    Baldwin (C. S.), *Ancient rhetoric and poetic*, New York, 1924.

Boissier    Boissier (G.), *La fin du paganisme*, Paris, 1891, 2 vols.

CSE    *Corpus scriptorum ecclesiasticorum latinorum*, Vienna.

Glover    Glover (T. R.), *Life and letters in the fourth century*, Cambridge, 1901.

   Haarhoff (T.), *The Schools of Gaul*, Oxford, 1920.

Halm    Halm (K.), *Rhetores latini minores*, Leipzig, 1863.

Keil    Keil (H.), *Grammatici latini*, Leipzig, 1870–1880, 7 vols.

Labriolle    Labriolle (P. de), *Histoire de la littérature latine chrétienne*, Paris, 1920.

Manacorda    Manacorda (G.), *Storia della scuola in Italia*, vol. I, *Il medio evo*, Milan, 1913 (2 parts in separate volumes).

Manitius    Manitius (M.), *Geschichte der lateinischen Literatur des Mittelalters*, Munich, 1911, 2 vols. (in Iwan von Mueller's Handbuch der klassischen Alterthums-Wissenschaft, IX. ii).

Monceaux    Monceaux (P.), *Histoire de la littérature latine chrétienne*, Paris, 1924 (Collection Payot).

MGH    *Monumenta Germaniæ historica* (cited by page of the appropriate volume).

PL    Migne, *Patrologia latina* (cited by volume and column).

Pichon    Pichon (R.), *Études sur l'histoire de la littérature latine dans les Gaules*, Paris (vol. 1), 1906.

Roger    Roger (M.), *L'enseignement des lettres classiques d'Ausone à Alcuin*, Paris, 1905.

## A. The Schools of Gaul

The need of the Church and of the Roman world for such forward counsels, the tenacity of sophistic among reactionaries and conformists, are amply exhibited by the last days of Roman Gaul. In the ancient province a cultivated leisure class, living in the twilight of a great past outworn and doomed, cherished the sophistic conception of elegance and the sophistic habit of education by rhetoric [1] as symbols of their Romanism. Provincials, they were sometimes more Catholic than the Pope; their writers and teachers would not risk being thought less literary than the capital of the world. But in fact Gaul of the fifth and sixth centuries was more Roman than Rome. It was the last territory of the ancient world.

### 1. Ausonius [2]

"The poetical fame of Ausonius," says Gibbon in a contemptuous postscript to a footnote,[3] "condemns the taste of his age." Whether or not Gibbon took too seriously the fourth-century habit in compliments, Ausonius at least reflects the taste of his age. Fading, therefore, long since to the shadow of a shade, hardly any longer an author, he is nevertheless an important document. Such fame as he may have had once is hardly even considered.

[1] ARP 90, 94, 96, 101.

[2] About 310–393; *grammaticus* and *rhetor* at Bordeaux, which was the greatest, perhaps, of the schools of Gaul.

Editions: Schenkl, Berlin (MGH, Auctores antiquissimi, V. ii), 1883; Peiper, Leipzig (Teubner), 1886; H. G. E. White, London & New York (Loeb series, 2 vols.), 1919–1921, with translation (used in this section), introduction, notes, and select bibliography; full bibliography in Marie José Byrne, *Prolegomena to an edition of the works of Ausonius*, New York, 1916.

[3] III. xxvii, last sentence of footnote 1.

Like the rhetors celebrated by Philostratus,[4] like those at Bordeaux whom he himself commemorates, he has ceased to be even a name. He is a collection of trivial fourth-century verses recalled only because they incidentally record contemporary preoccupations. Expert in the metric and the diction that he taught as *grammaticus*, he could turn a stanza on anything—on a city, a Cæsar, or a sage. Only he preferred topics that came handily in series: the order of the daily round or of noble cities, twelve Cæsars, seven sages, a roster of Trojan heroes. These are topics for Latin verses in school. Many of his poems are evidently, and others probably, school exercises. This in itself, the acceptance of themes as literature, is eloquent of the literary habit of sophistic.

For the work of Ausonius may be summed up as *declamatio*.[5] Its being mainly in verse hardly modifies its character beyond emphasizing *sententiæ*. The conciseness imposed upon some of his work by his predilection for epigrams is the balance and word-play of rhetoric, not the focus of poetry. That poetic was rhetoric applied to verse Ausonius was not the man to doubt. His praise of the Bordeaux rhetors for both alike [6] increases the probability that the two were in fact alike; and this is confirmed by his own verse. It is confirmed also by the appearance of several local celebrities now as *grammatici*, now as *rhetores*. The function of the former was traditionally both to teach elegant correctness and to expound the poets; of the latter, to train directly for oratory.

---

[4] Chapter I. B. 1.

[5] See Chapter I. B. 2, especially a. (1); and for the earlier *declamatio*, ARP 87–101.

[6] Palmæ forensis et camenarum decus. V. ii. 7.
Facundum doctumque virum, seu lege metrorum
Condita seu prosis solveret orsa modis. *Ibid*. iii. 3.

But the two functions thus distinguished by Quintilian seem in fourth-century Bordeaux to have been combined, or at least to have been exercised successively by the same person.[7]

Evidently the sophistic conception of style as dilation by decoration and literary allusion was still prevalent. To be literary was to dilate. Of this Ausonius sometimes shows a humorous awareness.

> I might tell thee outright; but for more pleasure I will talk in mazes and with speech drawn out get full enjoyment.[8]

But the humor of his address to his stenographer does not make the description of composing the less true to the habit of his time.

> I ponder works of generous scope; and thick and fast like hail the words tumble off my tongue. . . . I declaim, as now, at greatest speed, talking in circles round my theme. . . .[9]

The typical *declamator* appears in Exuperius, "majestic in gait and in great words." [10] Literary tags, especially in panegyric, come thick.

[7] Grammatice ad Scaurum atque Probum, promptissime rhetor. *Ibid.* xx. 7.

Grammatici in studio vel rhetoris aut in utroque. *Ibid.* xxv. 3.

Nos [i. e. Ausonius] ad grammaticen studium convertimus et mox Rhetorices etiam, quod satis, attigimus. I. i. 15.

[8] Possem absolute dicere,
Sed dulcius circumloquar
Diuque fando perfruar. Lines 7–9 of the poem in *Epist.* XII.

[9] Ego volvo libros uberes,
Instarque densæ grandinis
Torrente lingua perstrepo.

. . . . . . . .

Cum maxime nunc proloquor
Circumloquentis ambitu.

II. vii. 7.

[10] Incessu gravis et verbis ingentibus. V. xvii. 2.

> Who like you can approach the charm of Æsop, the sophis-
> tic perorations of Isocrates, the arguments of Demosthenes,
> the Tullian richness, or the felicity of our own Maro? [11]

The speeches and poems of these men, and of Ausonius
himself,[12] are typically occasional.  Their ideal of aptness
is sought by following the recipes for encomium.  Literature, long fixed, was to be attained by expert conformity.

Evidently too these encomiasts still had their reward.[13]  As official spokesmen they were appointed to
public office.  Ausonius himself rose with the fortunes of
Gratian.  From being his tutor he mounted by the steps
of *comes* and *quæstor* to be in 378 *præfectus Galliarum.*
Such a position dispenses a man from writing for posterity, and effectually prevents him from questioning the
permanence of an order of life and thought already spent.
Until the Roman world fell apart, it was satisfyingly en-
closed in the schools of Bordeaux.

## 2. Sidonius Apollinaris

Cherishing of the past, rhetorical education, obsession
of style—all this is embodied in the Roman prefect and
Christian bishop Sidonius Apollinaris.[14]  His letters and

---

[11] Quis ita Æsopi venustatem, quis sophisticas Isocratis conclusiones,
quis ad enthymemata Demosthenis aut opulentiam Tullianam aut
proprietatem nostri Maronis accedat?  *Epist.* ii.

[12] His most considerable prose piece is the *Gratiarum actio ad Gratia-
num.*

[13] Mox schola et auditor multus prætextaque pubes
　　Grammatici nomen divitiasque dedit.  V. xviii. 7.

[14] About 430–484; Bishop of Auvergne, 471; educated at Lyon.
Editions: Mohr, Leipzig (Teubner), 1895, and MGH.
Biography by Chaix (l'Abbé L.-A.), *St. Sidoine Apollinaire et son
siècle,* 2 vols., Paris, 1867; translation, with introduction and notes, by
Dalton (O. M.), Oxford, 1915.
For his influence see Manitius, Boissier, Roger.  It was doubtless

poems, current through the middle age as models of style, are consistently in the modes of sophistic. Commemorations, addresses of welcome or congratulation, above all panegyrics, they follow the tradition of *declamatio;* [15] and their allusions abundantly exemplify both the school practise of his day and the literary preoccupations.

Sending to Perpetuus his discourse at Bourges, Sidonius apologizes for its defects of style.

> Neither rhetorical division, nor oratorical urgency, nor the figures of *grammatica* have contributed to it appropriate ornament and virtuosity. For I did not give myself the pleasure of adjusting, after the habit of those who file their perorations, the weight of narrative, or the figures of poetry, or the sparks of the cadences practised in school. [16]

A long letter to Domitius, describing villa life in detail most interesting to the historian, contains a lively passage of description.

> How pleasant the sound of crickets chorusing at midday, frogs prating as twilight broods, swans and geese trumpeting their matings at night, cocks in concert crowing untimely!

So far Sidonius sounds as if he had a respite from style. The picturesqueness seems to spring from observation.

enhanced, if not revived, by *dictamen*, for which see below, Chaper VIII. Alain de Lille puts him beside Quintilian and Symmachus among "rhetoricæ auctores alii" (*Anticlaudianus*, III. iii). John of Salisbury refers to him in *Metalogicus* (PL. 199: 831 A, 865 D) and *Policraticus* (see the index to Webb's ed.).

[15] See above, Chapter I, B. 2. a. and ARP, IV. ii. A.

[16] Cui non rhetorica partitio, non oratoriæ minæ, non grammaticales figuræ congruentem decorem disciplinamque suppeditaverunt. Neque enim illic, ut exacte perorantibus mos est, aut pondera historica aut poetica schemata scintillasve controversialium clausularum libuit aptari. VII. ix. 1–2. The words *disciplina* and *controversialis* allude to the schools; *clausula*, to the study of closing cadences. Cf. VIII. iii. 3.

But habit is too strong to let him either stop there or dispense with literary allusions. He goes on:

> ominous ravens thrice saluting the ruddy torch of rising Aurora, and at daybreak Philomela whispering among the bushes, Progne chirping among the posts. To this symphony you may add the shepherds' reed music, which in rivalry of songs by night the unsleeping Tityri of our mountains practise among herds whose bells echo through the cropped pastures. But all the various melodies of voices and of songs will the more caressingly lure your sleep.[17]

Balance has never been pursued more anxiously. The teaching of Probus is praised for handing down:

> the loftiness of the epic poet and the wit of the comic, the lyrist's tunefulness and the orator's declamation, the historian's truth and the satirist's figure, the grammarian's regularity and the panegyrist's plausibility, the sophist's seriousness and the epigrammatist's liberty, the commentator's lucidity and the barrister's obscurity.[18]

The letter of welcome to Constans has a similar series of balanced contrasts.

[17] Hic iam quam volupe auribus insonare cicadas meridie concrepantes, ranas crepusculo incumbente blaterantes, cygnos atque anseres concubia nocte clangentes, intempesta gallos gallinacios concinentes, oscines corvos voce triplicata puniceam surgentis Auroræ facem consalutantes, diluculo autem Philomelam inter frutices sibilantem, Prognen inter asseres minurientem! Cui concentui licebit adiungas fistulæ septiforis armentalem Camenam, quam sæpe nocturnis carminum certaminibus insomnes nostrorum montium Tityri exercent inter greges tinnibulatos per depasta buceta reboantes. Quæ tamen varia vocum cantuumque modulamina profundius confovendo sopori tuo lenocinabuntur. II. ii. 14.

[18] Si quid heroicus arduum comicus lepidum, lyricus cantilenosum orator declamatorium, historicus verum satiricus figuratum, grammaticus regulare panegyrista plausibile, sophista serium epigrammatista lascivum, commentator lucidum iurisconsultus obscurum. IV. i. 2.

For days there was in each mind the paradox that your person, with the weight of age and the frailty of illness, lofty in rank and venerable in religion, with mind bent only on giving pleasure, broke so many bars, so many difficulties in the way of your coming: the journey's length, the shortness of the days; the snows' abundance, the poverty of provisions; deserts' wideness, narrowness of lodgings; in the roads chasms miry with the wetting of showers or rutted with the dryness of frosts; besides, either banks rough with rocks or rivers frozen slippery, hills rugged to climb or valleys scoured by the frequency of landslides. Through all these discomforts, because you sought not your private comfort, you brought back the public love.[19]

Such contrasts in series are sometimes made even more artificial by word-play.

> He responds as Pythagoras, discriminates as Socrates;
> evolves as Plato, involves as Aristotle;
> as Æschines soothes, as Demosthenes provokes;
> as Hortensius is in spring, as Cethegus in summer;
> hurries as Curio, lingers as Fabius;
> simulates as Crassus, dissimulates as Cæsar;
> has the suasion of Cato, the dissuasion of Appius, the persuasion of Cicero.[20]

[19] Obversatur etenim per dies mentibus singulorum quod persona ætate gravis infirmitate fragilis, nobilitate sublimis religione venerabilis, solius dilectionis obtentu abrupisti tot repagula, tot obiectas veniendi difficultates, itinerum videlicet longitudinem brevitatem dierum, nivium copiam penuriam pabulorum, latitudines solitudinum angustias mansionum, viarum voragines aut umore imbrium putres aut frigorum siccitate tribulosas; ad hoc aut aggeres saxis asperos aut fluvios gelu lubricos aut colles ascensu salebrosos aut valles lapsuum assiduitate derasas; per quæ omnia incommoda, quia non privatum commodum requirebas, amorem publicum rettulisti. III. ii. 3.

[20] Sentit ut Pythagoras dividit ut Socrates, explicat ut Platon implicat ut Aristoteles, ut Æschines blanditur ut Demosthenes irascitur, vernat ut Hortensius æstuat ut Cethegus, incitat ut Curio moratur ut Fabius, simulat ut Crassus dissimulat ut Cæsar, suadet ut Cato dissuadet ut Appius persuadet ut Tullius. IV. iii. 6. This is immediately followed by another series balancing the Fathers. Similar is the

This is the "pomp of Roman speech." [21]

> The aristocracy bent on discarding the scales of Celtic speech
> was indoctrinated now with the style of oratory, now with
> the modes of the Muses. [22]

Sidonius feels himself the representative of a great tradition. [23]    That tradition was generally ceremonious regard
for usage and a certain anxiety to exhibit culture by literary allusions and by command of the technic of style.
Generally, that is, the literary tradition of Gaul was sophistic.    Specifically it was *declamatio*. [24]    The school tradition celebrated by the elder Seneca, and made by him and
by the *declamatores* after him the exemplar of oratory, is
seen in the pages of Sidonius equally to monopolize the
schools and the platforms of Gaul.    This is rhetoric, and
there is no other.    It is fully displayed in the long letters
to Lupus [25] and to Claudianus Mamertius, [26] not only
in conclusive evidence of detail, but as a conception that
is pervasive because it is exclusive.    As in the letter above
to Probus, there is frequent use of the words *declamatio,
declamare, controversia*, etc.

> I remember that your boyhood was competently taught in
> the liberal schools; and I have satisfied myself that you often
> declaimed before an orator ardently and eloquently. [27]

invective in the letter to Thaumastus: iudicanda dictant, dictata
convellunt; adtrahunt litigaturos, protrahunt audiendos; trahunt ad-
dictos, retrahunt transigentes.  V. vii. 2.  So 3 and 5 in the same letter,
and 14 in the letter to Faustus, IX. ix.

[21] Sermonis pompa Romani.  IV. xvii. 2.

[22] Sermonis Celtici squamam depositura nobilitas nunc oratorio stilo,
nunc etiam Camenalibus modis imbuebatur.  III. iii. 2.

[23] Cui tamen sermonicari Latialiter cordi est.  IV. iii. 1.

[24] For sophistic, see Chapter I. B.; for *declamatio*, ARP 87-101.

[25] VIII. xi.                                    [26] IV. iii.

[27] Atqui pueritiam tuam competenter scholis liberalibus memini
imbutam et sæpenumero acriter eloquenterque declamasse coram oratore satis habeo compertum.  V. v. 2.

Now blows the epos of tragedies, now soothes gay comedy,
now flame satires and the oratory of debates on tyrants.[28]

He would vary prosopopœia according to the quality of
person, time, and place, and that in words not ordinary, but
thought out as great and beautiful. In debate assignments
[he was] strong and muscular.[29]

The most extended reference is the letter to Remigius
about the collection which had originally, perhaps, been
his desk-book at Rheims, and which had been revised
and copied for imitation.

A certain Auvergnat on his way to Belgium . . . filched
from your scribe or bookseller, whether you will or not, at a
price very large, though doubtless inadequate, the first draft
of your *Declamationes*. When he came back to us . . . I took
care to have them all copied. It was the universal opinion
that few such can now be spoken. For few, if any, bring to
such assignments even an approximately equal . . . aptness
in examples, authority in evidence; propriety in epithets, ur-
banity in figures; force in argument, weight in appeal; flow
of words, stroke of cadence. The structure, moreover, is strong
and firm, the very clever transitions woven with pauses that
cannot be resolved. Nor is it the less smooth, light, every
way rounded, and such as aptly to speed a reader's tongue
without making it stumble, or stutter over rough combinations,
or twist into the chamber of the palate. Finally all is liquid,
ductile, as when the finger runs without a scratch over a sur-

[28] Et nunc inflat epos tragœdiarum,
   Nunc comœdia temperat iocosa,
   Nunc flammant satiræ et tyrannicarum
   Declamatio controversiarum. VIII. xi. 3 (lines 26-29 of the en-
closed poem). Note that *declamatio* is here recognized as a literary
form.

[29] Ethicam dictionem pro personæ temporis loci qualitate variabat,
idque non verbis qualibuscumque, sed grandibus pulchris elucubratis.
In materia controversiali fortis et lacertosus. VIII. xi. 6. For prosopopœia see ARP, index, and Emporius in Halm, 561. For the use of
χαρακτήρ by Sidonius himself see the stock parasite in III. 13.

face of crystal or onyx. . . . There is no man now living
whose discourse your skill cannot easily outdistance and
surpass.[30]

Interesting as is the glimpse of the transmission and
traffic of books, it is quite overshadowed by the significance of such a collection. Evidently it was regarded
not only as a storehouse for imitation in school, but as a
work of literature. Similarly were collected early in the
sixth century the *declamationes* of Ennodius, Bishop of
Pavia.[31] The letter of Sidonius specifies, moreover,
those literary excellences which were sought alike in
teaching and in professional practise. What he means,
for instance, by firmness of *structura* is not cogency of
composition, but smoothness of style; and revision to this
end involves meticulous adjustment to tongue and ear.

[30] Quidam ab Arvernis Belgicam petens . . . postquam Remos
advenerat, scribam tuum sive bybliopolam pretio fors fuat officine
demeritum copiosissimo velis nolis declamationum tuarum schedio
emunxit. Qui redux nobis . . . curæ mihi . . . cuncta transcribere.
Omnium assensu pronuntiatum pauca nunc posse similia dictari. Etenim rarus aut nullus est cui meditaturo par affatim assistat dispositio
per causas, positio per litteras, compositio per syllabas; ad hoc opor-
tunitas in exemplis fides in testimoniis, proprietas in epithetis urbanitas
in figuris, virtus in argumentis pondus in sensibus, flumen in verbis
fulmen in clausulis. Structura vero fortis et firma coniunctionumque
perfacetarum nexa cæsuris insolubilibus, sed nec hinc minus lubrica et
levis ac modis omnibus erotundata quæque lectoris linguam inoffensam
decenter expediat, ne salebrosas passa iuncturas per cameram palati
volutata balbutiat; tota denique liquida prorsus et ductilis, veluti cum
crystallinas crustas aut onychitinas non impacto digitus ungue per-
labitur . . . non extat ad præsens vivi hominis oratio quam peritia
tua non sine labore transgredi queat ac supervadere. IX. vii. 1–4.

[31] 474–521; works in MGH and in CSE. The subjects of the *controversiæ* are from the usual stock; e. g.: In abdicatum qui patrem
necavit. In novercam quæ, cum marito privigni odia suadere non
posset, utrique venenum porrexit. In eum qui patri suo cibum sub-
traxit. His panegyric of Theodoric was delivered about 507.

A collection of *declamationes* was current under the name of Quintilian.

Other references show equally that the exercises of the schools were carried, as in the earlier imperial centuries, into public speaking and literature. The orator's achievement is not the persuasion of his fellow men; it is his own virtuosity.

> He spoke with order, weight, ardor, with great keenness, greater fluency, greatest skill.[32]

The climax of the praise is his *disciplina*. *Declamatio* teaches boys to develop an outline at length.

> So providing boys' themes with pieces to weave in, they understood that for youth expression consists rather in working out what is brief than in cutting down what is extended.[33]

But this is no less the achievement of the finished orator.

> So a great orator, if he essays an affair that is small, shows the more convincingly that his talent is large.[34]

The habit of dilation is carried into poetry. Is it not sanctioned by Horace?

> But if any one suggests that a poem so diffuse is to be blamed for exceeding the sparseness of epigram, he exposes himself as not having read the Etruscan baths, nor the Hercules of Sorrento, nor the locks of Flavius Earinus, nor the Tibur of Vopiscus, nor anything at all from the *Silvæ* of our Papinius; for all these ecphrases are not confined by the poet thus prejudged within the narrow bounds of distichs or quatrains. Rather as Horace, though a lyrist, teaches in his volume on the

----

[32] Dixit disposite graviter ardenter, magna acrimonia maiore facundia maxima disciplina. VIII. vi. 6.

[33] Sic adulescentum declamatiunculas pannis textilibus comparantes intellegebant eloquia iuvenum laboriosius brevia produci quam porrecta succidi. I. iv. 3.

[34] Sic et magnus orator, si negotium aggrediatur angustum, tunc amplum plausibilius manifestat ingenium. VIII. x. 3.

poetic art, he appropriately extends the matter he has undertaken by many, yes, and purple, patches from the common store.[35]

Horace is so misapplied because *declamatio* tends to merge poetic in rhetoric.[36] The poems of Sidonius differ from his prose in little but verse. Three of the longer ones are panegyrics; all are occasional; all show the same habits of style. The literary tags used to sum up the teaching of Probus [37] assign to poetry a kind of appropriateness which belongs to rhetoric. Sapaudus owes his literary reputation to his training in *declamatio* under Pragmatius, who used to "break the rhetoric benches" with a peroration.[38]

In short, the rhetoric and the poetic of fifth-century Gaul are seen in Sidonius to be following faithfully the sophistic tradition of *declamatio*. He knows all its recipes. From correctness conceived as archaism and elegance conceived as ceremony, through dilation by the Gorgian figures and by literary allusion, he is constant to the sophistic ideal of expert impressiveness.[39]  Augus-

[35] Si quis autem carmen prolixius eatenus duxerit esse culpandum quod epigrammatis excesserit paucitatem, istum liquido patet neque balneas Etrusci neque Herculem Surrentinum neque comas Flavii Earini neque Tibur Vopisci neque omnino quicquam de Papinii nostri silvulis lectitasse quas omnes descriptiones vir ille præiudicatissimus non distichorum aut tetrastichorum stringit angustiis, sed potius, ut lyricus Flaccus in artis poeticæ volumine præcipit, multis isdemque purpureis locorum communium pannis semel inchoatas materias decenter extendit.  Carmen XXII. 6 (prose epilogue).  The allusions are to Statius.  For the rhetorical cast of the *Ars poetica* itself, which is constantly quoted throughout the middle age, see ARP 245.

[36] ARP 100.

[37] Above, page 80.

[38] Nam debetur ab eo percopiosus litteris honor.  Hunc olim perorantem et rhetorica sedilia plausibili oratione frangentem. V. x. 2.

[39] See Chapter I. B. 2. a (3) and d (5).

tine had been the pioneer of the Christian future of rhetoric; Sidonius was a complacent reactionary of its decadent Roman past.

## 3. Textbooks

### a. GRAMMATICA AND DIALECTICA

In this period were written the Latin grammars author-itative throughout the middle age, those of Donatus and Priscian.[40] The former, used generally in two parts as an introductory manual, was so current, indeed, as to become common property and to reduce its author's name to a common noun.[41] Priscian came to be used as a second book.[42]

The ancient tradition including in the scope of *gram-matica* not only meters and some of the figures of speech,

[40] Both are in Keil, with two other grammarians of this period who seem to have had considerable currency, Fortunatianus and Victorinus. The names have occasioned some confusion. Keil calls the grammarian Atilius Fortunatianus, and distinguishes Maximus from Marius Vic-torinus. The latter has been regarded as the author of the widespread commentary on Cicero's *De inventione;* but Halm assigns this to Q. Fabius Laurentius Victorinus. The *Ars rhetorica* is generally assigned to Q. Chirius (or Curius) Fortunatianus. But the determination of persons is of little moment here. The works are all of this period and all current in the middle age.

Keil includes also the compends of Cassiodorus and Bede. His notes are valuable especially for locating correspondences and medieval use.

W. J. Chase's translation of the *Ars Minor* of Donatus reprints Keil's text and has an historical introduction (Univ. of Wisconsin Studies No. 36, Madison, 1926).

[41] E. g., in 1445 Panicali da Cingoli gave his *Flores grammaticæ* the sub-title *Donatellus;* and by then the English name for an elementary grammar was *donet.* Pecock uses the word, in the sense of primer, as a title for his handbook of morals.

[42] Priscian includes a translation of the elementary exercises of Her-mogenes (see above, Chapter I. B. 2. c).

but also the study of poetry through *prælectiones*,[43] is
recognized in several of the preliminary definitions.

> What is grammatica? The lore of interpreting poets and
> story-writers and the theory of writing and speaking cor-
> rectly.[44]

St Augustine refers to this induction into poetry as
habitual.

> Without some training in poetic you would not dare to at-
> tempt the function of grammarian. Asper, Cornutus, Donatus,
> and others without number are required, that any poet whose
> verse appears to seek the applause of the theater may be
> understood.[45]

For such teaching the favorite author was Vergil; the
favorite authority, the "Ars Poetica" of Horace.

From this period come also the standard medieval
textbooks of logic. The logic of Aristotle was mediated
to the whole middle age by the translations and com-
mentaries of Boethius. "He translated the Εἰσαγωγή of
Porphyry and the whole of Aristotle's *Organon*. He
wrote a double commentary on the Εἰσαγωγή and com-
mentaries on the *Categories* and the *De interpretatione*
of Aristotle, and on the *Topica* of Cicero. He also com-

[43] For *prælectio* see the index to ARP.
[44] Scientia interpretandi poetas atque historicos et recte scribendi
loquendique ratio.  Marius Victorinus, Keil VI. 188.  The same words
are found in Audax, Keil VII. 321; and substantially equivalent definitions in Servius on Donatus, Keil IV. 486; Asper, Keil V. 547; Dosi-
theus, Keil VII. 376.  Priscian's examples are mainly from poetry.
[45] Nulla imbutus poetica disciplina Terentianum Maurum sine magis-
tro adtingere non auderes. Asper, Cornutus, Donatus et alii innume-
rabiles requiruntur, ut quilibet poeta possit intellegi cuius carmina et
theatri plausus uiderentur captare.  *De utilitate credendi*, 17 (CSE,
S. August. vol. 6, 21. 25).
For later use of *prælectio* see the index to the present volume.

posed original treatises on the categorical and hypothetical syllogism, on Division and on Topical Differences." [46]
The medieval order of studies was: Porphyry's Introduction, the Categories, Interpretation, Syllogisms, Topics.

## b. RHETORICA

Quintilian was known to both Ausonius and Sidonius,
and doubtless generally to the rhetors of Gaul.[47] But
his work is addressed rather to teachers than to pupils.
More available for the schools was Cicero's youthful
compend *De inventione*. The early and continued use
of this is widely attested. Its contents are as follows:

*Book I*. i–vi scope, function, and relations of rhetoric; vii
its five parts; viii–xiii investigation (with *status* and *quæstio*);
xiv the parts of a speech; xv–xviii exordium; xix–xxi statement
of facts; xxii–xxiii division; xxiv–xli proof (with adaptation to
the persons and the case, and with the kinds of argument);
xlii–li rebuttal; lii–lv conclusion (with appeal to feeling).

*Book II* (expansion of I in pleading). i–iv introductory review, the Aristotelian type and the Isocratean type, the fields
of oratory, the determining of the issue (*status*); v–xvi issues
of fact (*status coniecturalis*) in relation to motive, person, evidence; xvii–xx issues of terms (*status definitivus*); xxi–xxxvi
issues involving more general considerations (*status generalis*);
xxxvii–xxxix profit (*præmium*) in relation to advantages in
themselves and to the person concerned, in general and with
reference to particular opportunities; xl–li disputed written
evidence; lii typical subjects of deliberative oratory; liii–lvii
honor, utility, necessity; lix encomium and invective.

[46] E. K. Rand's introduction to the Loeb *Boethius*, page ix.
    For the commented translation of the Analytics see Manitius I. 30;
for the resumption of the Analytics at Chartres, the section on John
of Salisbury's *Metalogicus* below, Chapter VI. C.
    [47] The history of the use of Quintilian is set forth in Fierville's edi-
tion of Book I (Paris, 1890). This has been reviewed and extended by
F. H. Colson in the introduction to his edition of Book I (Cambridge
University Press, 1924).

To this was added in general medieval use the *Rhetorica ad Herennium*, probably by Cornificius, but thought throughout the middle age to be Cicero's.[48] When this began its medieval vogue is difficult to determine. Since it is not mentioned by either Cassidorus or Isidore, it may not have been generally current before the Carolingian revival. Meantime the fourth century added, besides the commentary of Victorinus on the *De inventione*, the compendious catechism of Fortunatianus; [49] and the fifth century, the longer work of Julius Victor.[50]

## B. The Trivium in Compends of the Seven Liberal Arts

The relations of rhetoric to grammar on the one hand and to logic on the other must be considered in determining its function at any period of its history. The ancient *grammatica*, for instance, included at its best not only metric and some of the figures of speech, but a certain induction into poetry. Its field of composition was pretty definitely marked out in traditional elementary exercises.[51]  *Rhetorica* as conceived by Aristotle or by Cicero concerns itself of necessity with logic. With Quintilian not only proof and refutation, but that esti-

---

[48] The assignment to Cicero is as early as Jerome.  See Cornificius in Pauly-Wissowa.

Halm shows very little use of the *Rhetorica ad Herennium* during this period.  There is a full synopsis of this work in Wilkins's introduction to his edition of Cicero's *De oratore* (Oxford, 1893), page 56.  Faral shows in comparative tables that it is the source of the lists of figures in the medieval *artes poeticæ* (*Les arts poétiques du xiie et du xiiie siècle*, Paris, 1924), pages 52–54.

[49] *Ars rhetorica.*  It is praised by Cassiodorus.

[50] Julius Victor makes far the largest use of Quintilian.

[51] See Quintilian I. ix, and compare this and his II. iv with the exercises of Hermogenes above in Chapter I. B. 2. c.

mate of the whole line of argument for which he provides systematic analysis under the traditional head of *status*, are largely logical. Logic may be used for analysis without presentation. This, indeed, is abstractly its proper function, and indicates its relation to philosophy; but in actual practise, or in a given system of teaching, its relation may be rather to rhetoric, and conversely rhetoric, by yielding its field of *inventio* to logic, may be reduced to the study of style.

So the estimate of the rhetoric or the poetic of a given period must consider the contemporary view of the whole Trivium. This obligation is obvious where the Trivium is conceived as a unified group of studies; but it is no less important where the three studies are pursued without explicit relations. Indeed, one of the measures of effective functioning in any one of them is the fostering or the ignoring of their relations. A survey of the history of the Trivium in this aspect distinguishes the lingering of ancient educational traditions in the fourth and fifth centuries and their lapse in the sixth and seventh, then that increasing range of cathedral and especially monastic schools which received its historic impulse from Charlemagne. The great monastic schools come to their prime in the eleventh and twelfth centuries; in the thirteenth they yield to the universities. The dominant member of the Trivium in the earliest of these periods is the *rhetorica* of decadent antiquity; from the seventh into the tenth it is *grammatica;* from the eleventh on, it is *dialectica*.

## 1. Martianus Capella

The division of studies into seven liberal arts came to the middle age from Varro's *Disciplina* largely through

Martianus Capella.[52]    His *Marriage of Philology and Mercury* was widely current for centuries.   The allegory implied by his title is carried out in ornate verse and prose through two books.   In the other seven books allegory is reduced to the conventional description introducing each of the arts in turn with appropriate costume, symbols, and speech.   Thus the work divides sharply into a grandiose allegorical prelude of two books, with a similar prelude to each following book, and a sober, concise, pedestrian compend of *grammatica* (III), *dialectica* (IV), *rhetorica* (V), *geometria* (VI), *arithmetica* (VII), *astronomia* (VIII), and *harmonia* (IX).

*Grammatica*, the first of the language studies, claims its ancient territory, including the exposition of poetry. The subsequent treatment is conventional and incomplete.[53]

The Lady *Dialectica* is more assertive.

> I claim jurisdiction over whatsoever the other arts utter; for evidently neither *Grammatica* herself, whom your ears have approved, nor the second sister, renowned for the skill of rich utterance, nor she who reduces to line varieties of forms . . . can be explained without my theories.   Nay, in my domain and jurisdiction abide six norms, to which the other disciplines conform.   For the first concerns naming; the second, defining; the third, affirming; the fourth, concluding;

[52] The best edition of the *De nuptiis Philologiæ et Mercurii* is Dick's, Leipzig (Teubner), 1925.

[53] "Officium uero meum tunc fuerat docte scribere legereque; nunc etiam illud accessit ut meum sit erudite intellegere probareque."   III. 230.

Many of the usual topics are merely mentioned.   Marked agreement with this book is shown by Priscian, Diomedes, and Charisius; considerable agreement, by Marius Victorinus and Maximus Victorinus. See Dick's references *ad loc*.   It is used by Cassiodorus especially, and also by Isidore.   Bede's use may be through Maximus Victorinus.

the fifth, judging, which bears upon the interpretation of poets and their poems; the sixth, diction, which is adapted to rhetors.[54]

The fifth *norma* annexes that part of *grammatica* which was most remote from logic; the sixth trenches on *rhetorica*. The actual extension of *dialectica* into the ancient domain of rhetoric during the high middle age [55] may have found here some warrant. But Martianus himself does not include these items either in the prospectus immediately following or in the subsequent compend.[56]

*Rhetorica* enters Book V with such pomp and noise as to frighten some of the minor symbols.

> Interea sonuere tubæ raucusque per æthram
> Cantus, et ignoto cælum clangore remugit:
> Turbati expauere dii . . . .

But while the crowd of gods terrestrial was thus disconcerted, behold a woman of loftiest stature and great assurance, with countenance of radiant splendor, made her solemn entry. Helmeted and crowned with royal majesty, she held ready for defense or for attack weapons that gleamed with the flash of lightning. Beneath her armor the vesture draped Romanwise about her shoulders glittered with the various light of

---

[54] Meique prorsum iuris esse quicquid Artes ceteræ proloquuntur. Nam neque ipsam quam aures uestræ probauere, Grammaticam, neque alteram opimi oris præcluem facultate, uel illam formarum diuersa radio ac puluere lineantem sine meis posse rationibus explicari quis dubitat? Quippe in dicione mea iureque consistunt sex normæ, quis constant ceteræ disciplinæ. Nam prima est de loquendo, secunda de eloquendo, tertia de proloquendo, quarta de proloquiorum summa, quinta de iudicando, quæ pertinet ad iudicationem poetarum et carminum, sexta de dictione, quæ dicenda rhetoribus commodata est. IV. 336–338.

[55] See below, Chapter VI.

[56] The compend uses Cicero and Quintilian, Aristotle's *Topics*, but above all Aristotle's *Categories*. See Dick *ad loc.*

all *figuræ*, all *schemata;* and she was cinctured with most precious *colores* for jewels. The clatter of her weapons as she moved was as if thunder in the crash of a cloud aflame broke with leaping echoes. Nay, it seemed as if, like Jove, she herself could hurl the thunderbolt. For as queen in control of all things she has shown power to move men whither she pleased, or whence, to bow them to tears, to incite them to rage, to transform the mien and feeling as well of cities as of embattled armies and all the hosts of the peoples.[57]

After this fanfare *Rhetorica* settles down to drill. Though the predilection for *declamatio* transpires now and then even in this, the compend covers all five parts of the ancient program, and gives to *inventio* and *dispositio* more than twice the space granted to *elocutio*. There is room not only for character and the feelings ($\H\theta\eta$ and $\pi\acute{a}\theta\eta$), but for *status* and analysis of types of argument. Most of the examples are from Cicero. The rhetoric that Martianus preaches is quite distinct from that which he practises. Its proportions are those of the better ancient tradition. It does not even dilate

---

[57] Sed dum talibus perturbatur multa terrestrium plebs deorum, ecce quædam sublimissimi corporis ac fiduciæ grandioris, uultus etiam decore luculenta femina insignis ingreditur, cui galeatus uertex ac regali caput maiestate sertatum, arma in manibus, quibus se uel communire solita uel aduersarios uulnerare, fulminea quadam coruscatione renidebant. Subarmalis autem uestis illi peplo quodam circa humeros inuoluto Latiariter tegebatur, quod omnium figurarum lumine uariatum cunctorum schemata præferebat, pectus autem exquisitissimis gemmarum coloribus subbalteatum. Hæc cum in progressu arma concusserat, uelut fulgoreæ nubis fragore colliso bombis dissultantibus fracta diceres crepitare tonitrua; denique creditum quod instar Iouis eadem posset etiam fulmina iaculari. Nam ueluti potens rerum omnium regina et impellere quo uellet et unde uellet deducere, et in lacrimas flectere et in rabiem concitare, et in alios etiam uultus sensusque conuertere tam urbes quam exercitus prœliantes, quæcumque poterat agmina populorum. V. 426-27.

on *colores*.[58]  For all the rodomontade with which it is introduced, the ancient program is still comprehended.

## 2. Cassiodorus

The survey included by the monk Cassiodorus [59] in his *Institutiones* is hardly more than an enumeration. The seven arts are not considered in their larger aspects; and the Trivium is merely sketched. *Rhetorica*, after being summarily distinguished from *dialectica* and divided into its typical considerations and objects, is hastened through the parts of a speech into the emotions. Then defining it anew and dividing it into its traditional five parts, Cassiodorus enumerates *status*, reverts to the parts of a speech, cites Quintilian and Fortunatianus, and classifies arguments. The meager summary is not even clear. Nevertheless the influence of Cassiodorus in carrying forward the idea of the seven arts is attested by frequent reference.[60]

## 3. Isidore

In the seventh century, and for centuries afterward, a chief purveyor of the lore of the seven arts was the *Etymologiæ*, or *Origines*, of the Spanish bishop Isidore

[58] The sections on figures (523–555) are taken almost verbatim from Aquila Romanus. The preceding sections on *clausula* are based on Cicero. *Color* is used also (e. g. 471) as by Seneca Rhetor (ARP 98). The frequent agreement of Fortunatianus with this book is shown by Dick *ad loc.* In comparison with the medieval vogue of the whole work, the influence of this book seems small. John of Salisbury's *Metalogicus*, for instance, citing Martianus a dozen times, never refers to it.

[59] About 490–575.

[60] He is used, for instance, by Remi of Auxerre, and appears in the tenth-century library of Chartres (Clerval, 21). For other references see Manitius and Manacorda. The *Institutiones* are in MGH.

of Seville.[61]  The work is an aggregation of summaries, not only of the seven arts, which occupy only three books of the twenty, but of medicine, law, holy writ, history, the hierarchy celestial and terrestrial, zoölogy, geography, metallurgy, agriculture, and crafts.   Though it has no single guiding scheme, its brief chapters are grouped under headings fairly convenient for reference. It is a guide-book, rendering its first service when books were few and hard to get, and long continuing in vogue. In the thirteenth century Vincent of Beauvais,[62] under-taking more systematically a compend hardly less com-prehensive, his vast *Speculum*, transferred to it whole passages from Isidore.

Isidore appealed to the earlier middle age as a medi-ator not only of manifold lore, but especially of ancient tradition.

> The disciplines of the liberal arts are seven: first *grammatica*, i. e., skill in speaking; second, *rhetorica*, for the splendor and abundance of its eloquence deemed necessary especially in political questions; [63] third, *dialectica*, surnamed *logica*, which by subtlest arguments distinguishes the true from the false. I. ii.

Isidore's *grammatica* has the usual contents, including *schemata*, *tropi*, and metric.[64]   *Fabula* and *historia* reflect

---

[61] About 570–636; Bishop of Seville about 600.   *Etymologiœ* edited by Lindsay, Oxford, 1910.

To the usual general books of reference add Labriolle.

[62] See below, Chapter VI. D. 2.

[63] If Isidore's concision seems to involve him here in a non-sequitur, he is not the first, nor the last, to force the rhetoric that he heard under the rhetoric that he read.

[64] *Rhythmus* is defined vaguely as follows: "Huic adhæret rythmus, qui non est certo fine moderatus, sed tamen rationabiliter ordinatis pedibus currit; qui Latine nihil aliud quam numerus dicitur."   I. xxxix.

the ancient elementary exercises.[65]  His second book contains both *rhetorica* and *dialectica*.

" *Rhetorica* is the lore of speaking well on political questions to persuade [men of what is] just and good.  It is called by a Greek name ἀπὸ τοῦ ῥητορίζειν, i. e., from wealth of speech. For in Greek speech is called ῥῆσις, and an orator ῥήτωρ. *Rhetorica*, moreover, is connected with *grammatica*.  In the one we learn the lore of speaking correctly; in the other we perceive how to utter what we have learned.  II. i.

" This discipline was invented by the Greeks—Gorgias, Aristotle, Hermagoras, and transferred to Latin by Cicero and Quintilian. . . .  The perfect knowledge of this discipline makes the orator.  ii.

" The orator, then, is a good man skilled in speaking: good, i. e., in nature, breeding, education; skilled in speaking, i. e., in expert eloquence.  This consists of five parts (*inventio, dispositio, elocutio, memoria, pronuntiatio*) and in the function of persuading." . . . iii.

In the same summary fashion Isidore treats the three fields, *status*, simple or compound proposition, the four parts of a speech, the five sorts of cases, syllogisms, law, apothegm, proof and disproof, the school exercises *prosopopœia* and *ethopœia*, questions abstract and concrete.  The remainder of the section, somewhat more than one third, is devoted to *elocutio:* the three styles, the division into phrase, clause, and period, the typical faults of phrasing, and the figures.  As to the last he makes a distinction lost on his later medieval readers.  "Of these most have been noted above under *grammatica* as the *schemata* of Donatus.  Therefore only those should find place here which hardly occur in a poem, but freely in a speech."  II. xxi.

" *Dialectica* is the discipline designed for the discussion of cases (ad disserendas causas).  It is that species of philosophy which is called *logica*, i. e., the theory controlling definition, investigation and discussion.  For it teaches in many forms of questions how by discussion the true may be distinguished from the false. . . .  Therefore *dialectica* follows the dis-

[65] See the indexes to ARP and to this volume.

cipline of *rhetorica* because they have many things in common." II. xxii.

To distinguish the two, Isidore quotes from Varro a metaphor often quoted from Zeno; *dialectica* is the closed fist, *rhetorica* the open hand. The one is the more acute in discussing, the other the more fluent in imparting; the one is of the schools, the other of the forum; the one for scholars, the other for the people. xxiii.

A chapter (xxiv) inserted here groups all the seven arts under *philosophia*, which is threefold: [66] (1) *naturalis* (*physica*), (2) *moralis* (*ethica*), (3) *rationalis* (*logica*), "in which is discussed how in the causes of things or in the conduct of life truth itself may be sought." Isidore does not, however, pursue this larger scope of *logica*. Though he cites additionally Plato's use of the term to include both *dialectica* and *rhetorica*, he goes on to enumerate other divisions of philosophy, and then (xxv) to the usual items of *dialectica* as presented by Boethius: Porphyry's Introduction, Aristotle's Categories, interpretation, syllogisms, division and definition, topics.

The program for the Trivium keeps in the main the ancient proportions. Some usurpation of composition by *dialectica*, some leaning of *rhetorica* toward dilation and decoration, may be read into it; but each of the two studies clearly has its own function, and work enough for serious occupation. As in other parts of his aggregation, Isidore makes his summary of the Trivium a list of studies, not a group. He attempts no unified plan. Therefore his putting of *rhetorica* before instead of after *dialectica* should hardly be pressed for significance.

[66] For divisions of *philosophia*, see below, Chapter VI.

# CHAPTER IV

## POETIC, OLD AND NEW
## (FIFTH TO SEVENTH CENTURIES)

### REFERENCES AND ABBREVIATIONS

AH      Dreves and Blume, *Analecta hymnica medii œvi*, Leipzig, vol. 1, 1886; vol. 53, 1911.

ARP      Baldwin (C. S.), *Ancient rhetoric and poetic*, New York, 1924.

Britt      Britt (the Rev. Matthew, O. S. B.), *The hymns of the Breviary and Missal*, New York, 1922.

CSE      *Corpus scriptorum ecclesiasticorum latinorum*, Vienna.

Keil      Keil (H.), *Grammatici latini*, Leipzig, 1870–1880, 7 vols.

Mearns      Mearns (J.), *Early Latin hymnaries*, an index of hymns in hymnaries before 1100, Cambridge (University Press), 1913.

MGH      *Monumenta Germaniœ historica* (cited by page of the appropriate volume).

PL      *Patrologia latina*, Migne (cited by volume and column)·

## A. Claudian and Boethius

Lack of literary vitality must show itself conspicuously in poetry. Claudian [1] at the end of the fourth century is typical of the fashionable versified rhetoric. Poet of those who taught and quoted Vergil, but liked Lucan and Statius, he is imitative fluently, prettily, and, except for a certain monotony, expertly. His *Raptus Proserpinæ* had the longer life, doubtless, because the abundant allusions and decorative descriptions give literary atmosphere without taxing either memory or imagination, and because, though diffuse, it is briefer than much verse narrative current in its time. Most of Claudian's other poems were occasional, and faded with the occasion.

But the old modes, for all the trivial use of them, were not spent. Boethius [2] showed himself here too the last of the Romans. The man who interpreted to century after century the logic of Aristotle was a poet. Not only is the *Consolatio philosophiæ* poetic in conception; its lyric interludes are so far above the facile expertness of the time as to suggest comparison with the best Latin achievement. Nothing less was the inspiration of their firm and various technic. Though he seems at first like his contemporaries in looking backward to what was going or gone, he knew better than they what to look for in the Roman tradition. He is never either archaist or

[1] Claudian wrote about 400, mainly in hexameters and elegiacs. Sidonius refers to him; and he is often cited later as a model of verse.

[2] About 480–524. *Tractates* and *De consolatione philosophiæ*, text and translation, ed. Stewart (H. F.) and Rand (E. K.), London and New York, 1918 (Loeb Classical Library). For bibliography, see Manitius I; for introduction to the manifold significance, Stewart's *Boethius, an essay*, Edinburgh and London, 1891.

sophist.  Images of classical reminiscence are used with fresh realization of their source in the sounds and colors of sea and fields and clouds.  They are not tags, nor merely allusions, nor decoration.  So used, they have much the same freshness as of old, or as the poet's own immediate observation.

Visebat gelidæ sidera lunæ [3]

is at once old and original; and the last line of this poem focuses the whole in a pregnant phrase:

Cogitur, heu! stolidam cernere terram.

Conceived by him habitually in cosmical aspects, nature none the less struck his senses in distinct detail.  The philosopher was a poet.

Boethius thus revived the old poetic terseness, as in

Desuper in terram nox funditur, [4]

not merely because he was too original and too serious to be deviated by the literary habit of dilation, but because he grasped constructively the economy set forth in the *De sublimitate* [5] as a poetic principle.

> Ah! how sheer is the deep flooding my spirit!
> Light of my own is lost; alien darkness
> Daunts and deludes my soul.  Swollen by wind-storms
> Charged with vapors of earth, often returning,
> Care like a poison spreads infinite languor. [6]

[3] *De consolatione philosophiæ* I, Metr. ii. 9.
[4] I, Metr. iii. 6.                                          [5] ARP 126–127.
[6] Heu quam præcipiti mersa profundo
      Mens hebet et propria luce relicta
      Tendit in externas ire tenebras,
      Terrenis quotiens flatibus aucta
      Crescit in immensum noxia cura.
                                          I, Metr ii. 1–5.

Having thus suggested the mood of oppression through images of the blind frustration of man by the heavens and the earth, the lyric contrasts the first, joyous contemplation of nature "under the open sky," advances to the inevitable later pondering upon the causes of movements so stupendous, and returns to the unyielding inertia of environment, still sharply imaged, but now carried from mood to conviction. The essentially poetic composition of his lyrics saves them from what would otherwise seem too intellectual solutions. *Stolidam cernere terram* is, indeed, as some other closes of his, a logical conclusion; but it is not reached by a logical process, nor is it mere epigram. It is the final satisfying image of a composition intensely and progressively imaginative. The immense medieval vogue of the *Consolatio* must often have reminded apt spirits of the true method of poetry.

In detail also Boethius set a chastening example. The spiritual elevation of this very lyric may have suggested for hymns [7] a measure that otherwise would hardly have seemed available. Analysis reveals a fondness for cæsural effects of syncope, for rime, and for subtler recurrences. The next lines are:

> Hic quondam cælo liber aperto
> Suetus in ætherios ire meatus
> Cernebat rosei lumina solis,
> Visebat gelidæ sidera lunæ
> Et quæcumque uagos stella recursus
> Exercet uarios flexa per orbes,
> Comprensam numeris uictor habebat.
> Quin etiam causas unde sonora. . . .

[7] Hymns echoing this measure may be traced in *Mearns*. Bede cites two, which he erroneously ascribes to St Ambrose (*De arte metrica*, Keil VII. 255, 256).

But the italics exaggerate recurrences which to the ear
are not exaggerated. Boethius does not remind us of
literary devices. He never descends to word-play. His
rime [8] is neither insistent nor inclined to the later art
of stanzas. It is merged in the other suggestions of a
various harmony.

The third measure of the third book, echoed now and
then in hymns, slows its pace not only by the cæsural
pause, but by the predominance of spondees at the onset.

> Quamuis fluente     diues auri gurgite
>   Non expleturas     cogat auarus opes
> Oneretque bacis     colla rubri litoris
>   Ruraque centeno     scindat opima boue,
> Nec cura mordax     deseret superstitem,
>   Defunctumque leues     non comitantur opes.

Such reflective lyrics were so readily assimilated to medieval thought that their grave and restrained form must have
been instructive in the centuries of poetic transition.

## B. PRUDENTIUS, SEDULIUS, FORTUNATUS

Prudentius [9] devoted much capable and dignified verse
in many meters and in several distinct literary forms

[8] In this poem *or* recurs at the same place in 11, 13, 15, 17, 18, 19;
22 rimes with 24 on -*entis*. The rime of adjective with noun is frequent of course; but Boethius marks it by putting one at the cæsura,
the other at the end. His most frequent rimes of this sort are on -*as*.
For the recurrence of -*os*, -*us*, with neighboring -*o* see III. ii. 32–35.

[9] Aurelius Prudentius Clemens, Spaniard, 348—about 410; prepared
a complete edition of his works 405. Often cited in the middle age,
his works were printed in the sixteenth, seventeenth, and eighteenth
centuries, and have been studied often since. Lanfranchi reëdited the
Bodoni edition in 1894 (Turin, second ed., 1904).

See, besides Manitius, Boissier, Monceaux, and Glover: Puech,
*Prudence, étude sur la poésie latine chrétienne*, Paris, 1888; Lease, *A
syntaetic, stylistic, and metrical study of P.*, Baltimore, 1895; Maigret,

entirely to the service of religion.   The *Psychomachia*, in some nine hundred hexameters, is an allegory of the soul's warfare.   Such description as that which introduces Avarice [10] handed on from Roman antiquity to the middle age the poetic habit of presenting personified abstractions by appropriate costume, gesture, and speech. The habit is allegory in its most obvious form; the method is the descriptive ecphrasis [11] transferring to poetry the rhetorical doctrine of appropriateness.   It is the method of Martianus Capella in the same age and of Alain de Lille in the thirteenth century.[12]

Reviewing his life in the preface to the *Days* (*Cathemerinon*), Prudentius seeks a poetry proper to his old age in hymns.

Hymnis continuet dies,
Nec nox ulla vacet, quin Dominum canat.

The twelve poems that follow, cast in nine different measures, are lyric reflections on the daily recurrences of cockcrow, food or fast, lamplighting, sleep; or on the festal recurrences of Christmas or Epiphany.   They are poems of some length, not hymns in the specific sense to which the word was soon limited.   But stanzas selected from them were combined to make the Breviary hymns for Lauds on Tuesday, Wednesday, and Thursday, and for the feasts of the Holy Innocents, the Epiphany, and the Transfiguration.   Almost equally familiar in the middle age was the *Corde natus* [13] hymn taken from the ninth poem.

*Le poète chrétien P.*, Paris, 1903; Ermini (F.), *Peristephànon, studi Prudenziani*, Rome, 1914; Bergmann, *Aulus Prudentius Clemens, der grösste christlicher Dichter des Alterthums*, Dorpat, 1921–1924.

[10] 454.                                          [11] See above, page 17.
[12] For Martianus Capella see above, Chapter III; for Alain, below, Chapter VI.                              [13] See below, C. 2.

The *Crowns* (*Peristephanon*) is a group of fourteen poems commemorating martyrs. Some are even longer than those of the preceding group; and the narrative of St Romanus extends to eleven hundred iambic trimeters in five-line stanzas. Other lyric stanzas are pressed into the service of narrative, as well as the better adapted hexameter and elegiac. There is little narrative movement. What Prudentius sought was detailed description, the making of martyrdom vivid. This, rather than the vogue of *declamatio*,[14] explains a certain diffuseness and the violence of many physical horrors of torture and execution. His descriptive habit is utterly different from Claudian's. That he was not thinking of rhetoric seems sufficiently evident from his ignoring the recipes of encomium.[15]

The remaining verses of Prudentius, nearly four thousand hexameters, more than one-third of his work, present theology by exposition and argument.[16]

The main work of Sedulius [17] is a hexameter paraphrase

[14] Puech, however, calls Prudentius in the *Peristephanon* "l'un des derniers représentants de la déclamation latine," and perhaps with no more warrant, "le prédécesseur des peintres castillans ou valenciens du xvie ou du xviie siècle" (page 129).

[15] Nor has Prudentius, though he is fond of alliteration, much wordplay. His verse, rather strictly quantitative, seems undoubtedly to have been so composed, though later it was rendered accentually.

[16] *Apotheosis*, 1089 verses on the Incarnation; *Hamartigenia*, 974 on the origin of sin; two books *Contra Symmachum*, 1756 directly polemic. J. Bergmann regards him as a pioneer even in these poems. After pointing out the influence of the *Psychomachia* on the whole middle age, he adds that *Apotheosis* and *Hamartigenia* are "kühne Versuche, die kühnsten seit Lucretius' Tagen, Philosophie in Form einer Dichtung zu bieten." *Aulus Prudentius Clemens, der grösste christlichen Dichter des Alterthums,* Dorpat (Acta et Comment. Univer. II. 1), 1924.

[17] Fifth century; works in CSE and in PL.

Bede praises Sedulius for internal rime in hexameters. "Optima autem versus dactylici ac pulcherrima compositio est cum primis pæ-

of the Bible; but he is better known for his *Carmen pas-chale* because this gave to the Breviary two hymns.[18] Its rimes suggest increasing inclination toward regularity, forecasting the time when what the ancient prosody felt as a device of style was to become a device of composition, a recognized method of emphasizing words and of making stanzas.

But rime was recognized slowly as a composing principle. Fortunatus [19] in the next century used it often enough, indeed, to show intention, but still incidentally. His famous hymn *Vexilla regis*, ignoring rime in its first quatrain, ends every line of the second with the same sound, and three of them with double rime.[20]   Contemporary interest in meter appears in the poem replying to Gregory's request for Sapphics.[21]   Most of his many other graceful occasional poems are in elegiacs.   One other hymn achieved a fame second only to that of the *Vexilla regis*, the *Pange, lingua, gloriosi*.   These two great Passion hymns may be taken as typical of the transitional poetic of the time.   They are at once old and new.   Each is a veritable hymn, not adapted as were the

nultima ac mediis respondent extrema, qua Sedulius frequenter uti consuevit, ut

    pervia divisi patuerunt cærula ponti

et          sicca peregrinas stupuerunt marmora plantas . . . . Non tamen hoc continuatim agendum, verum post aliquot interpositos versus." *De arte metrica*, Keil VII. 244.

[18] *A solis ortus cardine* for Lauds on Christmas Day, and *Crudelis Herodes, Deum* for Epiphany Vespers (AH 50: 58).

[19] Venantius Honorius Clementianus Fortunatus, about 530–600; went from Italy to Gaul, 565; Bishop of Poitiers, 599.   Works, ed. Leo, MGH.

See, besides the general works, Elss, *Untersuchungen über den Stil und die Sprache des Venantius Fortunatus*, Heidelberg, 1907.

[20] Rime appears early in Irish hymns.   See AH 51, Part II.

[21] *Carmina* IX. vi.

selections from Prudentius, but composed in a popular measure for community singing. Turning back to them from their successors of the great medieval period, one almost inevitably renders them with the same strong stresses. So read, they seem not to lose, but to gain in emphasis and swing. Who shall prove that they were not so rendered in the poet's own time? But who shall prove that they were? Against such rendering is clear evidence that Fortunatus controlled expertly the ancient quantitative prosody. For it are, first, the measures themselves, which come from popular verse accentual even in ancient Rome, and, second, a shift of speaking habit spreading slowly through the new Roman world. Both these must now be examined.

### C. THE EARLIER LATIN HYMNS [22]

> O lux beata Trinitas
> Et principalis Unitas,
> Iam sol recedit igneus;
> Infunde lumen cordibus.
>
> Te mane laudum carmine
> Te deprecamur vespere;
> Te nostra supplex gloria
> Per cuncta laudet sæcula. [23]

[22] An excellent introductory summary is that of Blume (article *hymnody*) in the *Catholic Encyclopedia*, which may also be consulted for Ambrose, etc., and for some of the greater hymns. Britt makes the best known Latin hymns available in one volume, with carefully selected translations, trustworthy ascriptions, biographical and bibliographical notes, indexes, and brief historical introduction. But this admirable work, though otherwise constantly useful, does not give for most of the hymns the earliest known text. This will be found, through the invaluable index of Mearns, in AH. Other references will be found in Britt's preface.

[23] St Ambrose; Britt, 71; AH 51: 38.

Here is new poetry, and the beginning of a new poetic. Not graver than Boethius in rejecting decoration, not terser in rejecting dilation, it is more direct, more simply responsive. The communal expression, the imaginative answer of people united, is as distinct poetically from individual reflection as is the communal hope from pensive resignation. The hope that Boethius had, but did not express in his *Consolatio*, appears here as above all a communal inspiration. The hymns are popular essentially in being the poetry of a society, the kingdom of heaven. Often intensely lyric, they express typically in these earlier centuries the emotions of a community. Their poets, many of them soon forgotten, if ever known, without thought of individual fame sought to give voice to what all felt together. The wide and continued vogue of the early hymns testifies to the validity of their popular poetic.

Their popularity is conspicuous in their verse. The measure above may be found, indeed, among learned poets; but it is originally and usually the verse of common people. Latin popular verse, even in classical times, was probably accentual. Though still called by the grammarians dimeter, this particular measure is certainly accentual as it is used in hymns of later centuries, and as it is rendered later even in hymns of this early period. Is it accentual as rendered even here at the beginning of Latin hymnody? The answer, though still disputed, has been much advanced in the last fifty years. To begin with clear terms, *accentual* means controlled by stresses; *quantitative*, controlled by time. All verse beyond mere mechanical exercise and doggerel has both elements; but every verse has one or the other for its control, its rhythm. All verse is something like dance, something like song; but every verse is dominated by the one rhythm or the other.  In this sense English verse is accentual. Every expert English poet regards time also, as he is aware of alliteration or subtler recurrences, or as he uses rime; but he sets and holds his rhythm by stresses.  In this sense modern French verse is quantitative.  Though it regards other elements, including stress, it makes time, as English verse does not, essential in its pattern.  The same difference distinguishes the verse of Bernard of Morlaix from the verse of Vergil, and generally medieval Latin verse from ancient.  Medieval Latin verse has a different rhythm.  Probably the new rhythmical habit began early.

But when we try to determine dates, we should re- member that old verse habits give way to new gradually. Poetic does not progress by revolutions.  The decorative habit of the *Roman de la Rose*, though it is now a curious piece of antiquity, survived long after Chaucer had out- grown it and had even exploded it in satire.  In verse, too, the three centuries including Chaucer help us to understand the centuries from Sedulius to Bede.  With other court poets, Chaucer was bilingual.  He not only understood and spoke French; he had French verse in his subconscious mind.  True, the French verse of his time shows, more than that of to-day, awareness of stress. The two rhythms were so much less distinct that Chaucer could more easily turn French to the profit of his own development in metric.  None the less his rhythm is English.  In spite of his ready tolerance of a shift of stress in foreign words, and of the enhancing of his har- monies by long vowels, his rhythm, the pattern or con- trol of his verse, is consistently accentual.  The first great English poet, as he used French, indeed, but turned for his poetry to English, kept no less confidently English rhythm.

In the fourth century Latin verse showed distinctly side by side two rhythms. Quantitative verse, long confirmed by Greek example and often directly imitative of Greek models, held the field of culture. The verse of Horace, Vergil, Ovid, it imposed itself upon all educated poets. Its influence controlled the schools through the archaistic teaching of style; and its quantitative prosody continued for centuries to be taught as part of *grammatica*. But all this while another rhythm was heard from the mouths of soldiers in songs of marching beat. What is somewhat indefinitely known as Saturnian verse moved beneath and behind literature, sometimes broke in half-conscious echoes through learned poetry, then gained the ground lost by literary standards, and finally won recognition as valid poetry in the hymns.[24]

Eventually the manuals of metric, which in any age proverbially lag behind current habit, distinguished the new verse by a new application of an old name. They called it *rhythmus*. The ancient quantitative verse is generally referred to in the middle age as *metrum* (*metra*, *metricus*, etc.); the new Latin verse, as *rhythmus* (*rithmus rithmicus*, etc.). Bede's *De arte metrica*, written early in the eighth century and widely used as a textbook, distinguishes as follows:

> Rhythm is seen moreover to be like meter in that it is a harmonized pattern of words, not planned metrically, but

[24] Recognition of the two methods of verse may be indicated by a line of Fortunatus,
> Quæque sunt rythmis vel amica metris,
in stanza 11 of *Carm.* IX. vii (MGH, page 212); but the two words are not necessarily used with the distinction that is clear in Bede (below, in next paragraph).

adjusted by recurrence of syllables to the judgment of the
ear, as are the songs of popular poets.  Though there can be
rhythm without meter, there cannot be meter without rhythm.
The distinction may be stated more clearly thus: meter is
regularity with harmony; rhythm is harmony without regularity.  But often you will find in rhythm even regularity,
kept not by the modes of [ancient] art, but by the sound and
by the lead of the harmony itself.  This, though popular
poets must do it rudely, expert poets may do expertly.  In
this manner was most beautifully composed, with resemblance
to iambic meter, that famous hymn

> Rex æterne domine,
> rerum creator omnium,
> qui eras ante sæcula
> semper cum patre filius,

and other Ambrosians not a few.  So in the fashion of trochaic
meter is sung the alphabetical hymn on the day of judgment:

> Apparebit repentina
> dies magna domini,
> fur obscura velut nocte
> improvisos occupans.[25]

Bede is apparently feeling his way, and evidently trying to find warrant for a new poetic in ancient authority.
Victorinus, whom he is quoting,[26] may intend by *rhythmus*

[25] Videtur autem rhythmus metris esse consimilis, quæ est verborum
modulata compositio, non metrica ratione, sed numero syllabarum ad
iudicium aurium examinata, ut sunt carmina vulgarium poetarum.
Et quidem rhythmus per se sine metro esse potest, metrum vero sine
rhythmo esse non potest; quod liquidius ita definitur: metrum est
ratio cum modulatione, rhythmus modulatio sine ratione.  Plerumque
tamen casu quodam invenies etiam rationem in rhythmo, non artifici
moderatione servata, sed sono et ipsa modulatione ducente, quem vulgares poetæ necesse est rustice, docti faciant docte.  Quomodo et ad
instar iambici metri pulcherrime factus est hymnus ille præclarus . . .
et alii Ambrosiani non pauci.  Item ad formam metri trochaici canunt
hymnun de die iudicii per alphabetum . . . Keil VII. 258.
[26] The work, which is assigned by Keil to Maximus Victorinus, is

and *numerus* nothing more than their older, more general sense.   Bede's variations and additions make specific and unmistakable application to the verse of the hymns as distinct from *metra*.   The testimony, first to the new habit, and secondly to the recognition of it as a valid and beautiful poetic, is testimony to fact.   In a schoolbook of the early eighth century Ambrosians are exhibited as *rhythmi;* and *rhythmi* are recognized as a distinct, self-sufficient method of verse.

Though the change of verse habit was slow, though *metra* were composed long after *rhythmi* had won the field, and though on the other hand even early hymns that are metrically correct may have been rendered as *rhythmi*, the progressive prevalence of accentual composition can hardly be doubted; for it answers a shift in the habit of speech itself.   By the seventh century Latin was no longer spoken even by the learned, much less by the average monk in England or Spain, as it had been spoken by Cicero.   The change of speech tune, doubtless more rapid among men not born to the language, certainly unequal and gradual, seems to be a fact in the history of the language.[27]

headed *Ars Palæmonis de Metrica Institutione*.   It begins by defining *metrum*, and then goes on: "Metro quid videtur consimile? Rhythmus. Rhythmus quid est?   Verborum modulata compositio non metrica ratione sed numerosa scansione ad iudicium aurium examinata, ut puta veluti sunt cantica poetarum vulgarium.   Rhythmus ergo in metro non est? Potest esse.   Quid ergo distat a metro? Quod rhythmus per se sine metro esse potest, metrum sine rhythmo esse non potest.   Quod liquidius ita definitur, metrum est ratio cum modulatione, rhythmus sine ratione metrica modulatio.   Plerumque tamen casu quodam etiam invenies rationem metricam in rhythmo, non artificii observatione servata, sed sono et ipsa modulatione ducente."   Keil VI. 206.

[27] The importance of the music for the interpretation of a measure gives additional weight to what is in other respects the most specific exposition of the verse of the early hymns, that of Pierre Aubry

Some of the earliest verse generally recognized as *rhythmus* comes from Ireland.[28]  The earliest known hymn manuscript is the so-called Antiphonary of [Irish] Bangor,[29] which is not an antiphonary, but a collection of hymns, prayers, and canticles.  In poetic art these range all the way from measures of noble beauty, some of which appear to have been composed as *metra*, to mne-

in *Le rythme tonique dans la poésie liturgique et dans le chant des églises chrétiennes au moyen âge*, Paris, 1903.  For his conclusions as to verse, and more widely as to language, are supported by his expert knowledge of the early history of Church music.  They may be indicated by a few leading quotations.  "Évolution du langage parlé vers le principe tonique au quatrième et au cinquième siècle" (8).  "La rythmique antique est en voie de transformation . . . transformation même que subissent les langues de l'antiquité au seuil du moyen âge . . . un principe nouveau de vitalité linguistique: l'accent.  L'ancienne prosodie, qui reposait sur la distinction des syllabes en longues et en brèves, a disparu dans l'usage vers le même temps.  On ne connaît plus que des syllabes accentuées et des syllabes atones.  Un rythme d'intensité s'est substitué au rythme quantitatif.  L'accent vainqueur a tué la quantité" (54).  "Les langues liturgiques . . . ont dans chaque mot une syllabe affectée d'un accent tonique . . . .  À l'époque qui nous occupe, cet accent est toujours d'intensité . . . ni plus d'acuité, ni plus de durée, mais plus de force" (55).  "Un poète comme Claudien faisait des vers latins à la façon d'un amateur de vieux langage. . . .  L'accent tonique prend un rôle de plus en plus prépondérant. . . .  Au septième siècle cette transformation est un fait accompli" (57).  "Telles hymnes de saint Ambroise, *Consors paterni luminis* par exemple, ou de saint Grégoire le Grand, par exemple *Rerum Creator optime*, sont de pures strophes iambiques dimètres métriques, tandisque le principe tonique domine dans l'hymne ambrosienne *Vox clara ecce intonat*, et que dans cette autre, *Christe, Redemptor omnium*, il est assez malaisé de déterminer les règles suivies par le poète" (60).  But even readers inexpert in music and in some of the languages quoted will learn much by following the line of exposition throughout.

Aubry's position as to the dominance of stress is supported by Gastoué, *Les origines du chant romain*, Paris, 1907, chapter ii, pages 60–67.

[28] See AH 51, Part II, with Blume's introduction.

[29] 681–691; reproduced in facsimile and transcribed by F. E. Warren for the Henry Bradshaw Society, volume IV, London, 1892; edited and annotated by him in volume X, 1895.

monic jingle. The following hymn is probably of the fifth or sixth century:

Ignis creator igneus,
Lumen, donator luminis,
Vitaque vitæ conditor,
Dator salutis et salus,

Ne noctis huius gaudia
Vigil lucerna deserat,
Qui hominem non vis mori,
Da nostro lumen pectori.
Folio 11, *recto;* AH 51: 296.

On its face this is a *metrum*, the familiar iambic dimeter. Rendered as a *rhythmus*, it would freely disregard quantities, stress the final syllable of each line, and elsewhere generally stress the word-accent: ígnis creátor ígneús. Though either measure is satisfying, the safer assumption is that the composer intended a *metrum*.

Probably even older, on the other hand, is St. Sechnall's (Secundinus, fifth century) fervent but rude praise of St. Patrick in twenty-three stanzas beginning with the successive letters of the alphabet.

Audite, omnes amantes
　Deum, sancta merita
Viri in Christo beati,
　Patricii episcopi,
Quomodo bonum ob actum
　similatur angelis
Perfectamque propter vitam
　æquatur apostolis.

Beata Christi custodit
　mandata in omnibus,
Cuius opera refulgent
　clara inter homines,
Sanctumque cuius sequuntur
　exemplum mirificum,
Unde et in cælis patrem
　magnificant Dominum. . .
Folio 13, *verso;* AH 51: 340.

Here the ignoring of quantities is such as to preclude a *metrum*.[30] But accentual interpretation also is difficult. Read as a *rhythmus* based on the *Corde natus*

---

[30] Blume (AH 51: 345) calls it "der älteste uns bekannte rein rhythmische Hymnus;" but by "rein" he too probably means that it has no rhythm but syllabic equality. See note 33, below.

measure,[31] which was frequently thus used later, it moves tolerably in certain stanzas (e. g., 4 and 7), but in others, including the two quoted, intolerably violates word-accent. Read by word-accent as a *rhythmus* of three stresses, it makes extravagant use of two intervening unstressed syllables.[32]    Indeed, without some clearer clue than has yet been offered, we can hardly be sure what measure was intended.[33]    Much less should we regard it as representative of the early poetic capacity of *rhythmus*. That capacity is amply vindicated in other hymns of this very manuscript.

[31] See below, section 2.

[32] Nevertheless Benchuir bona regula (folio 30, *recto;* AH 51: 356) may well be reconsidered in this aspect, as well as the two later Irish hymns in AH 51: 351 and 352.

[33] A widespread explanation is that Irish hymns were often composed with no other rhythm than equality between lines in the number of syllables.    Even the support of W. Meyer (see especially *Spanisches zur Geschichte der ältesten mittellateinischen Rythmik*) and of Blume seems insufficient to establish this theory against two grave objections.    The first objection is that *mere* equality in number of syllables hardly con-stitutes a pattern.    It does not provide recurrences marked enough to guide either composer or hearer.    It is hardly verse.    The idea that a practise so mechanical actually became a habit is repugnant.    The second objection is that on this theory Irish Latin verse ignored not only quantities, but word-accent—ignored, that is, either speech-tune. The Irish monks of all men, the best linguists of Europe in this period, were hardly the ones to write Latin verse by ignoring the habit of the language.    And in fact the following of the word-accent will often re-veal a stress rhythm sufficient for the ruder mnemonic verses and satis-fying in the better ones.    Moreover this consideration is fortified by what we know of the music (see note 27 above), which leaned on the word-accent.    True, such rendering sometimes involves two unstressed syllables in succession, or conversely two stresses without intervention; but this variation is a natural means against monotony.    The pattern is kept by the unvarying number of stresses in each line; variety is secured by occasionally shifting their places.    The idea that in this period iambic or trochaic *rhythmi* admitted no effects similar to the substitution of dactyl or anapest in a *metrum*, or to a spondee, is an assumption unwarranted by either theory or fact.

## 1. Iambic

Examination of the early hymns measure by measure begins with St Ambrose, Bishop of Milan at the end of the fourth century. Both his own fame and the recognition of a typical stanza appear in the general use of the adjective Ambrosian to describe many hymns of unknown authorship and sometimes of uncertain date. The canon of his own hymns has, indeed, been determined; [34] but it is less important than his achievement of a type. His answer to a common need established a common form. He had the discernment, first, to select a popular measure often used accentually, and then so to use it as to obey both the popular stress habit and the learned poetic of quantity. That his hymns are valid either as *metra* or as *rhythmi* means, though his regard for word-accent shows that he foresaw the latter rendering, that they must have been composed in the former, and probably that time rhythm was still heard in speech. The increase of the stress habit gradually worked a transformation. The regular dactylic close hardly satisfying so short a line, the final syllable, which even in the ancient metric might be long sometimes, came to be stressed always. As a *metrum* the iambic

[34] Dreves (*Aurelius Ambrosius, der Vater des Kirchengesanges, eine hymnologische Studie*, Freiburg, 1893) settles on the following eighteen hymns, of which he prints the text and indicates the melodies.

| | |
|---|---|
| (1) Æterne rerum conditor, | (10) Inluminans altissimus, |
| (2) Splendor paternæ gloriæ, | (11) Agnes, beatæ virginis, |
| (3) Iam surgit hora tertia, | (12) Hic est dies verus Dei, |
| (4) Nunc sancte nobis Spiritus, | (13) Victor, Nabor, Felix, pii, |
| (5) Rector potens verax Deus, | (14) Grates tibi, Iesu, novas, |
| (6) Rerum, deus, tenax vigor, | (15) Apostolorum passio, |
| (7) Deus, creator omnium, | (16) Apostolorum supparem, |
| (8) Intende, qui regis Israel, | (17) Æterna Christi munera, |
| (9) Amore Christi nobilis, | (18) Iesu, corona virginum. |

dimeter ran *Ætērnĕ rērūm cōndĭtŏr;* as a *rhythmus* it became *Ætérne rérum cónditór.* The effect, though different, is not inferior. For the distinctive verse values of *rhythmi,* heard at their best in later hymns freely so composed, can be discerned even here in the earliest centuries by rendering as *rhythmi*—as in fact they came to be rendered—two of the most familiar hymns taken from the dimeters of Prudentius.

| | |
|---|---|
| Ales diei nuntius | Auferte, clamat, lectulos |
| Lucem propinquam præcinit: | Ægros, sopores desides: |
| Nos excitator mentium | Castique, recti, ac sobrii |
| Iam Christus ad vitam vocat. | Vigilate, iam sum proximus. |

. . . *Cathemerinon* i. 1: AH 50: 23.

| | |
|---|---|
| Salvete flores martyrum, | Quid crimen Herodem iuvat? |
| Quos lucis ipso in limine | Vos prima Christi victima, |
| Christi insecutor sustulit, | Grex immolatorum tener, |
| Ceu turbo nascentes rosas. | Palma et coronis luditis. |

. . . *Cathemerinon* xii. 125: AH 50: 27.

The accentual habit spread slowly and intermittently as a change of control from one element of verse to another. Both elements continued in the better hymns to vary and enhance what must otherwise become monotonous or bald; but the control, the rhythm, gradually changed from time to stress. Variety through shifting the places of stress [35] appears in several hymns of the sixth century. The Ambrosian quoted by Bede as an example of *rhythmus* [36] even begins with a stress; [37] and the probable following of word-accent often gives a dactylic opening.

[35] Compare *Ignis creator igneus* above, page 114, and the latter part of note 33.

[36] Above, page 111.

[37] Blume *ad loc.* notes that this opening is not unusual. The hymn is mentioned by Cæsarius of Arles.

Réx ætérne, Dóminé,
Rérum creátor ómniúm,
Qui éras ánte sǽculá
Sémper cum pátre fíliús,

Qui múndi ín primórdió
Ádam plasmásti hóminém,
Cuí tuaé imáginís
Vúltum dedísti símilém; . . .

AH 51: 5.

Similar variations appear in the "Versus Flavii ad Mandatum."

Téllus ac ǽthra iúbilént
In mágni céna príncipís,
Quæ prótoplásti péctorá
Vítæ purgávit férculó.

Hac nócte fáctor ómniúm
Poténti sát mystérió
Cárnem súam cum sánguiné
In éscam tránsfert ánimæ. . . .

AH 51: 77.

Though possible lingering or revival of a sense of quantities, and the shifting pronunciation of proper names, leave uncertainties (as above, for example in *Adam* and *vitæ*), there is little doubt that such variations were not only accepted, but even sought.    They often relieve dubious measures; and conversely they are sometimes used in ruder *rhythmi* so excessively as to blur the verse pattern.    One of the Bangor hymns seems to run best as follows:

Médiæ nóctis témpus ést;
Prophética vóx ádmonét,
Dicámus laúdes út Deó
Pátri sémper ac fílió

Sáncto quóque spírituí.
Perfécta énim trínitás
Úniúsque substántiæ
Laudánda nóbis sémper ést. . . .

Folio 11 *verso;* AH 51: 3.

If so, the syncope in line 2 serves to emphasize *vox.*    But the verse of this hymn is inferior.[38]    The better hymns use the variations with better art.

[38] So is that of the commemorative Bangor hymn *Sáncta sanctórum óperá* at the end of the manuscript (folio 36 *verso;* AH 51: 357).

## 2. Trochaic

More immediately suggestive of accentual rendering
was another soldiers' measure used by Prudentius in the
first poem of his *Crowns (Peristephanon)*, a commemoration of two soldier martyrs.  It was better known through
a hymn taken from the ninth poem of his *Days*.

> Corde natus ex parentis ante mundi exordium,
> A et O cognominatus, ipse fons et clausula
> Omnium quæ sunt, fuerunt, quæque post futura sunt,
>
> Ipse iussit, et creata; dixit ipse, et facta sunt:
> Terra, cælum, fossa ponti, trina rerum machina,
> Quæque in his vigent sub alto solis et lunæ globo,
>
> Corporis formam caduci, membra morti obnoxia
> Induit, ne gens periret primoplasti ex germine,
> Merserat quem lex profundo noxialis tartaro. . . .
>
> *Cathemerinon* ix. 10.[39]

Rendered as a *rhythmus*, as in the hymn quoted by Bede,[40]
the measure, besides ending with a stress, was often
divided at the cæsura, to make stanzas of six four-stress
lines; for the original line is long to handle singly; it
tends to break.  None of the other hymns taken from
this poem of Prudentius is so familiar and so stirring as
this of Fortunatus:

> Pange, lingua, gloriosi prælium certaminis,
> Et super crucis tropæo dic triumphum nobilem,
> Qualiter redemptor orbis immolatus vicerit.

[39] The meter is $- \smile - - - \smile - - - \smile - - - \smile \smile$ (with $- \smile$
permissible instead of $- -$)  For other combinations of stanzas in hymns
taken from this poem see AH 50: 25–27.

[40] *Apparebit repentina*, above, page 111.

De parentis protoplasti fraude factor condolens,
Quando pomi noxialis morte morsu conruit,
Ipse lignum tunc notavit, damna ligni ut solveret. . . .

*Carmina* II. ii; MGH 27.[41]

Possibly Fortunatus composed this as a *rhythmus;* more probably he thought of the soldiers' marching stresses as reinforcing his *metra*. The long Bangor hymn ascribed to St. Hilary of Poitiers, and probably very old,[42] is quoted with admiration by Bede [43] as a *metrum.*

Hymnum dicat turba fratrum,
  hymnum cantus personet;
Christo regi concinnantes
  laudem demus debitam.

Dextra patris, mons et agnus,
  angularis tu lapis,
Sponsus idem vel columba,
  flamma, pastor, ianua.

Tu Dei de corde verbum,
  tu via, tu veritas,
Iesse virga tu vocaris,
  te leonem legimus.

In prophetis inveniris
  nostro natus sæculo;
Ante sæcla tu fuisti
  factor primi sæculi. . . .

Folio 3 *recto;* AH 51: 264.

It has the deeper significance of exhibiting an early form of medieval symbolism.

The very different trochaic measure of the sixth-century Irish "breastplate" hymn, with abrupt pauses and rime, seems clearly a *rhythmus*, and deserves attention least of all for its art.

[41] Part of this, but also used separately, is *Lustra sex qui iam peregit.*
[42] The evidence is reviewed by Blume, AH 51: 269–271.
[43] *De arte metrica*, Keil VII. 258.

*Lorica sancti Gyldœ Sapientis*

Suffragare,   *   trinitatis unitas,
Unitatis   *   miserere trinitas.

Suffragare,
  quæso, mihi posito
Maris magni
  velut in periculo,
Ut non secum
  trahat me mortalitas
Huius anni
  neque mundi vanitas.

Et hoc idem
  peto a sublimibus
cælestis mi-
  litiæ virtutibus,
Ne me linquant
  lacerandum hostibus,
Sed defendant
  me iam armis fortibus. . . .

AH 51: 358.

## 3. Other Measures

Less popular, more literary measures, though some of them were used early in the hymnaries, seem to have been interpreted as *rhythmi* more slowly. This, indeed, is what one would expect; but the evidence is not decisive. The Sapphic stanza, the beautiful meter of the second poem of Boethius,[44] even iambic trimeter, were in time transformed. But in hymns they were comparatively infrequent; and for other uses they were revived with what seems clearly quantitative intention and achievement. Either rendering is beautiful for one of the few Sapphic poems that are essentially hymns, a hymn for Sunday Lauds.

Ecce iam noctis tenuatur umbra;
Lucis aurora rutilans coruscat;
Nisibus totis rogitemus omnes
  Cunctipotentem,

Ut Deus nostri miseratus omnem
Pellat languorem, tribuat salutem,
Donet et patris pietate nobis
  Regna polorum.

[44] *De consol. philos.* I, Metr. ii. See above, page 101.

> Præstet hoc nobis deitas beata
> Patris et nati pariterque sancti
> Spiritus, cuius reboatur omni
>   Gloria mundo.
>
>                   AH 51: 31.[45]

The most striking verse in the Bangor manuscript is that of the familiar Communion hymn.

> Sancti, venite,   Christi corpus sumite
> Sanctum bibentes,   quo redempti, sanguinem,
>
> Salvati Christi   corpore et sanguine,
> A quo refecti   laudes dicamus Deo,
>
> Hoc sacramento   corporis et sanguinis
> Omnes exuti   ab inferni faucibus.
>
> Dator salutis,   Christus filius Dei,
> Mundum salvavit   per crucem et sanguinem;
>
> Pro universis   immolatus Dominus
> Ipse sacerdos   exsistit et hostia. . . .
>
>                 Folio 10 *verso;* AH 51: 298.

The spondaic opening and the marked cæsura may be reminiscent of the *Quamvis fluente dives auri gurgite* of Boethius; [46] and the composition is far superior to the Bangor habit in sense of time values.   Not only Irish and

---

[45] Blume rejects the ascription to St. Gregory the Great; and the hymn may belong to the next period. Cf. *Nocte surgentes vigilemus omnes,* page 136.  Any one who will render in time rhythm the most familiar of all Sapphics, the "Integer vitæ" of Horace, then sing it to the familiar college tune, then render it as a *rhythmus,* will realize practically much of what is involved in interpreting a given text of this period of transition.  Greenough's *Accentual rhythm in Latin* (Harvard Studies IV. 105) pointed out in 1893 that quantitative correctness in medieval use of the Sapphic does not preclude accentual preoccupation.

[46] *De consol. phil.* III, metrum iii; quoted above, page 103.

popular, but probably much older than this manuscript,[47] the hymn may have been composed as a *metrum*. By either rendering it is unusually, and at the same time expertly, free. Though the spread of stress rhythm carried some verse that is rude and mechanical, as in this manuscript, it did not of itself forfeit time values, and it opened in the old language new effects of verse.

## 4. Poetic Conceptions

But the newness of the verse is at best less significant than the newness of the poetry. A jaded world has been refreshed by new imaginative expression. Bede's exhibition of Christian poetry is not merely pious; nor is it either timid or complacent. He is convinced of a new Latin poetry. As Augustine redeemed rhetoric, so Ambrose transformed poetic, by new motives. The tender image of the Holy Innocents playing with their palms and crowns [48] is neither old nor new; it is the timeless language of individual lyric. But the habitual conceptions of Prudentius and Ambrose, of Hilary and Gregory, are not individual; they are communal. The lyric of the hymns exalts the common emotions of common observance. It is the poetry of aspirations shared not only with all Christians everywhere, but with immediate companions turning work into worship. It expresses the visions of a fellowship.

[47] See Blume *ad loc.* He admits the possibility, which seems far from a probability, of reading this as a senarius, but prints it with conviction as a four-verse stanza (dividing at the cæsura) after the analogy of other Irish hymns. Some of these are in this manuscript; but none is equal in art, and this one is not so written. I think it must have been sung *Sáncti, veníte, Chrísti córpus súmité*, though *Sáncti, veníte* is a more frequent rhythmical opening.

[48] Second stanza of *Salvete flores martyrum*, above, section 1.

No exception is found in the early hymns commemorating martyrs. The triumph is not personal. The individual heroism passes into the common hope of released energy and of the triumph of the kingdom of God. As early churches were built over the tombs of martyrs, and later additions made the nave look both down to the original *confessione* and up to the high altar, so the martyr hymns express both a common gratitude and a common devotion. So a hundred images of light, suggestions of dawn, noon, stars, the ordinary lamp, the candle in church, lead not to individual emotion, but to the poetry of theology.

In every light is the light of the world. The night-light (*vigil lucerna*) leads up to the giver of light, the creative fire (*Ignis creator igneus, Lumen donator luminis*).[49] Poetry discerns a new earth because of a new heaven, and finds both one. The poets of the hymns do not, as the Stoics, look down on the material world; they look through it. They neither belittle physical reality nor bow to it; they go on from it. Life in the hymns is not an urgent present and a visioned future; it is all one. The frame of the Christian year opens in the hymns on eternity. Eternal life begins now, and is not survival, but progressive release of human energy by God. Thus the Incarnation is revealed by Prudentius not in versified theology, but in poetic truth. It becomes a cosmic vision.

Though this conception was widespread through the Prudentian hymn *Corde natus*,[50] and though Prudentius was quite as much philosopher as poet, literary influences are insufficient to account for the consistent continuity of the hymns as thought. Even Fortunatus, who cer-

[49] Above, page 114.                    [50] Page 119.

tainly was no philosopher, was uplifted by common visions. The single line *Hymnum dicat turba fratrum* [51] might be taken as a formula for the poetic of the early hymns. Hilary discerned also the communal appeal of the symbolism of the Old Testament, as Ambrose had discerned a communal verse; but though the hymns owe much to individuals, the character of their lyric grows from unifying communal conceptions of life.

[51] Page 120.

# CHAPTER V

# THE CAROLINGIANS AND THE TENTH CENTURY

## REFERENCES AND ABBREVIATIONS

AH   Dreves and Blume, *Analecta hymnica medii œvi*, Leipzig, vol. 1, 1886; vol. 53, 1911.

ARP   Baldwin (C. S.), *Ancient rhetoric and poetic*, New York, 1924.

     Clark (J. M.), *The abbey of St. Gall* . . . Cambridge University Press, 1926.

Ermini  Ermini (F.), *Poeti epici latini del secolo X*, Rome, 1920.

Halm  Halm (K.), *Rhetores latini minores*, Leipzig, 1863.

Keil   Keil (H.), *Grammatici latini*, Leipzig, 1870–1880, 7 vols.

Manitius Manitius (M.), *Geschichte der lateinischen Literatur des Mittelalters*, Munich, 1911, 2 vols. (in Von Mueller's Handbuch der klassischen Alterthums-Wissenschaft, IX. ii).

MGH  *Monumenta Germaniæ historica* (cited by page of the appropriate volume).

PL   Migne, *Patrologia latina* (cited by volume and column).

### A. THE TRIVIUM IN THE GREATER MONASTERIES

Hibernia, Northumbria, Francia were successively the seats of learning in the period of readjustment after the invasions. Men born to Celtic speech, to English, to Frankish learned the Latin culture and transmitted it to the middle age. In the circumstances the writers of the eighth, ninth, and tenth centuries were primarily teachers; and their chief field was *grammatica*. The language of learning was no longer for any of them common speech; it had to be acquired even by Italians and Gauls as a second language and a superior. In compensation it was universal, halted by no frontiers. The whole western world of culture was a *quartier Latin*. *Scoti*, as the Irish Celts were commonly called, wrote and taught in it by Humber, Rhine, or Loire; Bede wrote in it his *Church History of the English People;* Alcuin was brought from the school of York to apply it to the education of the Frankish empire, and his companion and successor was the Bishop of Orléans, Theodulf, a Goth from Spain.

*Grammatica* became thus more important than ever. It opened not only learning in general, not only literature, but especially the interpretation of the liturgy, the offices, the creeds, and the Scriptures. Charlemagne's care was to secure a clergy that should be first educated and then educating. The mission of the Church to teach through the universal language of western Christianity was exercised partly through the cathedrals, mainly through the monasteries. In these centuries rose such great monastic schools as Fulda, St Gall, and Tours. As the physical preservation and circulation of texts depended on the *scriptoria*, so on the masters of the

monasteries depended not only specific training for
the religious life, but much of the more general training
in divinity and most of the seven liberal arts.

The monastic slant suggests a narrowing of culture.
But the restriction of the seven arts must have been due
quite as much to those other conditions which gave the
preponderance to *grammatica*. The achievement of the
age was preparatory. That the age of preparation was
also an age of revival is witnessed best by the outstanding
teachers. The *Scoti* who fled from the Danes to the
Continent were remarkable no more for their preservation of the last vestiges of Greek than for their intellectual
eagerness. They were a stirring leaven. The greater
schools founded during this period, such as that at Wearmouth to which English Benedict had brought store of
books from Rome and Vienne, show an impressive succession of teachers: Bede, Alcuin, Rabanus, Loup,
Remi, Gerbert.[1] The former three are sufficient assurance that culture was safe; the latter, that it was advancing.

A work on the Elements of Philosophy, ascribed to
Bede, closes with the following list:

> The order of learning is as follows. Since *eloquentia* is the
> instrument of all teaching, they are instructed in it first. Its

[1] Bede (c. 673–735), Wearmouth.
Alcuin (c. 735–804), York, Schools of the Palace, St. Martin's at
Tours.
Rabanus (c. 780–856), Fulda.
Loup (805–862), Fulda, Ferrières.
Remi (841–908), Auxerre, Reims.
Gerbert (c. 940–1003), Reims. See Julien Havet's *Lettres de Gerbert*
(*983–997*), with his valuable introduction, Paris, 1889. For a suggestive
summary of the greater schools and their teaching, with valuable
bibliographical notes, see Ermini, vi–xvi, 69–70.

three parts are correct writing and correct delivery of what is written; proof of what is to be proved, which *dialectica* teaches; figures of words and sentences, which *rhetorica* hands down. Therefore we are to be initiated in *grammatica*, then in *dialectica*, afterward in *rhetorica*. Equipped with these arms, we should approach the study of philosophy. Here the order is first the quadrivium, and in this first *arithmetica*, second *musica*, third *geometria*, fourth *astronomia*, then holy writ, so that through knowledge of what is created we arrive at knowledge of the Creator.[2]

Toward the close of the tenth century the same order of studies, except for the transposition of *geometria* and *musica*, appears in the school at Speier. Though the details of the reminiscences prefixed by Walter of Speier to his *Passion of St. Christopher*[3] are obscured by figurative language, allusions, and other devices of style, he shows unmistakably, after his first lessons in psalmody, a full course of *grammatica*, including much metric. His references seem also to indicate both the elementary exercises beginning with *fabula*, and *prælectiones* on Vergil, Ovid, Horace's *Ars poetica*, and the *metra* of Boethius. *Dialectica*, which he entered by the door of Porphyry, he recalls less distinctly. *Rhetorica*, though remembered in her usual garb of flowers, evidently included *declamatio*. By the end of the tenth century, then, a typical monastic

[2] *Opera*, Basel, 1563 (whence PL), vol. II, page 343, end of the last book (IV, περὶ διδάξεων) of *De elementis philosophiæ*.

Loup's first letter to Einhard puts *rhetorica* second (MGH, *Epist.* tom. VI, pars prior, page 8); and so does Rabanus, *De clericorum institutione*, III. xviii (PL 107: 395 B).

[3] *Passio S. Christophori, carmen rhythmicum*, rec. C. Strecker, MGH, Poet. lat. med. æv., vol. IV, Part II. 809.

The introduction is included among the selections printed in Ermini.

Walter's reference to psalmody is at line 15; to *fabula*, at 55; to *prælectio*, at 91; to *declamatio*, at 140. For all these, except the first, see the indexes to ARP and to the present volume.

school, though still spending most time on *grammatica*, seems to have offered an ample trivium.

## B. GRAMMATICA

Donatus and Priscian, with the other grammarians of the declining Empire,[4] kept their authority. They were successively adapted to changing needs in manuals by Bede, Boniface, Paulus Diaconus, Alcuin, Loup, Remi, Gerbert, Abbo, Ælfric. That *grammatica* thus engaged the best teachers of the time is evidence of its cardinal importance. At Chartres, by the tenth century, *grammaticus* was the usual name for headmaster.[5]

The study of figures, both those usually included in *grammatica* and those assigned to *rhetorica*, was applied to the interpretation of holy writ. Augustine[6] had pointed out that the Scriptures not only use figures, but explicitly mention allegory and parable. Bede's brief summary *De schematibus et tropis sacræ scripturæ*[7] is thus typical both of elementary teaching and of medieval habit of reading.

## 1. Poetic

That neither Bede nor Alcuin specifically defines *grammatica* in the traditional terms as including the

[4] See above, page 87. Alcuin's verses on York (MGH, *Poet. lat. æv. Carol.* I. 169) enumerate in the eighth-century library there: Donatus, Eutyches, Phocas, Pompeius, Priscian, Probus, Victorinus, Servius, The ninth-century library of St. Amand had Eutyches, Marius Plotius [Sacerdos], Priscian, Servius, and Victorinus (Desilve, *De schola Elnonensi Sancti Amandi*, Louvain, 1890, page 51).

[5] Clerval, *Les écoles de Chartres*, 22; and, for the eleventh century, 47, 48, 56, etc.

[6] *De doctrina christiana*, III. xxix.

[7] PL. 90: 175; Halm, 607.

study of Latin poetry may mean no more than that neither wrote comprehensively on the whole subject. The *prælectio* can hardly have been neglected by the *Scoti*, or by Bede himself. The definition of Rabanus in the ninth century [8] not only resumes the whole ancient scope, but puts the interpretation of the poets first. That Boethius was added to the list of classics [9] is significant of the influence of his *metra* even on the hymns.

When Bede tells his boys to look at all the first syllables [10] of a manuscript page of hexameters, because these syllables must be long, he is not precluding either nicer points of metric or wiser consideration of poetry; he is very practically teaching Latin quantities. His book offers much more; and though its subject is only metric, it takes pains to distinguish rhythmic,[11] and closes with that classification of poetry by Diomedes which was to be often repeated.

Since we have discussed at length poems and meters, it is to be observed finally that the kinds of poetry are three. For it is active, or imitative, what the Greeks entitle *dramaticon* or *mimeticon;* or narrative, what the Greeks style *exegematicon* or *apangelticon;* or common, i. e. mixed, what the Greeks call

[8] Grammatica est scientia interpretandi poetas atque historicos et recte scribendi loquendique ratio. Hæc et origo et fundamentum est artium liberalium. *De clericorum institutione,* III. xviii (PL, 107: 395 B).

[9] Above, section A, close.

[10] *De arte metrica* (PL, 90: 156. 4; Keil, VII. 234).

[11] Above, page 110. The distinction seems to be made by Walafrid Strabo, *Libellus de exordiis et incrementis rerum ecclesiasticarum* (840–842), cap. 26, pp. 506–508 (MGH, *Capitularia regum francorum,* II, Appendix); and by Hucbald (IXth century):

Astipulare meis, quia non sunt carmina, rhythmis . . .
Quod si, ut puto, nequit carmen jam jure vocari,
Sit satis huic saltem censeri nomine rithmi.

Quoted by Desilve, *De schola Elnonensi Sancti Amandi,* p. 57.

*cœnon* or *micton*. That is *dramaticon*, or active, in which the
*personœ* are presented as speaking without the intervention
of the poet, as in tragedies and fables, for drama is called in
Latin *fabula*. In this kind is written "Quo te Moeri pedes?
an quo via ducit, in urbem?" as also among ourselves the
Song of Songs, where the voice of Christ and of the Church
are clearly found to alternate without the writer's intervention.
That is *exegematicon*, or narrative, in which the poet himself
speaks without the intervention of any *persona*, as three books
of the Georgics and the first part of the fourth, as well as the
poems of Lucretius and others like them. In this kind our
literature shows Proverbs and Ecclesiastes, which are composed metrically in their own language. *Cœnon* or mixed,
is the kind in which the poet himself speaks and also the *personœ* are presented as speaking. So are written the Iliad and
Odyssey of Homer, the Æneid of Vergil, and with us the story
of blessed Job, though this in its own language is written not
entirely as poetry, but partly as prose, partly in *metra* or in
*rhythmi*.[12]

Far as this is not only from Aristotle, but from Vergil,
the shift of emphasis from composition to style remained
for centuries characteristic of medieval Latin poetic,
and opened the way for the confusion of poetic with
rhetoric.

### a. LATIN HYMNS

### (1) Iambic

The best known hymn of this period is by Rabanus
(ninth century).

| | |
|---|---|
| Veni creator, Spiritus, | Qui paracletus diceris, |
| Mentes tuorum visita, | Donum Dei altissimi, |
| Imple superna gratia | Fons vivus, ignis, caritas |
| Quæ tu creasti pectora. | Et spiritalis unctio. . . . |

AH 50: 193.

[12] Keil, VII. 259. The passage in Diomedes is in Keil, I. 482.

This keeps generally the quantities of the metrical dimeter.[13] Rime is insistent in ruder hymns. The two following, Irish of the eighth century, though substantially correct as *metra* in some stanzas, seem to be *rhythmi*. The first is alphabetical; the second, a *lorica*. As *rhythmi* they are relieved by shift of stress in the places indicated, and probably intend it elsewhere; i. e., they are most satisfactorily read by word-accent.

R. Assint nobis sublimia
Sancti Petri suffragia.

Audite, fratres, famina
Petri pastoris plurima.
Baptismatis libamina
Fudit veluti flumina.

Bís refúlsit ut fulmine
Sacro sanctorum agmine;
Fléntes dúxit ex ordine
Gentes divino carmine. . . .

AH 51: 347.

O rex, O rector regminis,
O cultor cæli carminis,
O persecutor murmuris,
O Deus alti agminis.

Curet caput cum renibus
Méis átque cum talibus,
Cum oculis et genibus,
Cum auribus et naribus,

Aido, mech Prich, benevola
Posco puro precamina,
Út refrígeret flumina
Méi cápitis calida;

Cum ancylis euntibus,
Cum fistulis sonantibus,
Cum lingua atque dentibus,
Cum lacrimarum fontibus.

Sanctus Aid altus adiuvet,
Meum caput ut liberet,
Ut hoc totum perseveret
Sánum, átque pervigilet.

AH 51: 315.

[13] Iamb for spondee in the third foot, as in line 8, is a liberty adopted from classical verse by Bede (*Adesto, Christe, vocibus*) and by Paulus Diaconus (*Fratres, alacri pectore*). Even Sedulius Scotus, as to whose metrical expertness there can be no doubt, uses this liberty in a classical poem (*Ventosa cum desæviat*, MGH, *Poet. lat. Car.* III. 162). Rendered rhythmically, their hymns often suggest the shift of stress that seems to be intended in the Irish hymns.

## (2) Trochaic

Rhythmical use of the *Corde natus* measure [14] is suggested by frequent disregard of the distinction in the original meter between trochee and spondee within the line, and of the dactyl at the end.[15] The popular swing of this *rhythmus* is felt in a well known hymn of the eighth century:

> Urbs beata Hierusalem, dicta pacis visio,
> Quæ construitur in cælis vivis ex lapidibus,
> Et angelis coornata ut sponsata comite!
>
> Nova veniens e cælo, nuptiali thalamo
> Præparata ut sponsata, copulatur Domino.
> Plateæ et muri eius ex auro purissimo;
>
> Portæ nitent margaritis, adytis patentibus
> Et virtute meritorum illuc introducitur
> Omnis qui pro Christi nomine hic in mundo premitur. . . .
>
> AH 51: 110.[16]

[14] See above, page 119.

[15] Nos dicamus Christo laudem genitoris unico,
Mundi legitur librorum qui creator paginis,
Cuius fine clemens venit liberare perditos. . . .
　　　　　Petrus Diaconus, MGH, *Poet. lat. Carol.* I. 48.

Sensi, cuius verba cepi exarata paginis,
Nam a magno sunt directa, quæ pusillus detulit;
Fortes me lacerti pulsant, non imbellis pueri. . . .
　　　　　Paulus Diaconus, *ibid.* 49.

The interesting application of the measure by Paulinus of Aquileia to extended narrative, though generally keeping the final dactyl, pays otherwise no more regard to quantity.

Fuit domini dilectus languens a Bethania
Lazarus beatus sacris olim cum sororibus,
Quas Iesus æternus amor diligebat plurimum,
Martha simul et Maiiam felices per sæcula. *Ibid.* 133.

These are all of the eighth century. Compare, in the ninth, Rabanus (Claras laudes ac salubres, posco, fratres dicite, *ibid.* II. 235; AH 50: 203), and Sedulius Scotus (Conditor supernus orbis imperator omnium, *ibid.* III. 159).

[16] The hymn has nine stanzas; but the latter part, beginning *Angularis fundamentum*, is also sung separately.

Freer use, with both end-rime and occasional internal rime,[17] as in lines 3 and 5 above, appears in an Irish hymn ascribed to St Cuchuimne.

Cantemus in omni die
   concinnantes varie,
Conclamantes Deo dignum
   hymnum sanctæ Mariæ.

Maria de tribu Iuda,
   summi mater Domini,
Opportunam dedit curam
   ægrotanti homini.

Bis per chorum, hinc et inde,
   collaudemus Mariam,
Ut vox pulset omnem aurem
   per laudem vicariam.

Gabriel advexit verbum,
   sinu patris paterno
Quod conceptum et susceptum
   in utero materno. . . .

                            AH 51: 305.

A Septuagesima hymn in a tenth-century manuscript is so united by the iteration of *Alleluia* that the poet felt no need of rime.

    Alleluia, dulce carmen, vox perennis gaudii,
    Alleluia laus suavis est choris cælestibus,
    Quod canunt Dei manentes in domo per sæcula.

    Alleluia læta, mater, concinis, Ierusalem,
    Alleluia vox tuorum civium gaudentium;
    Exsules nos flere cogunt Babylonis flumina. . . .

                          AH 51: 52.

A much simpler trochaic measure is heard in one of the most popular of medieval hymns. Found in a manuscript of the ninth century, it may well be earlier.

Ave, maris stella,
Dei mater alma
Atque semper virgo,
Felix cæli porta.

Sumens illud Ave
Gabrielis ore,
Funda nos in pace
Mutans nomen Evæ. . . .

                          AH 51: 140.

---

[17] Interesting use of rime both as occasional echo and as regular correspondence is heard in the hymn, from a tenth-century manuscript, *O redemptor, sume carmen*, AH 51: 80.

### (3) Other Measures

Sapphics, which of course exercised the skill of the learned,[18] are occasionally convincing in a hymn.

Nocte surgentes vigilemus
    omnes,
Semper in psalmis medite-
    mur atque
Viribus totis Domino canamus
    Dulciter hymnos,

Ut pio regi pariter canentes
Cum suis sanctis mereamur
    aulam
Ingredi cæli simul et beatam
    Ducere vitam.

Præstet hoc nobis deitas beata
Patris et nati pariterque sancti
Spiritus, cuius reboatur omni
        Gloria mundo.   AH 51: 26.

One Sapphic, doubtfully ascribed to Paulus Diaconus, had currency enough to furnish later a memory stanza for the notes of the scale.

UT queant laxis REsonare fibris
MIra gestorum FAmuli tuorum,
SOLve polluti LAbii reatum,
        Sancte Iohannes. . . .
        MGH, *Poet. lat. Carol.* I. 83.

The striking measure of *Sancti venite* [19] is not forgotten.

[18] E. g., Sedulius Scotus. Blume suggests that the hymn above is by the author of *Ecce iam noctis*, page 121.

Alcuin's Sapphic *Christe salvator hominis ab ore* (MGH, *Poet. lat. Carol.* I. 313; AH 50: 154) is less scrupulous in quantities than might be expected of him if he intended a *metrum*. It is entitled *Ymnus*.

[19] Chapter IV. C. 3.  Compare, in the same volume of MGH, *Refulget omnis luce mundus aurea* (137); in volume III, *O tu qui servas armis ista mœnia* (703, late eighth century); in AH 51: 121, *Adnue, Christe, sœculorum Domine;* and, in Duemmler's *Rhythmorum eccl. œvi carolini specimen* (Berlin, 1881), *Audi me deus, peccatorem nimium* (6), and *Agnus et leo, mitis et terribilis* (12). These instances taken together seem to me to make against W. Meyer's different reading (*Spanisches zur Geschichte der ältesten mittellateinischen Rythmik,* 111) of the poem below as a "rhythmic pentameter."

Felix per omnes festum mundi cardines
Apostolorum præpollet alacriter
Petri beati, Pauli sacratissimi,
Quos Christus almo consecravit sanguine:
Ecclesiarum deputavit principes. . . .

        MGH, *Poet. lat. Carol.* I. 136; AH 50: 141.

The second measure of Boethius, exhibited by Bede in
two poems,[20] is echoed in the *Tanquam præcipitans turbo
regentes* of Sedulius Scotus[21] and appears in a fine Assumption hymn of the ninth century.

      O quam glorifica luce coruscas,
      Stirpis Davidicæ regia proles,
      Sublimis residens, virgo Maria,
      Supra cæligenas ætheris omnes!

      Tu cum virgineo, mater, honore
      Angelorum domino pectoris aulam
      Sacris visceribus casta parasti;
      Natus hinc Deus est corpore Christus. . . .

                      AH 51: 146.

In a few hymns of this period the measure seems to be
derived from one used twice by Prudentius.[22]

[20] Ascribed erroneously to St Ambrose (*De arte metrica*, Keil VII.
255). For the poem of Boethius, *Heu quam præcipiti mersa profundo*,
see above, Chapter IV. A.

[21] MGH, *Poet. lat. Carol.* III. 158. So *Vestri tecta nitent luce serena*,
III. 169, and others.

[22] *Cathemerinon* v and in the preface to Book I *Contra Symmachum*.
The meter is – – – ‿ ‿ ‿ – ‿ ‿ – ‿ ‿. Compare the first ode
of Horace. So Paulus Albarus in an acrostic poem on St Eulogius,
*Almi nunc revehit festa polifera* (MGH, *ibid.*, III. 139). Boethius uses
the measure with a shorter alternate line (III, *metrum* viii); and it is
otherwise varied, by a shorter line at the end of the stanza, in the eighth-
century hymn *Sanctorum meritis inclyta gaudia* (Britt, 159), and in the
ninth-century hymn *Festum nunc celebre magnaque gaudia* (MGH, *ibid.*
II. 249). All these hymns are exceptionally correct in quantities; and
the measure, unusual in hymns, may well have been composed metrically.

En cæli rutilant lumine splendido,
Testantur dominum nascere parvulum,
Qui format minima et qui creat ardua;
Regni sceptra tenens, est Deus atque homo. . . .
                    MGH, *Poet. lat. Carol.* II. 247.

A *rhythmus* of uncertain date is most plausibly assigned to tenth-century Verona.[23]

O Roma nobilis, orbis et domina,
Cunctarum urbium excellentissima,
Roseo martyrum sanguine rubea
Albis et virginum liliis candida,
Salutem dicimus tibi per omnia,
Te benedicimus, salve per sæcula.

Petre, tu præpotens cælorum claviger,
Vota precantium exaudi iugiter;
Cum bis sex tribuum sederis arbiter,
Factus placabilis iudica leniter
Teque petentibus nunc temporaliter
Ferto suffragia misericorditer.

O Paule, suscipe nostra precamina,
Cuius philosophos vicit industria;
Factus œconomus in domo regia
Divini muneris adpone fercula,
Ut, quæ repleverit te, sapientia
Ipsa nos repleat tua per dogmata.
                    AH 51: 219.

To read this as a rhythmical senarius disregards not
only many quantities, as might be expected, but also
many word-accents.  The measure of the hymn just above
is suggested by the doubly dactylic close and the generally long and stressed opening.  But so to render it is

---

[23] See Traube (in *Philolog. Untersuch. aus dem Mittelalter*, Munich
1891), who associates with it *O admirabile Veneris ydolum*.
    Cf. Abelard's *O quanta qualia sunt illa sabbata.*  AH. 48: 163.

again to violate many word-accents, including almost all those of the characteristic second foot. The word-accent is generally kept by rendering:

Ó Roma nóbilis, órbis et dómina.[24]

It is hard not to think that at least the final rhythmical dactyls were in the composer's mind. If so, we have rhythmical dactyls not only as occasional substitutions, but as constituent; and the easiest rendering makes them constitute the whole measure.

Carolingian hymn-writers ranged in art all the way from the expert and fluent metrist Sedulius Scotus to the undisciplined Gottschalk,[25] who would write twelve stanzas on a single rime such as *Christe, mearum/Lux tenebrarum,*[26] or *Spes mea, Christe,/Rex benedicte.*[27] Thus he rimes even Sapphics. With much diffuseness and jingle he has sometimes a lyric appeal that forecasts the more sentimental hymns of later centuries, and is as far from the gravity of the elder habit.

Hymnody is typically communal and popular. Such poetic opportunities inspired and authorized in the Carolingian period some verse more valid as devotion than as poetry. Here and there manuscripts have preserved local commemorations which make little pretense beyond grateful mnemonic. But hymns of higher achievement show that the new Latin verse given by the Church to the last days of the Empire was appreciated and car-

[24] The recollection that Poe wished thus to render the first ode of Horace might well give pause, were it not that Poe, though doubtless an ignoramus in Latin metric, was a poet and was interpreting Horace rhythmically.

[25] Godescalc (822–870) is in MGH, *Poet. lat. Carol.* III. 724.

[26] AH 50: 220.                    [27] *Ibid.* 221.

ried forward as poetry; and the rhythmical adaptations of measures not used before evince an active, and often an expert, poetic.

### b. NARRATIVE HEXAMETERS AND ELEGIACS

But the characteristic verse of the period is hexameter or elegiac. Thus Theodulf composed even the familiar Palm Sunday hymn.

> Gloria, laus et honor tibi sit, rex Christe redemptor,
> Cui puerile decus prompsit osanna pium. . . .
>
> MGH *Poet. lat. Carol.* I. 558.

Alcuin devotes fifty-five hexameters to a *conflictus* between spring and winter, and celebrates York in over sixteen hundred.[28] The elegiacs may seek Ovidian recurrences.[29]

> *Præsul amate, precor*, huc tu diverte, viator:
> Sis memor Albini ut, *præsul amate, precor*.
> *O mea cara domus*, habitatio dulcis, amata,
> Sis felix semper, *O mea cara domus*.
>
> Alcuin, *ibid*. 250.

> *Ordiar unde tuos*, sacer O Benedicte, triumphos?
> Virtutum cumulos *ordiar unde tuos?*
> *Euge beate pater*, meritum qui nomine prodis!
> Fulgida lux secli, *euge beate pater!*
>
> Paulus Diaconus, *ibid*. 36.

Of the many narrative poems employing these measures the commonest were the *passiones*, or saints' legends, usually with at least a rhythmic bent, and by the tenth century habitually *rhythmi* with internal rime. The tenth-century *Vita et passio sancti Christophori* of Walter of Speier, though it abundantly exemplifies both the

[28] *Ibid.* 270, 169.                                    [29] ARP 217.

metrical training and the study of Latin poets that he mentions in his introduction, shows also the trend of the time.

> More quidem regum gestabat sceptra Syrorum
> Fascibus indignus publicis rex, nomine Dagnus,
> Celans corda lupi simulatis vultibus agni,
> Et dum plumatam portarent colla coronam,
> Texerat occulte serpentem forma columbæ.
> Iam quid plura querar? Tigribus rabidis fuit is par.
>
> II. 1–6; Ermini, page 82, 240–245.[30]

Some, at least, of these longer poems were cumulative school exercises. A promising theme in the imitative verse that was commonly part of the study of the Latin poets would be commented by the *grammaticus*, revised according to his criticism, and kept by him for later re-handling or extension.[31] Thus the verse, even with the rhythmical habit established, attended to Latin quantities. Thus also classical reminiscences, especially Vergilian, are frequent; and Walter shows the continued vogue of Prudentius. For the hexameters most typical of the period are literary exercises.

## C. DIALECTICA

Logic followed the Boethian tradition handed down by Isidore.[32] Alcuin, though his manual is meager, repeats in his tract on the Trinity St Augustine's view

[30] Riming hexameters appear generally, though not always, throughout Ermini: in the Latin *Gesta Apollonii* versifying the romance of Apollonius of Tyre (113); in Uffing's *Carmen de sancto Liudgero* (131); even in the accomplished Hrotsvitha.

[31] Ermini xvi, xviii, 43, 74, 110, 111. In the following century, school exercise in prosopopœia is suggested by some of the verse of Baudry de Bourgeuil (1046–1130); e. g., the Ovidian XLII, XLIII, CLIX, CLX, pages 29, 39, 141, 145 in the edition of Phyllis Abrahams, Paris, 1926. [32] Above, Chapter III. B.

of the importance of this study [33] for the defense of the faith. Rabanus makes it theoretically central.

> *Dialectica* is the training of the reason to investigate, define, and express, and to be able to distinguish the true from the false. This, then, is the training of trainings; it teaches how to learn. This exhibits and unfolds the nature, aim, and scope of reason itself. It knows; its aims and virtue are both to know and to make knowers.
>
> *De clericorum institutione* III. xx; PL 107: 397 C.

But the turn of *dialectica* to dominate the Trivium was not yet.

## D. RHETORICA

Alcuin's adaptation of the *De inventione* of Cicero, Walafrid Strabo's enumeration of the five ancient parts of rhetoric, do not prove the use of the whole ancient program. Even the ancient texts would not of themselves carry on the ancient method. The "*quæstiones civiles*" often quoted from Cicero's opening definition could hardly carry their ancient content either in a society disturbed by the invasions or in a society reorganizing under feudalism. Moreover the teaching of *rhetorica*, even when it kept touch with Roman method, was likely to lean on the *declamatio* handed down by the schools of Gaul.[34] For all these reasons the ancient lore naturally most sought and most used was *elocutio*, the counsels of style. The function of *rhetorica* is usually described by some such verb as *ornare*.

Little beyond this is suggested by the summary of Rabanus. Repeating once more that the field of rhetoric is *quæstiones civiles*, he adds:

[33] *Libellus de sancta Trinitate*, cited by Gaskoin, *Alcuin*, 127.
[34] Above, Chapter III. A.

Nevertheless [rhetoric] is not outside the scope of training for the Church. For whatever an orator or preacher of the divine law sets out capably and fitly in teaching, whatever he expresses aptly and elegantly in letters, conforms to this art.
*De clericorum institutione* III. xix; PL 107: 396 C.

The passage is reminiscent of St. Augustine's *De doctrina christiana;* [35] and eight later chapters (xxix–xxxvi) follow this closely, sometimes continuously and word for word. But Rabanus is at once less specific and narrower as to style. As to composition in the large he says hardly anything; and he seems to miss the cogency of Augustine's own order.

The larger and more vital conception of rhetoric, which was at least before the eyes of Rabanus, seems more to beckon Loup de Ferrières. Man of letters in his intellectual eagerness [36] as well as in his style, and teacher as well, he makes requisitions on the libraries of his friends. The Quintilian that he needs is not the volume of selections, but all twelve books; [37] the Cicero, not only the common *De inventione*, but also the book whose recovery by Poggio in the fifteenth century was one of the literary events of the Renaissance, the *De oratore*. [38] If these two cardinal works of the better an-

[35] Book IV; see above, Chapter II.
[36] "Erinnert an die Tätigkeit der italienischen Humanisten." *Manitius* I. 486.
  The letters of Loup are in MGH (*Epist.* VI, Pars Prior, ed. Duemmler, 1900). See also Levillain, *Étude sur les lettres de Loup de Ferrières,* Bibliothèque de l'École des Chartes 72 (1901): 445–509; 73 (1902): 69–118, 289–330, 537–586.
[37] *Epist.* 62, to Altsig about 849: "Quintiliani institutionum oratoriarum libros xii." Cf. *Epist.* 103, to Benedict III.
[38] *Epist.* 1, to Einhard: "Tullii de rhetorica liber . . . eiusdem auctoris de rhetorica tres libri in disputatione ac dialogo de oratore." The latter is unmistakable. It is sufficient evidence even if the "Tullium de oratore" of *Epist.* 103 be regarded as uncertain.

cient tradition were not much sought, at least they were available.

The "three styles" seem already to have been transferred in school from rhetoric to poetic, and exemplified from Vergil.[39]   Mature practise was already attentive to prose rhythm.   Abbo of Fleury, much preoccupied with this, was also fond of alliteration, and sometimes marked his balances with rime.

> Qua peracta pœnitentia, populos suæ dioceseos mandat, mandando convocat, convocando suppliciter persuadet, ut triduano jejunio a se divinæ indignationis iracundiam removeant, removendo avertant, quatenus sacrificio spiritus contribulati placatus Dominus illi suam gratiam concederet, qua corpus beati martyris tangere et lavare auderet; qui licet tantis virtutibus floreret in mundo, vili tamen et sibi incongruo continebatur mausoleo.
>
> *Abbonis Floriacensis Passio Sancti Edmundi.*[40]

Though the extremes of this passage go beyond Abbo's normal practise, they appear also in tenth-century ceremonious letters.[41]

[39] The misapplication, very common later (see the index), seems to be intended by Walter of Speier.

> Præterea triplicis succincta veste coloris
> Omnibus excellens docuit nos musa Maronis.
> *Vita et Passio Sancti Christophori* I. 104.

For the "three styles" see ARP 56, 57–59, 228; and above, 56, 67.

[40] In *Memorials of St. Edmund's Abbey,* ed. T. Arnold (Rolls Series, 96), I. 22.  See the references to Abbo in G. H. Gerould's *Abbot Ælfric's rhythmic prose,* Modern Philology 22 (May, 1925): 352–366; and, for the prose of Loup de Ferrières, W. Meyer, *De clausula in Lupi epistolis rhythmica,* Gött. gelehrt. Anzeig., 1893, page 22.

[41] E. g., Summæ sanctitatis, scientiæ, pietatis et ordinis culmine sublimato domino. . . . Nunc ergo puerum istum, viscera mea, filium consobrinæ meæ, solam et maximam curam meam, commendo quibus estis plenissimi visceribus misericordiæ vestræ, ut vestram vitam et vos 'primis miretur ab annis,' mansuetudinem vigore decoratam, doctrinam operibus commendatam, austeritatem dulcedine tempera-

### E. The Poetic of Germanic Epic

This is the period also of Germanic epic: the Anglo-
Saxon *Beowulf* (probably eighth century), *Waldere*,
*Finnsburgh*, and *Maldon*, the *Hildebrand* (early ninth
century) of the continental Germans, the Scandinavian
"Elder Edda." [42] Though little connection is apparent
between these verse narratives and the Latin poetic
with which they are contemporary, there may have been
some. [43] Anglo-Saxon epic is of the time of Bede. The
Walter legends are known largely through the Latin
hexameters of Ekkehard; [44] and other learned clerks

tam, taciturnitatem modestam, locutionem utilem vel necessariam,
victus et somni parcitatem, mediocritatem vestitus, ieiuniorum et
orationum per dies et noctes instantiam, largitionem elemosinarum,
susceptionem hospitum, solamen lugentium, peregrinis et egentibus,
plebibus et clero, monachis et virginibus, viduis et orphanis, comitibus
et regibus, servis et liberis, coniugibus et continentibus, mediocribus et
maximis, Iudæis et gentilibus vos unum omnia perdiscat effectum.
Quod si aliquid apud vos, ubi omnes proficiunt, doctrinæ morumque
profectus, Deo largiente, ceperit, debitorem vobis de eo Christum facitis,
qui eum talem educaveritis, ut non solum sibi, sed et aliis possit utili-
tati fieri. MGH, Legum sectio v, formulæ, 409 (Collectio Sangallensis
Salomonis III tempore).

For prose rhythm in medieval letters see below, Chapter VIII. C.

[42] The poetic of Irish epic during this period is more difficult to determine. From the existing forms, which are later, we may divine that
its conceptions were at once mythical and romantic, and that its incidental verse—its main course was in prose—had already an elaborate
technic.

The generally typical epic traits are suggestively presented by W. P.
Ker, *Epic and Romance*, London, 1897; the specifically Anglo-Saxon
ones, by R. W. Chambers, *Beowulf*, Cambridge, 1921. Both give ex-
tracts and references.

[43] Chambers, reviewing the parallels with classical epic explored by
Klaeber, finds "no tangible or conclusive proof of borrowing. But the
influence may have been none the less effective for being indirect" (330).

[44] Ekkehard I of St. Gall, *Waltharius*, MGH, *Script*. II. 117. For
other editions, translations, and studies see Ermini, who reprints considerable selections.

found native epic worth while not only as history, but as literature.

What has been preserved shows the primary epic appeal of legend not exotic and imported, but handed down in folklore still orally active. This is not at all to say that they are history as opposed to fiction. Their historical value, however great, is accidental. Their facts, already centuries old, have been shaped by tradition. Their Sigurd or Hildebrand is seen through a magnifying mist. Epic is never, in our modern sense, history. It is the glorification in song of a hero; and primary epic has its own authentic appeal from singing a hero that still belongs to the poet and to his hearers and still beckons their communal dreams.

Thus Germanic epic, taking us farther back through legend into myth, gives a more immediate sense of oral tradition. There is even an eery likeness, as of the most ancient poetic repeating itself, between the minstrel in the *Beowulf* and the minstrel in the *Odyssey*.

But after they had put from them the desire of meat and drink, the muse stirred the minstrel to sing the songs of famous men, even that lay whereof the fame had then reached the wide heaven, namely the quarrel between Odysseus and Achilles, son of Peleus. . . . Then Odysseus of many counsels spake to Demodocus, saying: "Demodocus, I praise thee far above all mortal men, whether it be the Muse, the daughter of Zeus, that taught thee, or even Apollo; for right duly dost thou chant the faring of the Achæans, even all that they wrought and suffered, and all their travail, as if, methinks, thou hadst been present, or heard the tale from another. Come now, change thy strain, and sing of the fashioning of the horse of wood, . . . even the guileful thing that goodly Odysseus led up into the citadel, when he had it laden with the men who wasted Ilios!" . . . So spake he, and the minstrel, being stirred by the god, began and showed forth his min-

strelsy.  He took up the tale where it tells how the Argives
of the one part set fire to their huts, and went aboard their
decked ships and sailed away, while those others, the fellowship of renowned Odysseus, were now seated in the assembly-
place of the Trojans, all hidden in the horse, for the Trojans
themselves had dragged him to the citadel.  *Odyssey* viii.
72–75, 484–504 (Butcher and Lang's prose translation).

So Hrothgar's minstrel is represented as singing songs
of former heroes to awaken joy in hall along the mead-
bench.  Among those thus inserted in the *Beowulf* is
the lay of King Finn, which has come down also in another form.  As the Greek minstrel turns old songs to
the praise of the hero present before him, so the warriors
celebrating in hall Beowulf's killing of Grendel turn
the legend of Sigmund.

At times one of the king's thanes, whose memory was full
of songs, laden with vaunting rhymes, who knew old tales
without number, invented a new story, closely bound up with
fact.  The man deftly narrated the adventures of Beowulf,
and cunningly composed other skilful lays with interwoven
words.  *Beowulf*, 867–874 (Tinker's prose translation).

In such passages we seem to be near the roots of verse
narrative.

The verse narratives of the Germanic peoples during
this period are poetically homogeneous.  *Hildebrand*,
indeed, is more stinted than *Beowulf*, and the north in-
clines more than the west toward lyric; but they all
have essentially the same poetic.[45]  Their epic conception is typically not of a progressive story, but of a situation.  The hero is imagined in a crisis.  Sometimes
abrupt or stinted, they nevertheless prevail by unity.

[45] "For purposes of poetry there was only one nation—the Germanic—
split into many dialects and groups, but possessed of a common metre,
a common style, a common standard of heroic feeling."  Chambers, 99.

This mainspring of their poetic is their habitual means toward tragic intensity.[46]    Even more constant is their movement in detail.   The verse consists of two staves separated by a marked cæsura, but corresponding by alliteration.   The alliteration is not, as in Latin verse, an added suggestion; it is constituent; it makes the verse.

> Him ða Scyld ʒewat to ʒescæphwile
> felahror feran on frean wære;
> hi hyne þa ætbæron to brimes faroðe,
> swæse ʒesiþas, swa he selfa bæd,
> þenden wordum weold wine Scyldinʒa,
> leof landfruma lanʒe ahte.
> þær æt hyðe stod hrinʒedstefna
> isiʒ and utfus, æþelinʒes fær:
>
> *Beowulf*, 26–33 (Wülcker's revised text)

No less essential is the two-stave movement, so strong in Germanic habit that it may well have been influential in handling even Latin hexameters with cæsura reinforced by rime.[47]    In Anglo-Saxon the staves show distinct recurrent types; and the verses generally tend, as above, to "run on," whereas the Old Norse are oftener composed in the fashion of the "closed couplet."   But these differences are unimportant beside the constant binary movement.   The verses are not equal in number of syllables; their stress rhythm is patterned in alliterated pairs.

> Then departed Scyld at his appointed hour,
> glorious to go unto God's keeping.
> Together they bore him to breaking surges,
> bosom companions, as he bade himself
> while he wielded words, warden of Scyldings,
> loved land-ruler, long their master.

---

[46] For the tragic tendency see Ker, 86.    [47] See above, page 140.

At the roadstead bode his ringèd bow,
icy, eager, atheling's ship.
They laid him there, beloved chieftain,
bringer of booty, on the breast of the ship,
mighty by the mast.  There were many treasures
from long voyages laden beside him.
Ne'er heard I that comelier keel provided
hacking weapons and harness warlike,
brands and byrnies.  On his bosom lay
store unstinted that must start with him
on the flood's realm to float outward.[48]

*Beowulf, 26–42.*

All primary epic is thus concrete.  It speaks habitually
in the immediate terms of the five senses.  But the habit
of images crystallized among the Germanic poets in a
conventional epic diction.  Their style is deliberately
removed from common speech.  Its most obvious traits
are designation by descriptive compounds and accompaniment by descriptive epithets.  A lord is "land-ruler,"
as above, or "prize-giver," or "hoard-ward."  His war-
rior is "hall-counselor," "earl's hope," "rugged-in-war."
The ominous raven is "sallow-brown, swarthy."  Ships
especially command a whole store of such phrases as
those of the seventh and eighth lines above.  Germanic
epic has a distinct poetic language.

[48] The beginning of the passage is quoted above in the original.  The
object of this rendering is to follow exactly, verse by verse, the original
rhythm.  Though such imitation must sooner or later break down, for
short stretches it indicates specifically the salient verse habits.

# CHAPTER VI

## RHETORIC AND LOGIC IN THE TWELFTH AND THIRTEENTH CENTURIES

REFERENCES AND ABBREVIATIONS

ARP      Baldwin (C. S.), *Ancient rhetoric and poetic*, New York, 1924.

Clerval    Clerval (l'Abbé A.), *Les écoles de Chartres au moyen âge, du Ve au XVIe siècle*, Chartres, 1895 (Mémoires de la Société Archéologique d'Eure-et-Loir, XI).

Haskins    Haskins (C. H.), *The renaissance of the twelfth century*, Harvard University Press, 1927.

Manacorda   Manacorda (G.), *Storia della scuola in Italia*, vol. I, *Il medio evo*, Milan, 1913 (2 parts in separate volumes).

Mignon    Mignon (l'Abbé A.), *Les origines de la scolastique et Hugues de Saint-Victor*, Paris, 1895, 2 vols.

PL      *Patrologia latina*, Migne (cited by volume and column).

Poole    Poole (Reginald Lane), *Illustrations of the history of medieval thought*, London, 2d ed., 1920. See also his important biography of John of Salisbury in Dict. Nat. Biog., his article in Eng. Histor. Rev., July, 1923, and his communication, March 27, 1924, to the British Academy (Proceedings, xl) on the early correspondence.

150

## A. The Trivium at Chartres, Eleventh and Twelfth Centuries

At the fall of Rome the Trivium was dominated by *rhetorica;* in the Carolingian period, by *grammatica;* in the high middle age, by *dialectica.* The shift of emphasis to logic probably began in the eleventh century. Even Chartres, renowned for its teaching of *grammatica*, shows hints of this under Fulbert.[1] In the next century the theory of logic was fortified by commanding in Latin translation those parts of Aristotle's *Organon* which had not been available; and its practise became more urgent through the historic debates as to universals. By offering thus the most active training in composition, logic confirmed the restriction of rhetoric to style. John of Salisbury, after giving full scope to *grammatica*, focuses his great book on *dialectica. Rhetorica* he merely mentions; it claims none of his thought. Nor does any other leader of the high middle age treat rhetoric as active in the intellectual processes of composing. Rhetoric has no educational vitality. The vital study that taxes and develops men's minds is logic.

In detail, *grammatica* at Chartres[2] during the great

[1] Fulbert, c. 960–1028. His distinguished successor Ives, who ruled Chartres 1090–1115, had been, with Anselm, a pupil of Lanfranc at Bec, and had himself taught there (Clerval, 146).

That Chartres had the whole *Organon* even before Gilbert de la Porrée, Richard l'Evêque, and John of Salisbury is shown by Clerval, 244 seq.

Haskins notes in the twelfth century the primacy of the cathedral schools (Laon, Tours, Chartres, Orléans, Paris) over the monastic. (*The Normans in European History*, 177; *The Renaissance of the Twelfth Century*, 49.)

[2] The traditional manuals and authors continue: Donatus, Priscian, Martianus Capella (not much used), Bede, *De arte metrica;* Livy, Valerius Maximus, Orosius, Gregory of Tours; Vergil, Ovid, Horace, Terence, Statius; Fortunatus, Sedulius, Arator, Prudentius, Boethius.

century of the school (about 1050–1150), shows a full development of *prælectio* and distinct cultivation of rhythmic.[3] *Rhetorica*, except in *dictamen* and in some application of the larger ancient precepts of composition to preaching, is at a standstill.[4] The more significance therefore attaches to a short poem of Fulbert summing up the differences between rhetoric and logic: the one concrete, current, reasoning in enthymemes, aiming at persuasion; the other abstract, syllogistic, aiming at conviction.[5] This giving of the full ancient scope to rhetoric in theory may be a reminder, may be even a protest. At any rate the practise had no such scope. The Chartres manuscript [6] containing these verses is an eleventh-century collection of traditional

*Prælectio* appears at its best in John of Salisbury's account of the teaching of Bernard of Chartres (below pages 160–164). See the admirable summaries, period by period, in Clerval.

The library at Bec in the twelfth century had Priscian, Isidore, Martianus Capella (with Remi's commentary), Anselm *De grammatica*, and Claudian (PL 150: 775–782).

[3] Clerval, 111–113, suggests an influence on the earlier forms of liturgical sequences.

[4] Colson (ed. of Book I, Cambridge, 1924) finds no clear indication of Quintilian in the eleventh century; and the large use of him by John of Salisbury in the twelfth (below, page 169) is not specifically related to rhetoric. Cicero is limited to *De inventione* and the commentary of Victorinus (Clerval, 115). The *Rhetorica ad Herennium* is the source of the *Colores* of Onulf, who taught at Speier c. 1050. The Bec library had in the twelfth century "utraque rhetorica" (i. e., *De inv.* and *Ad Herenn.*), Cicero, *De partit. orat.*, Suetonius, and the letters of Sidonius. At Chartres Thierry cites Quintilian and, according to Clerval, 233, Cicero, *De oratore*. The latter, with Quintilian, appears in *A list of textbooks from the close of the twelfth century*, Haskins in Harvard Stud. Class. Phil. 20:92.

[5] Clerval, 115–116.

[6] * 100 as described in Clerval, 117. Besides Fulbert's verses, it has (* 10) two short treatises: *De rhetoricæ cognatione*, and *Locorum rhetoricorum distinctio*. The *Topica*, of course, are common ground between rhetoric and logic.

materials for the study of logic. The study was advanced by Gilbert de la Porrée.[7] Thierry's collection[8] of the traditional writers on the seven arts, *Bibliotheca septem artium*, or *Heptateuchon*, gives 190 leaves to *grammatica*,[9] 88 to *rhetorica*,[10] 154 to *dialectica*.[11] The remaining 160 leaves of the two large volumes are devoted to the Quadrivium. Thierry's prologue,[12] summarizing the functions of the several arts *viâ* Martianus Capella, distributes those of the Trivium as follows: through *grammatica*, elegance; through *dialectica*, logical coherence; through *rhetorica*, ornament. Oral composition, as distinct from revision for style, seems to have no pedagogy except through logic.

## B. THE TRIVIUM IN HUGH OF ST. VICTOR

Hugh of St. Victor's [13] *Lore of teaching* (*Eruditio didascalica*, or *Didascalicon*) is neither a compend nor a pro-

[7] Gilbertus Porretanus, c. 1075–1154, Chancellor at Chartres 1126, teacher at Paris 1141, Bishop of Poitiers 1142; *Liber sex principiorum, Comment. IV libr. Boeth., Liber de causis*. See Clerval, 163–168, and Poole. Clerval suggests that Gilbert, as well as Thierry and Bernard Silvester, had relations with the Toulouse translators of Arabic books into Latin.

[8] Terricus Carnotensis, Breton, *scolarum magister* at Chartres 1121, taught rhetoric at Paris c. 1140, died c. 1150; *Comment. De invent.* and *Rhet. ad Herenn.; Heptateuchon* c. 1141 (Chartres MSS. **497, 498) described in Clerval, 220 seq., with a synoptic table of contents.

[9] Donatus and Priscian.

[10] Cic. *De invent.* and *Partit. Orat., Rhet ad Herenn.*, the summary of Severianus, and Martianus Capella.

[11] The usual Boethian items.    [12] Translated in Clerval, 221.

[13] Hugh of St. Victor, Saxon, c. 1096–1141, entered the Abbey of St. Victor at Paris c. 1116 and taught there; works PL 175–177. See especially Mignon, whose second chapter is a good summary of studies before Hugh. A critical study of the MSS. by Hauréau (B.), *Les œuvres de H. de St. V.*, Paris, 1886 (a revision of a study published in 1859), shows that *Eruditio didascalica* has only six parts, the seventh added

gram; it is a concise philosophical survey of education. Though his primary concern is with what is to be studied, and to what ends, he sometimes gives also acute hints of method. Book I (*De studio legendi*), a preliminary survey of typical directions of study, ends (xii) with *logica*, Hugh's general term for the Trivium as a group, i. e., for all language studies. Considering language as expression (*logica sermocinalis*), these are indeed the usual three; but considering language as thought (*logica rationalis*), they are only two, *dialectica* and *rhetorica*. Book II (*De discretione artium*) expands the exposition to determine the places of all seven arts in a scheme of philosophy. First the Quadrivium, then the manual arts, are classified under the traditional threefold division:[14] theory (1) of thought, (2) of morals, or conduct, (3) of technical skill. Outside this division remains the Trivium, Hugh's *logica*, as a fourth and final group. Though *logica* may be divided simply, as in Book I, Hugh now offers a more philosophical division by function in composing. By the latter we have (a) *grammatica* by itself as having no such function, and (b) *rhetorica* and *dialectica* together as both involving investigation (*inventio*) and the processes of arrangement, and revision (*iudicium*). These two composition studies are thus seen to belong, as probable proof (*probabilis*), between absolute, or abstract proof (*demonstratio*) and plausible, or illegitimate proof (*sophistica*).

in PL being a separate work.  See also Fourier Bonnard, *Histoire de l'abbaye royale et de l'ordre des chanoines réguliers de St. Victor de Paris,* Paris (n. d.); and the index to Manacorda.  John of Salisbury refers to Hugh, and uses part of his classification.

[14] The division, which is common in the middle age (e. g., John of Salisbury, *Metalogicus,* II. ii), is in Quintilian, *Inst. Or.* XII. 2. 10.

## PHILOSOPHIA

| | | | |
|---|---|---|---|
| *theorica*<br>(*specula-*<br>*tiva*) | theologia<br>mathematica<br>physica | (the Boethian  intellectibilis)<br>(  "       "     intelligibilis)<br>(  "       "     naturalis) | arithmetica<br>musica<br>geometria<br>astronomia |

*practica* (*activa, ethica*)

*mechanica:* the seven manual arts, e. g., lanificium, agricultura

| | | |
|---|---|---|
| *logica*<br>I | rationalis | dialectica<br><br>rhetorica |
| | sermocinalis | grammatica (scientia loquendi sine<br>   vitio)<br>dialectica (disputatio acuta, verum<br>   a falso distinguens)<br>rhetorica (disciplina ad persuaden-<br>   dum quæque idonea) |
| *logica*<br>II | grammatica | |
| | ratio disserendi | demonstratio<br><br>probabilis (involving          { dialectica<br>inventio and iudicium)      { rhetorica<br>sophistica |

From these classifications Hugh proceeds in Book III to practical considerations: of studies as training (*disciplina*), of the interrelations of the seven arts, of a scheme of reading (*ordo legendi*), of meditation, etc. The three remaining books deal with sacred studies.

Hugh's term *logica* expresses a conception of the Trivium as an integrated group. Less obvious, but hardly less significant, is the importance given implicitly to logic (*dialectica*). Though rhetoric is recognized as having theoretically a function in composing, it receives otherwise but little more attention than in the cardinal treatise of medieval pedagogy, the *Metalogicus*.

## C. The *Metalogicus* of John of Salisbury

The most extensive reasoned medieval survey of the Trivium is the *Metalogicus* [15] of John of Salisbury. Though this devotes most space to logic and to the logical aspects of other language study, it is a unified and carefully coherent presentation of all teaching that deals with words. Statesman as well as scholar, more widely known, perhaps, than any other man of his time, and more widely conversant with its movements in church and state, secretary to two archbishops of Canterbury, rounding out his life as Bishop of Chartres, he devoted his best thought to the *Metalogicus*. The classification underlying its first two books is that of Hugh of St. Victor. [16]

[15] About 1159. For John see Poole, the index to Clerval, and the antiquated, but still suggestive study of Schaarschmidt, *J. S. nach Leben und Studien* . . ., Leipzig, 1862. Webb (C. C. I.) has edited the *Policraticus*, Oxford, 1909, with an introduction especially valuable for John's reading, and announced an edition of the *Metalogicus*, for which meantime the only available text is in PL 199, referred to in this section by column. The letters, also in PL 199, were printed with Gerbert's and Stephen of Tournai's in 1611 (Paris, Ruette). The *Historia pontificalis*, printed in MGH as anonymous, has been edited by Poole, Oxford University Press, 1927. *Policraticus* IV, V, VI, with selections from VII and VIII, are translated, with an introduction, by Dickinson (J.) as *The statesman's yearbook of J. of S.*, New York, 1927.

[16] See the preceding section. John mentions Hugh at 833 A, 924 B. The word *disserere* Hugh and John may have taken, as John took other things at the opening of Book II, from Isidore (see above, page 97); but the ultimate source of the phrase *ratio disserendi* is probably Cicero's *Topica:* "omnis ratio diligens disserendi duas habet partes, unum inveniendi alteram iudicandi." *Top.* 2. Cf. *Fin.* 1. 7. 22; *Fat.* 1. 1. *Disserere* seems limited to *dialectica* in *De orat.* I. 9 (see Wilkins's note); but using the same word in II. 157, Cicero points out that the proper function of *dialectica* is analysis (*iudicium*, not *inventio*). In *Orator* 113, discussing the common ground of rhetoric and logic, he says "utrum-

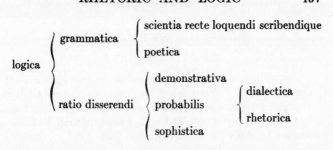

By the conception of the Trivium as twofold, *rhetorica* is theoretically subordinated; and in John's working out of the scheme it is ignored.  Barely mentioned,[17] it appears to have no distinctive composing function. Part of its ancient function seems to be implied now and then under *grammatica;* more is certainly transferred to *dialectica*, with which John connects most of what he discerns of composition as a study.  His scheme can be comprehended only as a whole and in sequence.  The survey of *logica* in Books I and II is not primarily an analysis.  Rather it develops the functions of language studies in progressive stages.  This procedure, too, as well as some of its important details, may have been suggested by Quintilian.[18]  John is concerned less with division than with order.  His own order is so significant and so carefully marked [19] that it should be followed step by step.

que in disserendo est," and goes on to distinguish logic as *ratio disputandi* from rhetoric as *ratio dicendi*.  *Dicere* is generally his word for rhetoric. Quintilian, whom John uses largely, probably has in mind the same distinction in X. 1. 81, though in other places he uses *disserere* more generally.

[17] I. xvii (847 C), xxiv (854 B), II. x (868 B).

[18] For John's use of Quintilian, see below, page 169.

[19] In this respect *Metalogicus* is conspicuously different from *Policraticus*.

## DIGEST OF *METALOGICUS*

### Book I. *GRAMMATICA*

i–vi. The opening takes occasion from certain opponents of the Trivium.[20] "When *logica* was derided, and its envious opponent provoked me, in spite of my indignation and protests, by almost daily disputes, at length I accepted trial, and have studied to reply to his calumnies" (824 A) . . . "Since I have undertaken the defense of *logica*, the book is entitled Metalogicon."

vii–ix. Eloquence is natural, not in the perverted sense that the full exercise of speech is instinctive, but only to the extent that speech is the peculiar opportunity of mankind,

x (837 B). "*Logica*, then, to show the widest meaning of the word, is the theory of speaking or of discoursing. Sometimes it is contracted to the extent of limiting the force of the word to theories of discourse. Whether, therefore, it teaches the ways of reasoning or offers a rule for all speech. they are evidently unwise who call it useless; for either [the narrower or the wider scope] is taught by most famous theory as necessary. The twofold meaning of the word comes from its origin in Greek; for there λόγος means now speech (sermo), now theory (ratio). But that its meaning may be extended most widely, let us assign to it at present the control of all speech, so that nowhere it may be proved useless, and so that in its more general sense it may appear as a whole very useful and necessary."

xi. The idea of any art is to further nature by theory.

xii (839 C). "But since *artes* are of many kinds, the first of all for a mind bent on wisdom are the *artes liberales*. All these are included in the theory either of the Trivium or of the Quadrivium; and so great efficacy they are said to have achieved among the ancients, who taught them assiduously,

[20] These "Cornificians" are mentioned 825 C, 827 A, 852 B, 857 A. See Clerval 182, 211, 227.

that they opened all reading, roused the mind to everything, and sufficed to resolve the difficulties of all questions which can be settled. They to whom the theory of the Trivium expounded the secrets of all speech, the law of the Quadrivium the secrets of all nature, needed no teachers to explain their books or resolve their questions."

xiii (840 A). "Of all these the first is *logica*, in that part of it which deals with the first teaching of speech. . . . This is *grammatica*, the lore of speaking and writing correctly, the origin of all liberal disciplines . . . the cradle of all philosophy . . . the first nurse of all literary study."

xiv–xvi. *Grammatica* imitates nature by keeping congruity of thought.[21] For instance, it does not tolerate adjectives of secondary application with nouns of primary application.

xvii (847 A). "In other things, too, *grammatica* imitates nature; for the precepts of *poetica* set forth the habits of nature and exact of the craftsman in this art that he follow nature— to that degree, indeed, that the poet shall not depart from the footprints of nature, but apply himself to stick to them in manner, gesture, even word. Moreover the theory is to be kept not only in feet or tenses, but in ages, places, seasons,[22] and other details beyond our present purpose; for all these come from the workshop of nature. Indeed, *poetica* stays so close to the things of nature that many have refused to include it in *grammatica*, asserting that it is an art in itself, pertaining no more to *grammatica* than to *rhetorica*,[23] though so far related to both as to have precepts in common. Let them snarl about this who will. I will not keep up the dispute; but under favor of them all I think that *poetica* is to be as-

[21] Quadam proportione rationis, 841 B.

[22] This poetic is none the less rhetoric for being confirmed by quotations from Horace (*Ars poetica*, 102–105, 108–111; see ARP 245). The general doctrine of appropriateness was the basis of the specific recipes for *encomium* (above, page 31).

[23] Cf. Vincent of Beauvais below, section D. 2.

signed to *grammatica* as to the mother and nurse of its study.
. . . Either *grammatica* will hold on to *poetica*, or *poetica*
will be turned out from the number of the liberal disciplines."

xviii–xx.  *Grammatica* deals both with precision and with
imagery, both with denotation and with connotation.  It
includes letters, syllables, phrase, sentence-form, punctuation,
figures, metric—everything that can be taught verbally.

xxi–xxiii.  It has occupied persons no less eminent than
Cæsar and Cicero.  It is a practical guide to utterance and to
learning.  The objection derived from Seneca is insufficient.
For the practise of philosophy and of virtue the important
approaches are reading, teaching, meditation.  Of these the
root and foundation is *grammatica*.

xxiv.  Actually the *prælectio* is vindicated by such a *grammaticus* as Bernard of Chartres.[24]

(853 C)  "He, then, who aspires to philosophy, let him
lay hold of reading, teaching, and meditation, with the practise of good works, lest God be angry and what he seemeth
to have be taken from him.  But since *lectio* is equivocal,
applicable both to the practise of teacher and learner and to
the absorption of one studying writings for himself, let the
one, the interchange of teacher and learner, be called, to use
Quintilian's word, *prælectio*, the other, applied to the scrutiny
of meditation, simply *lectio*.  On the authority, then, of
Quintilian, the *grammaticus* in his *prælectio* ought to attend
to such details as to ask to have the verse analyzed into the
parts of speech and the appropriate feet, which ought to be
known in poems.  He should take exception to barbarisms.
improprieties, or other transgressions of the law of speaking—
not, however, that he should find fault with poets for metrical

[24] The following translation renders entire the most specific extant
account of *prælectio* in the middle age.  Long selections from it in French
translation will be found in Clerval, 225–227; a shorter selection, with
the corresponding Latin text, in Faral, *Les arts poétiques du xiie et du
xiiie siècle*, Paris, 1924, 99–101.  Haskins, 135, has a short selection in
English translation.

For *prælectio*, see the index to ARP and to this volume.

necessities which, though faults in prose, are called virtues in verse, since force of necessity commonly wins the praise of virtue for what cannot be denied without sacrifice. Metaplasm, sentence variation, figures of speech and such various iterations as may be present, the theory underlying this way of speaking or that—all these the *prælectio* should point out and impress upon the hearer's memory by frequent warnings.

(854 A) "The *prælectio* should make authors yield, without holding them up to ridicule, the feathers with which, crow-fashion, they have decked their works from various disciplines, to make the style more becoming. The more disciplines the teacher is imbued with, and the more abundantly, the more fully he will discern the elegance of authors, the more clearly he will bring it out in teaching. For they by the *diacrisis* which we may call illustration [25] or visualization, when they had undertaken in bare outline story, plot, fable, or whatever else it might be, would develop it with such abundance of disciplines and such charm of sentence and style that the work when completed seemed the image of all the arts.

(854 B) "*Grammatica* and *poetica*, indeed, are entirely fused and control the whole surface of what is expounded. *Campologica*, as it is called, contributing descriptive amplification of proof,[26] looses its theory in a blaze of gold; and *rhetorica* with store of persuasions and brilliance of style rivals the brightness of silver. Mathematics is borne on the wheels of its Quadrivium and, hard on the heels of the others, has woven

[25] *Illustratio* is Quintilian's word (and Cicero's, he says) in VI. ii. 32, where he is exhibiting the same sort of development as is here indicated by John. For *historia, argumentum, fabula* see the index. That these were elementary school exercises suggests that the subject of this sentence (*Illi*) refers not to authors, but to schoolboys engaged in developing a *materia;* but the reference can hardly be determined in PL, in which the whole sentence seems to me dubious.

[26] *Probandi colores.* The word *colores* in this sense, unusual at this time, is characteristic of Seneca Rhetor, to whom John refers in II. viii. But the solution of a passage apparently corrupt may well await a better text.

its own figures and charms in manifold variety. Science, having searched the counsels of nature, brings from its own storehouse manifold charm of figures. Moreover that which rises above the other parts of philosophy—I mean ethics—without which not even the name of philosopher abides, surpasses all the others in the gift of ornament that it brings. Sound Vergil or Lucan, and there, whatever philosophy you profess, you will find its making. In proportion, therefore, to the capacity of the pupil, or to the industry and diligence of the teacher, the fruit of the *prælectio auctorum* is constant.

(854 C) "This used to be the habit of Bernard of Chartres, in our modern times the most overflowing spring of literature in Gaul. In his reading he would show first what was simple and regular. Grammatical forms, rhetorical figures, quibbles of sophistry, relations of the passage to other disciplines, he used to bring out clearly—not, however, by teaching everything at every point, but by adjusting to the capacity of his pupils and to the time of the instruction. Since appeal of discourse is either in precision, that is in the nice adjustment of adjective or verb to noun, or in imagery, that is in passing by comparison from one sense to another, he used to inculcate these in the minds of his hearers whenever he found occasion. Since memory is strengthened and talent is sharpened by practise, he would spur some by exhortation, others by punishments, to imitate what they had heard. Each of them was required to account on the following day for what he had heard on the preceding, some more, some less. For with them the preceding day always taught the following.[27]

(855 A) "The evening exercise, which was called *declinatio*,[28] carried such abundance of grammar that any one keeping at it for a whole year, provided he were not too stupid, would control the principles of speaking and writing and could

[27] Cf. III. vi (904 C). Et sicut juxta ethicum: discipulus prioris est posterior dies.

[28] *Declinatio* is the eighth item, under Priscian, in the list from Thierry's *Heptateuchon* cited above, page 153.

not remain ignorant of the meaning of expressions in common
use. But since no school, nor any day, should be without
religion, such a subject was proposed as would upbuild faith
and morals and animate the group, as by common discussion,
toward good. The final item, moreover, of this *declinatio*, or
rather of this philosophical discussion, exhibited the foot-
steps of pious remembrance. The souls of the departed, by
devout offering of the sixth penitential psalm [*De profundis*]
and the Lord's Prayer, were commended to their Redeemer.

(855 B) "For those whose assignments were elementary
exercises in imitating prose or poetry he set poets or orators
and prescribed close imitation after showing the art of connection and of sentence close.[29] If a boy had brightened his
work by sewing on a piece from some one else, he would show
that the theft was detected, but very often would inflict no
punishment. But if the borrowing was misplaced, with
modest kindliness he bade the boy come down to express his
author's likeness; and his own practise was such that in imitating his predecessors he became a model for his successors.
He also taught among the elements and fixed in mind the
force of composition,[30] the achievement of thought and of
phrase, the character of the style, whether thinness or plausible abundance, extravagance or just measure.

(855 C) "Stories and poems, he used to say, were to be
read carefully, not on the run; and of each pupil he required
as a daily task something memorized with careful attention;
But superfluous reading, he would add, should be shunned.
famous authors are enough. To follow what every one, however unimportant, has ever said is to regard oneself either too
meanly or too boastfully. It holds back and obstructs minds
which would otherwise make better use of their leisure; and
what displaces something better is so far unavailing that it
cannot even be called good. To explore all papers and ponder

[29] For *clausula* see the indexes to ARP and to this volume; for John's
own cadences, below, Chapter VIII.
[30] Oeconomia.

all writings, even those not worth reading, is no more to the purpose than to attend to old wives' tales. For, as Augustine says in his *De ordine:* 'Who shall call that man uncultured who has not heard of the flight of Dædalus, or a liar for asserting it, or impudent for questioning it? I always feel deep pity for those of our friends who are accused of ignorance if they have not answered what was the name of the mother of Euryalus, and who dare not call the people who ask such questions shallow, impertinent, and curious.' So says Augustine both neatly and truly. Therefore it was rightly reckoned by the ancients among the virtues of a *grammaticus* that there should be some things which he did not know.

(856 A) "Since in all the preliminary exercises nothing is more useful than to accustom oneself to what ought to be done expertly, Bernard's students would daily write prose and verse and practise themselves by exchange of criticism. Nothing is more useful than this exercise for expression, nothing more promotive of learning; and its greatest contribution is to the conduct of life, provided this insistence be controlled by charity, and progress in literature contribute to humility."

The last chapter (xxv) quotes at length the *laus grammaticæ* of Quintilian I. iv. 5–6.[31]

## Book II. *Demonstrativa* and *Dialectica*

*Proem.* "The course of the former book has sufficiently, I think, disengaged the truth that *grammatica* is not useless, and that without it not only eloquence falls short, but the way toward the other expressions of philosophy is not open."

i. *Logica,* being the theory of discourse, embraces both investigation and judgment.[32]

ii. Knowledge of truth being for them the highest good, the Peripatetics divided philosophy into two parts: natural,

---

[31] See below, page 170.

[32] For *inventio* and *iudicium* see Hugh above, page 154, and note 16. Quintilian III. iii. 5 objects to the application of this to rhetoric.

or physical, and moral, or ethical.[33]    But the difficulties arising
from insufficient control of discourse " demonstrated the need
of determining and publishing a lore which should distinguish words and concepts [34] and dissipate the mists of fallacies.
Here, indeed, as Boethius asserts in his second commentary
on Porphyry, is the origin of the *logica disciplina*.    For there
had to be a lore which should distinguish the true from
the false and teach which reasoning holds the path of [ab-
solute] truth, which of probable, which of assumed,[35] and
which should be distrusted.    Otherwise truth cannot be found
by reasoning (858 C). . . .    The rules of the art were seized
and handed down finally by Aristotle."

iii. (859 C)  "Later in time than the other disciplines of
philosophy, this is first in place.    For beginners in philosophy
it is a prerequisite, as the interpreter of words and concepts,
without which no item of philosophy comes precisely to light.
He who thinks that philosophy is taught without *logica*, i. e.,
by [direct] cultivation of wisdom, may as well do away with
theory in everything, since this is the domain of *logica*. . . .
The very name comes from its being an aid and a test of
theory.    Plato divided it into *dialectica* and *rhetorica;* but
those who estimate its efficacy higher give it more, i. e., *demonstrativa*, *probabilis*, *sophistica*.    *Demonstrativa* begins in the
first stages of training, and passes on into the next.    It is
satisfied only by necessity; provided a thing ought to be so,
it pays little attention to whether or not it appears to be so.
This becomes the philosophical majesty of those who are
teaching precisely, a majesty grounded, quite apart from the
assent of an audience, on its own will.    *Probabilis*, on the
other hand, is occupied with what appears to be so to all, or
to many, or to intelligent observers, with what is best known
and most probable to them, or with what follows therefrom.

[33] See Hugh's division above, page 155.
[34] Vocum et intellectuum.
[35] Ficta, hypothetical?  Sophistica seems to be intended in the following clause.

This includes *dialectica* and *rhetorica*, since logician and orator alike striving to persuade, the one an opponent, the other a judge, think the [abstract] truth of their arguments makes little difference, provided they keep what seems to be true. But *sophistica*, which is apparent and not serviceable wisdom, assumes the likeness either of probability or of necessity, little caring what this or that may be, while it involves whatever is discussed in fanciful images and deceptive shadows. *Dialectica*, that member of the Trivium which all approach from this side and from that, but few, in my judgment, really pursue, neither aspires to dogma, nor is drowned in the waves of politics, but analyzes truth by prompt and reasonable probability."

iv.   *Dialectica*, moreover, is the art of effective debate.

v–viii.   *Logica* has for its distinctive function to serve as effective instrument. It is not an end in itself. So perverted, it becomes the absurd and deplorable occupation of senility.

ix–xi. (866 C)   "*Dialectica*, which among the servants of eloquence is most alert and prompt, avails each man according to the measure of his knowledge. . . . Deprived of the strength of the other disciplines, it is maimed and almost useless; thriving with their vigor, it is strong to overthrow all falsehood, and always suffices at least to reach a probable conclusion." From my own teachers, to whom I returned years after they had schooled me, I conclude that "as *dialectica* advances other disciplines, so if it remain alone, it lies bloodless and sterile, and does not engender the fruit of philosophy in a soul not impregnated from other sources." Of itself it can only despatch issues, not rise to others.

xii.   *Dialectica* operates in all disciplines wherever the issue is abstract.[36] It leaves to *rhetorica* whatever is hypothesis, i. e., whatever involves concrete circumstances: who, what, when, why, how. It makes no address to the public, expects no legal decision.

[36] Thesis.

xiii–xv.  Though each division of philosophy has its own field of inquiry and its own principles, yet *logica* supplies methods common to all, as it were theory in a nutshell.  A problem in *dialectica* considers choice and avoidance, truth and knowledge, whether for itself or as aiding inquiry where opinion divides.

xvi–xvii.  Review of the value and place of Aristotle, of the right use of Porphyry's Introduction, and of other typical cases in teaching.  Bernard (875 D) of Chartres and his followers took great pains to heal the breach between Plato and Aristotle; "but in my opinion they came late and labored in vain to reconcile in death those who differed as long as they lived."

xviii–xix.  Certain errors of those who profess Aristotle can hardly be overlooked: the burdening of tender shoulders, the making of Porphyry cover the whole ground, the misinterpretation that simplifies Aristotle by substituting Plato or something remote from both.

xx.  The last chapter, much the longest, presents Aristotle on genus and species.

## Book III.  *Topica*

i–iv.  A survey of the teaching of categoriæ, prædicamenta, and interpretatio as preliminary begins with general advice (890 D).  "The exposition of every book should be such as to furnish most readily the knowledge of what is written.  No occasion should be sought of introducing difficulty; everywhere the way should be opened.  That was the practise, I remember, of Abelard . . . (891 A).  Thus Porphyry should be read so that the significance of the expressions in question may be retained and the sense of the words got from the surface.  He will be sufficiently introductory so, and conspicuous for being quickly intelligible . . . (891 D).  For the text is to be searched mannerly, not bitterly racked, as if it were a prisoner, until it gives up what it has not taken."  This preliminary closes with a reminiscence (900 C).  " Bernard of Chartres used to say that we, like dwarfs on the shoulders of giants, can see more and farther not because we are keener and taller, but because of the greatness by which we are carried and exalted."

v–x. Forecasting the rest of the program, John wonders why Aristotle's *Topica* should have been so long neglected (903 A). "Single words of it, in both rules and examples, are valuable not only for *dialectica*, but for almost all the disciplines. It comprises eight books, each more potent than the last." The following digest, book by book, iterates (910 C) the general value. "The precepts of all eloquence seem to be derived originally from it as from the primary source. For it is indubitably true, as Cicero and Quintilian say, that rhetors and rhetoricians have found in it not only an aid, but a source."

## Book IV. *Analytica*

In contrast to the ten long chapters of III, IV is divided into forty-two short ones: i–v, *analytica* in general; vi–viii, *demonstrativa;* ix–xx, the progress of knowledge: sensus, imaginatio, prudentia, ratio, intellectus; xxi–xxiii, *hypothetica, sophistica;* xxiv–xlii, critical review: objectors to Aristotle the place of *logica* in teaching, typical conceptions of ratio, and of truth and error, the relation of ratio to veritas.

This last book iterates the importance of correlation (xxviii. 932 B). "But though *logica* is useful generally, he who is ignorant of other arts [37] is not so much helped by it toward philosophy as he is hindered by a habit of verbosity and presumption. For *logica* is almost useless if it be alone.    It stands out when it shines by the power of correlated studies."

John's slighting of rhetoric cannot be explained merely by his preoccupation with logic.  Why was he thus preoccupied in a consistent and progressive scheme of the

[37] Reading *aliarum.*

whole Trivium?  He begins with a *logica* embracing all
studies of words; he devotes a whole book to *grammatica;*
in his last pages he is speaking of an *organon* that shall
be a minister to *eloquentia*.  Yet *rhetorica* he merely
mentions when he must.  That he was aware of its ancient importance in such a scheme as his is evident from
his large use of Quintilian's *Teaching of Rhetoric*.  No
other medieval writer gave this work more attention.
The much-quoted chapter (I. xxiv) on *prælectio* uses
not only Quintilian's ideas, but his very words; [38] and
other correspondences are no less significant.  The following list, though not complete, is typical.

QUINTILIAN, *INST. ORAT.*        *METALOGICUS*

I. iii. 3–5        II. viii. 865 B–C
Illud ingeniorum . . decrescit. Hoc est quod . . decrescit.

I. viii. 13–14        I. xxiv. 853 D–854 A
In prælegendo grammaticus . . In prælegendo grammaticus . .
memoriam agitet.        memoriam auditorum.

17–21        855 B–D
Præcipue vero illa . . .        Id quoque inter prima . . .
aliqua nescire.        aliqua ignorare [with substitu-
        tion of Augustine for Didymus,
        who is relegated to 864 C].

The correspondences above, verbatim for considerable
stretches, involve here and there transpositions or other
variations.  The following are quotations or adaptations.

[38] This is pointed out by Colson in his edition of Quintilian's first
book, Cambridge, 1924, page 1, note 2.  It is the stranger that the
quotations should not have been noticed before since John himself
calls attention to them: "ut verbo utamur Quintiliani," "ab auctori-
tate ejusdem Quintiliani" (I. xxiv. 853 D).

| I. iv. 5-6 | I. xxv. 856 D |
|---|---|
| Quo minus sunt ferendi . . quam ostentationis. Ne quis igitur . . . scientiam possit. | in libro *De institutione oratoris* . . Ait ergo: "Ne quis [and the two sentences are quoted in reverse order]." |

| II. iii. 3 | II. vii. 864 D |
|---|---|
| Propter quod Timotheum . . . | Refert Quintilianus [quotation with slight verbal variation]. |

| II. iv. 5-7 | IV. xxviii. 932 B |
|---|---|
| Nec unquam . . quod exculpi. | Teneræ tamen ætati . . . improbitas conquiescat [correspondence evident in idea, occasionally in word]. |

| X. i. 83 | II. ii. 859 A |
|---|---|
| Quid Aristotelem? . . . clariorem putem. | quid de eo dicat Quintilianus: "Quid Aristotelem? . [exact quotation]." |

| X. i. 125-131 | I. xxii. 852 B |
|---|---|
| Ex industria Senecam. . . quod voluit efficit. | [Discusses Quintilian's view ("ut pace Quintiliani loquar") with occasional reminiscence of his words.] |

Even if these correspondences were confined to Quintilian's first and second books, there would still be no sufficient ground for the inference that John, consulting him primarily for *grammatica* and further for his general ideas on education, did not think of him as a rhetorician. For Quintilian not only presents rhetoric from the beginning; he frequently in these first books cites and quotes Aristotle as a rhetorician. But the matter seems to be put beyond doubt by the use of Book X. It is only fair to assume of so careful a scholar reading the first books and one of the last, and occupied with Quintilian's idea of educational sequence, that he read the whole work.[39]

Having read and admired one of the chief ancient works on rhetoric, why did he leave rhetoric out of his own scheme? The answer is probably in the contemporary conditions to which the *Metalogicus* is adjusted, and especially in the contemporary state of rhetoric. It seems not to have been in the twelfth century worth more than mention from a John of Salisbury seeking a vital sequence of studies. It lacked what he sought above all, vital relations. If he had known Aristotle's *Rhetoric*, he might conceivably have sought to recall the ancient study to its better ancient aim. What he found vital in Quintilian's rhetoric he transferred to *grammatica* or to *dialectica*, partly, no doubt, because the transfer was actually going on, partly, one may think, because he saw in these other studies the real opportunities of his time for composition. The current lore of ornament which passed for rhetoric could hardly detain his consideration.

What he discerns in *grammatica*, and had found in the teaching of Bernard, is of course training in precision. But though he makes much of this, he does not slight the value of concreteness for presentation; he sees the importance of studying style by imitation; and he adopts from Quintilian a word not common in medieval treatises, *œconomia*. All these point to composition; and composition seems to have been one of the essential applications of the master's analysis. The *prælectio* as John describes it is tinged with Quintilian because it

---

[39] *Illustratio* in I. xxiv (854 A/B) is probably a reminiscence of Quintilian VI. ii. 32, to judge not only from the word, but from the context in both passages. Cf. 844 A, 851 C, 860 C, 910 D.

realizes fully the ancient function of *grammatica* with
the poets.

In the rapidly expanding teaching of *dialectica* also
he sees opportunity for composition.  To this end, very
likely, he urges repeatedly that the debates of the schools
keep touch with reality by insisting on subject matter
through correlation with other studies.  Above all he
desires that language studies be unified and progressive,
that they call for expanding correlation of *inventio* and
*iudicium*.  The study that in his time actually demanded
and exercised these was not *rhetorica*, which was by way
of ignoring both; it was *dialectica*.

## D. Thirteenth Century Surveys

### 1. The *Anticlaudianus* of Alain de Lille

The allegorical survey entitled by Alain [40] *Anticlaudianus* has but superficial likeness to the *De nuptiis philologiæ et Mercurii* [41] of Martianus Capella.  Each presents
the seven liberal arts in allegory; each is in nine books;
but there is no real resemblance, nor any indication of
Alain's having used Martianus except as a stock source.
The allegory of Martianus is confined to his first two
books, and is purely decorative; the allegory of Alain
pervades his whole work as a controlling idea.  That idea

[40] Alanus de Insulis (about 1128–1202), Cistercian at Citeaux, sometimes called "doctor universalis," wrote mainly on theology.  *Anticlaudianus* was edited by Wright in the second volume of his *Anglo-
Latin Satirical Poets and Epigrammatists of the Twelfth Century*, London,
(Rolls Series), which contains also *De planctu naturæ*.  The latter has
been translated by D. M. Moffat in Yale Studies in English, New York,
1908.

The citations in this section are by column from PL 210.  For the
*Summa de arte predicatoria* see below, Chapter IX. C.

[41] See above, Chapter III. B. 1.

is the function of education in the redemption of mankind.  The subtitle "de officio viri boni et perfecti" is
akin to Hugh's [42] "animæ perfectio."  The consistent,
elaborate theological symbolism shows some force of
conception and, in spite of occasional excursions into
style, some ardor and elevation.  The four thousand
hexameters are usually above the medieval fatal fluency
in this verse.  The survey, though it has not Hugh's
originality and does not attempt John's unification, is
equally serious.

> The seven arts are summoned to provide *Prudentia* with a
> chariot for her quest on behalf of man.  *Grammatica* supplies
> the pole; *Logica*, the axle, which *Rhetorica* adorns with gems
> and gold; the Quadrivium, the four wheels.  The horses, the
> five senses, are then harnessed by *Ratio*.  When the upward
> journey has reached the term of human powers, *Prudentia*,
> leaving her chariot, is conducted by *Theologia* into the empy-
> rean, to the saints, to Mary, to God himself.  Obtaining of
> God the formation of the new man, *Prudentia* returns to seek
> gifts for the *anima creata*.  *Natura* gives it a body.  *Concordia*
> and *Pudicitia*, *Ratio* and *Honestas*, coöperate in gifts with the
> seven arts.  The dubious gifts of *Fortuna* are assisted by *Ratio*.
> Thereupon the vices declare war, which is concluded by the
> victory of the opposed virtues.

Alain incidentally defines the character of each of the
seven arts, and summarizes its scope.  Each has its
function—except *rhetorica*.  The other members of the
Trivium [43] provide the car of Prudentia with essential
pole and axle; the Quadrivium supplies essential wheels;
but all that *Rhetorica* has to offer is quite unessential

---

[42] For Hugh, see above, page 153.
[43] Alain's order is the usual (1) *grammatica*, (2) *dialectica*, (3) *rhetorica*.  His *logica* is *dialectica*, not the inclusive term of Hugh and John.
Its *auctores* (III. ii. 510 A) are Porphyry, Aristotle, Zeno, Boethius.

adornment. Though Alain rehearses the traditional
parts of her ancient lore,[44] he sums up her actual occupation in two lines of cardinal significance.

> Supremasque manus apponit, opusque sororum
> Perficit, atque semel factum perfectius ornat.
>
> III. ii. 511 D.

In other words, rhetoric is not operative as composition,
but only as style after the fact. Her gifts to the soul
are only *colores, decor, clausula*.

> Adsunt rhetoricæ cultus floresque colorum,
> Verba quibus stellata nitent; et sermo decorem
> Induit, et multa splendescit clausula luce.
>
> VII. vi. 554 D.

Alain's own use of rhetoric is consistent with this
point of view. Each of his allegorical figures is introduced
with the conventional descriptive ecphrasis; and his
diffuseness arises from the idea that *poetica* involves
decorative dilation by those *colores* of which Cicero and
Vergil are equally patterns.

> Verbi pauperiem redimit splendore *colorum*
> Tullius, et dictis ornatus fulgura donat.
> Virgilii musa mendacia multa *colorat*,
> Et facie veri contexit pallia falso.
>
> I. iv. 491 C.

## 2. The *Speculum Doctrinale* of Vincent of Beauvais

The vast *Speculum* of Vincent of Beauvais [45] is a
compend of all knowledge. Its second part, *Speculum
doctrinale*, Mirror of Teaching, devotes two books to the

[44] III. ii. 512–513.
[45] About 1190–1264. The *Speculum* was printed at Strasburg in
1473, and by the Benedictines at Douai in 1624.

Trivium. *Grammatica,*[46] including metric, follows Isidore. The following book [47] devotes ninety-eight chapters to logic (*logica*), ten to rhetoric, twenty-three to poetic. The proportion is significant; and *poetica*, taken from under the ægis of *grammatica*, appears as a separate, co-ordinate section. For rhetoric Vincent, still following Isidore,[48] repeats the classical definition and division. The following chapters (101–108) deal briefly with the elements of a speech, the ideals of oratory, the types of cases, status, syllogisms, *loci rhetorici*, style.

Vincent then goes on to *poetica,*

which Alphorabius [49] in his book on the division of the *scientiæ* puts last among the parts of *logica*, and which in his book on the origin of the *scientiæ* he describes thus: "*Poetica* is the lore of ordering meters according to the proportion of words (*dictiones*) and the times of feet and of their rhythms (*numeri*)." Again he says in the former book: "It belongs to *poetica* to make the hearer through its locutions image something as fair or foul which is not so,[50] that he may believe and shun or desire it. Although certainly it is not so in truth, nevertheless, the minds of hearers are roused to shun or desire what they image." Moreover poetry has seven species: *comedia, tragedia, invectio, satyra, fabula, historia, argumentum.*[51]

[46] Book III (II in the Benedictine edition).

[47] Book IV (III in the Benedictine edition).

[48] Vincent refers in Chapter 100 to Quintilian. "Tullius in libro de oratore" (100 and 127) is probably not a reference to *De oratore*. In 101 "Tullius in rhetorica prima," and in 127 "idem in rhetorica secunda," are the usual references to *De inventione* and *ad Herennium*. For the references to Quintilian see Bassi, *Giornale storico*, XXIII, 186, and Colson's introduction to his edition of Quintilian's first book, page lii.

[49] Farabi. For translations from Arabic see above, page 153, and Haskins, Chapter IX.

[50] Compare Alain above in the quotation on page 174.

[51] For the three school exercises that conclude this list see the indexes to ARP and to this volume; for the rest of the classification, Bede, above, Chapter V. B. 1.

*Comedia* is poetry reversing a sad beginning by a glad end; but *tragedia* is poetry lapsing from a glad beginning to a sad end (109). The function, then, of the poet is in this, that with a certain beauty he converts actual events into other species by his slanting figures (end of 110).

Except meter, which belongs under *grammatica*, and the two forms of drama, which are not thought of as forms of composition, there is nothing to distinguish this poetic from rhetoric.

### 3. St Bonaventure *de Reductione Artium ad Theologiam*

St Bonaventure [52] distinguishes four "lights": (1) the exterior light of a manual art, illuminating with regard to artistic form; (2) the inferior light of knowledge through the senses, illuminating with regard to the patterns of nature; (3) the interior light of philosophical knowledge, illuminating with regard to truth comprehended intellectually; (4) the superior light of grace and revelation, illuminating with regard to truth as a means of salvation.[53] For (3), the "interior light," his division is stated first in its commonest form. *Philosophia* is: (a) *rationalis* (i. e., *sermonum*), (b) *naturalis*

---

[52] 1221–1274.  The *Opusculum de reductione artium ad theologiam* is number 4 (pages 317–325) in volume 5 of the Works edited by the College of St Bonaventure, Quaracchi (Florence), 1891.

[53] (1) Lumen exterius artis mechanicæ illuminat respectu figuræ artificialis;

(2) lumen inferius cognitionis sensitivæ illuminat respectu formæ naturalis;

(3) lumen interius cognitionis philosophicæ illuminat respectu veritatis intellectualis;

(4) lumen superius gratiæ et sacræ Scripturæ illuminat respectu veritatis salutaris.

(i. e., *rerum*), (c) *moralis* (i. e., *morum*). This division [54]
he then repeats in another form and order:

(a) *physica*, for knowing the causes of being;
(b) *logica*, for knowing the theory of understanding;
(c) *practica*, for knowing the conduct of living.

Finally he considers it in a third aspect. The domain
of *moralis* is motive; of *physica* is self-limited and self-
sufficient; of *sermocinalis* is interpretation. The last
item he subdivides into:

*grammatica*, for expression, regarding reason as apprehension, seeking the appropriate;
*logica*, for instruction, regarding reason as judgment, seeking the true;
*rhetorica*, for persuasion, regarding reason as motive, seeking the ornate.[55]

Bonaventure does not use the word *dialectica*. His
word for this, not for the whole Trivium,[56] is *logica*.
Though his *movendum* and *motivam* suggest association
of rhetoric with morals, and remind one of Aristotle's

[54] For the classifications of Hugh of St Victor and John of Salisbury
see above, sections B and C.
[55] (a) moralis regit motivam;
  (b) naturalis regit se ipsam;
  (c) sermocinalis regit interpretativam:
    (1) grammatica ad exprimendum respicit rationem ut appre-
        hensivam . . congruum;
    (2) logica ad docendum respicit rationem ut iudicativam . .
        verum;
    (3) rhetorica ad movendum respicit rationem ut motivam
        . . ornatum.
[56] That he does not intend *logica* in the larger sense of Hugh and John
will be clear from comparative study of the three forms of his division, and also from *Collationes in hexaëmeron* (in the same volume),
IV. 18–25. This briefly sums up *rhetorica* according to its ancient topics,
including the three fields and the five parts. Here again *dialectica* is
not used, and *logica* merely supersedes it.

conception, and Cicero's, and Quintilian's, he is content
to give rhetoric the narrow and barren field of *ornatus*,
assigning *docendum* and *verum* to logic.

## 4. The *Trésor* of Brunetto Latini

The Old French *Trésor* of Brunetto Latini [57] devotes
a far larger proportion of space than Vincent's *Speculum*
to rhetoric.  Book I, surveying the seven arts,[58] includes
history, geography, and the zoölogy of the bestiaries.
Book II adds to Aristotelian ethics a collection of
moral apothegms.[59]  Book III opens politics with
rhetoric.

> Here begins the third book of the *Treasure*, which speaks
> of the teachings of good speech and of the government of
> towns and cities. . . .  Cicero says that the highest lore for
> governing a city is rhetoric.[60]  467.
> They are mistaken who think that to tell fables or old
> stories . . is matter of rhetoric. . . .  [Rather rhetoric is
> concerned with] what is said by word of mouth  or sent by
> letter to induce belief, to praise or blame, to advise . . . in
> something that demands decision.  471.

[57] 1230–1294.  The *Trésor* is edited, with an introduction, by Cha-
baille in the Collection des documents inédits sur l'histoire de France,
Paris, 1863.  References in this section are to the pages of this edition.
The Italian version, also widely current, is edited by L. Gaiter, Bologna,
1878.  See also F. Maggini, *La rettorica italiana di B. L.* (Pub. del R.
Istituto di studi superiori), Florence, 1913.

[58] The proem, beginning with theology as the highest  lore of *theorica*,
makes the usual enumeration under *mathematica*, divides *practica*, "la
seconde science de philosophie," into "éthique . économique . politi-
que," and so arrives at rhetoric, but with some confusion as to logic.

[59] See Chabaille, xv.

[60] Villani may be merely repeating this when he says: "Egli fu comin-
ciatore e maestro in digrossare i Fiorentini, e farli scorti in bene parlare
et in sapere guidare e reggere la nostra repubblica secondo la politica."
VIII. x.

The following chapters present the ancient division
into five parts and the lore of *status* and *quæstio*.[61] But
at this point the distinctive ancient function of rhetoric
begins to fade. After saying that the main division of
all expression is into prose and rime, he adds that "the
teachings of rhetoric are common to both," save for the
restrictions of meter.[62] The section on *dispositio*, the
ordering of a speech, takes from Martianus Capella not
his sober survey, but a single passage which Brunetto
perverts by subdivision and by transfer to narrative.

> To exploration of the material [of a speech], with discern-
> ment of its value for persuasion, is to be joined the ordering
> of the points, which is the part commonly called *dispositio*. . . .
> The scheme may be either the natural order or devised by
> the orator's artifice; natural, when after the beginning comes
> the statement of facts, then the division, proposition, proof,
> conclusion and epilogue; by the orator's artifice, when the
> things that must be said have been distributed through the
> parts of the speech.[63]

Here Martianus is apparently extending to the whole
plan of a speech the commonplace of ancient rhetoric
that the *narratio* (statement of facts) might be either
continuous as a single, distinct part, or distributed for

[61] Brunetto's main source is Cicero *De invent*.

[62] La grans partisons de touz parleors . . en prose . . en rime;
mais li enseignement de rectorique sont commun andui, sauf ce que la
voie de prose est large et pleniere, si comme est ore la commune parleure
des gens; mais li sentiers de rime est plus estroiz et plus fors.  481.

[63] His igitur ad fidem faciendam prudenter inuentis ordo rerum est
sociandus, quæ pars *dispositio* uocitatur . . duplex igitur huius
partis est ratio; aut enim naturalis est ordo aut oratoris artificio com-
paratur: naturalis, cum post principium narratio, partitio, propositio,
argumentatio, conclusio epilogusque consequitur; artificio oratoris, cum
per membra orationis quæ dicenda sunt digerimus.  V. 506 (Teubner,
ed. Dick, 248).

the sake of giving salience to its separate items.  Brunetto's further extension is not his own; it is common stock of the contemporary *artes poeticæ*.[64]  These manuals make much of "natural" and "artificial" order, subdivide each, and apply both to narrative.  Brunetto is typical.

> "Order [means] everything in its place; but this order is in two manners, one which is natural and another artificial. . . . The artificial order is divided into eight manners":
> (1) to say at the beginning what was at the end,
> (2) to begin with what was in the middle,
> (3) to base your story on the beginning of a proverb,
> (4) to base it on the middle of the proverb,
> (5) to base it on the end of the proverb,
> (6) (7) (8) so for three uses of an example.  482.

The mechanical division reflects a wide abeyance in theory, not only of poetic shaping and movement, but even of the *dispositio* of ancient rhetoric; for its real concern is not with composition at all, whether in prose or in verse, but with the phrasing of certain patterns.

Brunetto's preoccupation with style, and with style mainly as decorative dilation, soon appears in "how to dilate one's tale in eight ways . . . which are called colors of rhetoric."[65]  Among these *colores*, under *demonstrance* (*demonstratio*), is his celebrated, but entirely conventional, ecphrasis on Yseult.

The traditional parts of a speech (exordium, etc.)

---

[64] See below, Chapter VII. B.

[65] "Comment l'om puet acroistre son conte en viij manieres . . qui sont apelees color de rectorique."  The first of these, *aornement*, is defined so bluntly that the humorous implication may be intentional: "tout ce que l'om porroit en iij moz ou en iiij, ou a mult po de paroles dire, il les acroist par autres paroles plus longues et plus avenans qui dient ce meisme."  486.

are used [66] as an approach to *dictamen,* of which Brunetto appears to be thinking through much of what follows. The concluding chapters on statecraft are far from a discussion of politics. Rather they set forth the conduct of a seigneur. Thus they fail to carry out the relations of rhetoric to government which in his opening he borrows from Cicero. Book III, then, of the *Trésor* lapses further and further from the ancient conception of rhetoric with which it begins. The rhetoric which it actually presents, and which it applies to poetry as well as to *dictamen,*[67] is a meager, though pleasant, review of style.[68]

What rhetoric appears in these surveys to lack most is distinct function. Writers as different as John of Salisbury and Brunetto Latini seem to think of it as polishing, decorating, especially dilating, what has been

---

[66] 490.      [67] For *dictamen,* see below, Chapter VIII.

[68] Jean d'Antioche in his introduction to the translation of *De inventione* and *Rhetorica ad Herennium* (end of XIIIth century) has two divisions of *Philosophye:* (A) into *ethique morale, rationele,* and *naturele;* (B) as follows:—

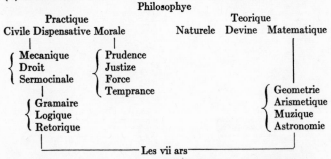

Delisle in *Notices et Extraits,* 36:216.

Neither *Le mariage des sept arts* nor Henri d'Andeli's *Bataille des sept arts* contains any information about teaching.

already expressed. It comes in after the real job is done; it has lost its ancient function of composing. The ancient lore of *inventio* kept rhetoric in contact with subject matter and with actual presentation. This had so much less scope in feudal society that the lore easily lapsed, or was perverted. The only large field for its exercise was preaching. Education, therefore, naturally threw its weight on *grammatica* for boys, on *dialectica* for men. Between the two rhetoric was crowded into narrow room. Whether it would still have vindicated itself if it had been the rhetoric of Aristotle, or oftener the rhetoric of Quintilian, can be only conjectured. Actually it was the rhetoric of *De inventione* and *ad Herennium*, and inculcated the sophistic of Sidonius. That may explain why there was no medieval rhetorician who really advanced the study.

# CHAPTER VII

## LATIN POETIC IN THE TWELFTH AND THIRTEENTH CENTURIES

REFERENCES AND ABBREVIATIONS

AH          Dreves and Blume, *Analecta hymnica medii œvi*,
            Leipzig (vol. 1, 1886; vol. 53, 1911; sixty volumes
            proposed).

ARP         Baldwin (C. S.), *Ancient rhetoric and poetic*, New
            York, 1924.

Britt       Britt (the Rev. Matthew, O. S. B.), *The hymns
            of the Breviary and Missal*, New York, 1922.

F           Faral (E.), *Les arts poétiques du xiie et du xiiie
            siècle*, recherches et documents sur la technique
            littéraire du moyen âge, Paris, 1924.

Manacorda   Manacorda (G.), *Storia della scuola in Italia*,
            vol. I, *Il medio evo*, Milan, 1913 (2 parts in sep-
            arate volumes).

Mari        Mari (G.), *I trattati medievali di ritmica latina*,
            Milan, 1899, pages 35–80, for the latter part of
            the *Poetria* of Johannes de Garlandia; for the
            former part, Romanische Forschungen XIII
            (1901–1902), pages 883–965.

Misset-Aubry  Misset (l'Abbé E.) and Aubry (P.), *Les proses
            d'Adam de St Victor*, texte et musique, pré-
            cédées d'une étude critique, Paris, 1900.

## A. *Poetica* included in *Grammatica*

The *grammatica* of this period continued the traditional inclusion of metric and of certain figures of speech;
and the master's *prælectio* on the Latin poets involved
at Chartres, as two centuries before at Speier,[1] imitative
writing of Latin verse.   About 1200 appeared two hexameter summaries: the *Doctrinale* [2] of the Norman Alexandre de Villedieu, and the *Græcismus* [3] of the Flemish
Évrard de Béthune.   The former had so long and wide a
vogue that it may be called the standard medieval
mnemonic of *grammatica*.   Reviewing successively inflections, syntax, metric,[4] accents, figures, it includes
under the last the lists of Greek terms that show at once

[1] Pages 129, 152.

[2] In 1199; represents the new school of Paris as against the conserv-
atives of Orléans; 2645 hexameters; in use at Troyes, 1436 (Carré (G.),
*L'enseignement secondaire à Troyes*, Paris, 1888, pages 18, 19, 49).

First printed at Venice by Wendelin of Spires, 1470; more than 160
editions by 1500 (Allen (P.), *The Age of Erasmus*, page 41), though meantime attacked by Valla and Sulpitius Verulanus.

Ed. Reichling (D.) Berlin, 1893, with an introduction of 300 pages,
including the researches of Thurot.   See also Manacorda, index.

Generally speaking, the *Doctrinale* was current throughout Europe
for three hundred years.

Fierville (Ch.) exhibits the interesting return to Priscian of a thirteenth-century grammarian evidently dissatisfied with the method of
Alexander (*Une grammaire inédite du xiiie siècle* . . Paris, 1886).

[3] About 1212, *Græcismus de figuris et octo partibus orationis, sive grammaticæ regulæ versibus latinis explicatæ;* mentioned by Henri d'Andeli
(ed. Paetow, 49, 50); by Reginald Pecock, *Reule* (ed. Greet, E. E. T. S.,
251); printed 1487, Paris; reprinted in Corpus grammaticorum latinorum medii ævi, vol. I, Wratislaviæ, 1887.   See Manacorda, index.

[4] In this part (III) he makes bold to say (1559): "Cum sim Chris-
ticola, normam non est mihi cura / de propriis facere quæ gentiles posu-
ere."   In the next part also (IV, accents) he insists on the habit of the
actual Latin verse of the time (2295): "hos solos usu debes servare
moderno"; and again (2329) "Accentus normas legitur posuisse vetus-
tas; / non tamen has credo servandas tempore nostro."

a preoccupation of the time and the shifting boundary between *grammatica* and *rhetorica*.[5]

## B. *POETRIA*

Distinctive of this period is the separate *ars poetica*, or *poetria*. Often itself in verse, this sort of manual differed from Bede's, first in being less a reference book for the study of meters than an exercise book for the actual writing of Latin verse, and secondly in giving less space to prosody than to poetic diction. The four most conspicuous [6] may be assigned approximately to the half-century divided by 1200 (c. 1175-1225).

## 1. Matthieu de Vendôme, *Ars Versificatoria* (before 1175)

Matthew's prose manual, though it omits prosody, is otherwise connected even more obviously than the others with the teaching of *grammatica*. Not only is he known to have been *grammaticus* at Orléans; his book is inclined throughout in the direction of such

[5] The first list (2365), pleonasmos, is: acyrologia, cacosyntheton, eclipsis, tautologia, amphibologia, tapinosis, macrologia, perissologia, cacenphaton, aleoteta.

The second, metaplasmus (2405), appears as: prothesis, epenthesis, paragoge, auferesis (syncopa, apocopa), systola, ectasis, etc.

The third, schema (2445), is: prolempsis, zeugma, sylempsis, hypozeuxis, anadiplosis, epanalempsis, epizeuzis, anaphora, paronomœon, schesis onomaton, homoteleuton, paronomasia, polyptoton, etc.

The fourth, tropi (2497), is: metaphora, metonomia, antonomasia, catachresis, onomatopœia, synodoche, allegoria, hyperbole, etc.

[6] F, cardinal for these *poetriæ*, and a most important contribution to medieval poetic, studies dates, ascriptions, and relations, provides analytical tables of contents, sums up in its introduction the common rhetorical doctrine, and for three of these authors establishes critical texts. The fourth and latest, Johannes de Garlandia, will be found in Mari.

teaching,[7] and it contains specimen school exercises. The grammatical slant is most obvious in those on adjectives in *-alis, -osus, -atus, -ivus, -aris*.[8] The longer examples of descriptive verse may well be such successively revised themes as were seen earlier at Speier.[9] The use of Horace's "Ars poetica" is so extensive, even for the time, as to suggest that Matthew's book may have begun in his *prælectiones* on that poem. Whatever degree of probability may be attached to these suggestions, there is no doubt of Matthew's intention and preoccupation. His book seeks to further the writing of Latin descriptive verse. The idea behind it is that poetry is mainly description, which in turn proceeds mainly by dilation. Style, which is his only concern, is conceived as decoration. Though his lists of figures for this purpose (III) generally agree with those of the *Doctrinale*,[10] rhetoric is evident not only in the phrase *colores rhetorici*,[11] but as a constant preoccupation. That *poetica* as style is identical with *rhetorica* he assumes; that it is distinct as composition can hardly have entered his head, but composition in either field is beyond his scope. His sections on beginning (I. 3–16) refer not to introducing the subject, but to phrasing the first sentences. The faults then enumerated (I. 30–37) are of style. Description is expounded (I. 38–113) as appropriateness of phrase

---

[7] Ad informationem puerilis disciplinæ quasdam dictiones quæ cooperativæ sunt . . interserui. II. 12 (F 154). Qui in scolastico exercitio fabulas circinantes poeticas. IV. 1 (F 180). In scolastico versificandi exercitio. IV. 16 (F 184).

[8] II. 15–26 (F 155–160). He adds: "sunt et aliæ terminationes adjectivorum; sed in prælibatis ornatior verborum festivitas et elegantior junctura potest assignari " (F 155).

[9] I. 50–58, 107–111 (F 121–132, 146–149). For the practise at Speier, see above, page 141.

[10] See note 5, above.          [11] III. 45.

to condition, age, place, etc., and as the seeking of "attributes" in a person's physical and mental habit, his deeds, his speech,[12] or in the cause, quality, and time of an event. Reference to subject, thought, or composition goes no further; the rest of the book is purely verbal.

## 2. Geoffroi de Vinsauf, *Poetria Nova* (c. 1210)

The extraordinary vogue of Geoffrey's two thousand hexameters in itself suggests that his too is an exercise book. To suppose that it was cherished for its literary achievement is to impute to several centuries a larger and more general appetite for bombast than other evidence warrants. As school mnemonics his verses are more tolerable. As exercises in synonyms they have excuse for their redundancy. As suggestions and examples in the pursuit of figures they have more warrant for exaggeration as a means of distinctness. Caricature, which can never have been the intention of a man devoid of humor, has before Geoffrey's time, and since, resulted from sheer overemphasis. His own incessant word-play is so anxious as to verge sometimes on *reductio ad absurdum*. Or were some of these tirades made to order by his students? May they be such progressively revised composite themes as the earlier schools assigned in similar hexameter tasks? [13] At any rate, a probable explanation of the portentous style, as well as a charitable one, is that the *Poetria nova* was a museum for boys.

After bowing to the ancient *inventio* and *dispositio*, neither of which is in point and neither handled as a

[12] Sunt igitur attributa personæ undecim: nomen, natura, convictus. fortuna, habitus, studium, affectio, consilium, casus, facta, orationes, I. 77 (F 136). Both the topics and their application are descended from the encomium of sophistic. See above, page 31.

[13] Above, note 7, and page 141.

process of composing, Geoffrey devotes most of his book to the rhetorical means of dilation. This is the aim of the *colores*, not only of verbal expansions in general, but in particular of two sorts of deliberate interpolation: apostrophe and description.

> To go farther afield, let apostrophe be the fourth means of lingering by which you may detain the subject.
> Seventh comes description, pregnant with words, to dilate the work.[14]

Chaucer,[15] whose ironical homage has made Geoffrey a laughing-stock, was exploding the use of these figures in verse narrative. In oratory also of a certain sort he exhibits their deviation in the specimen preaching of the Pardoner because they are perennial in sophistic. Geoffrey's description is precisely the ecphrasis cultivated throughout the Empire in *declamatio*.[16] In a word,

[14] Latius ut curras, sit apostropha quarta morarum
   Qua rem detineas et ubi spatieris ad horam. 264.

   Septima succedit prægnans Descriptio verbis,
   Ut dilatet opus. 554.

A hundred lines later Geoffrey can still say:

   Restat adhuc aliud quod linguam reddit opimam.

So certain is he of dilation as the mode of poetry that he demands support for it even of Horace.

   Multiplice forma
   Dissimuletur idem; varius sis et tamen idem. 224.

The doctrine is no less insistent in his prose treatise, also printed in F. See especially II. 2. A. (F 271–284).

[15] Tale of the Nun's Priest, 521 (B 4531). The allusions are to *Poetria* 326 (Anglia regnorum regina), 375 (O Veneris lacrimosa dies). For the significance of Chaucer's satire here, see below, Chapter X. D. 3. Chaucer's use of the contemporary rhetorical fund is discussed in Manly's "Chaucer and the Rhetoricians," London, 1927 (British Academy, Warton Lecture on English Poetry XVII, read June, 1926).

[16] See in general Chapter I, and in particular the index. Faral acutely notes Geoffrey's mention of Sidonius.

Geoffrey's poetic, as Alain's, Vincent's, Brunetto Latini's,[17]
is mainly the rhetoric of dilation. The sophistic of the
ancient encomium, walking the schools once more, is
now called Poetria.

### 3. Évrard, *Laborintus* (c. 1213)

The *Laborintus*[18] is at once briefer and more inclusive. Opening with rueful mock-heroic on the lot of a
schoolmaster, it glances through the seven arts in a
series of allusions, and expands upon *grammatica*. Thus
poetry is reached by the traditional approach.[19] Most
space, however (269–598), is given to exemplifying rhetorical ornament, especially figures. Though the list,
as usual, is long, the manufactured or borrowed examples
are short. Évrard's plan of tucking away each within
a closed hexameter-pentameter couplet is carried out
with some ingenuity. Though he has to take more room
for *demonstratio* (573–594), he generally abjures Geoffrey's
dilating upon dilation. His examples are rather mnemonics than exhibitions. The fourth section (599–686)
is a list of authors for school reading.[20] The order, though
not obviously progressive, suggests: (1) certain brief mor-

[17] See above, Chapter VI. D. Geoffrey presents Lady Poetry (61)
substantially as Alain presents Lady Rhetoric (*Anticlaudianus* III. ii,
quoted above, page 174); and Alain tags with the same *colores* Cicero
and Vergil in two successive lines (I. iv, above, page 174).

[18] Composed in some thousand elegiacs, to which are appended specimens of various *rhythmi*. The author is called by Faral, to distinguish
him from Évrard de Béthune, Évrard l'allemand.

[19] Nostra comes fida, Poesis, 224.
  Grammaticæ famulans subit ingeniosa Poesis, 253.

  [20] Viribus apta suis pueris ut lectio detur,
      Auctores tenero fac ut ab ore legas. 599.
The following titles, which are sometimes given allusively, are indicated
in F.

alizing works for elementary study, i. e., a "Cathonet" (the so-called "Distichs of Cato"), a "Théodolet," or "Theudlet" (the allegorical verse dialogue entitled *Theodulus*),[21] an "Ysopet," or collection of fables;[22] (2) the classics and their imitators, with Vergil applied as the exemplar of all "three styles";[23] (3) the Latin summaries of the Trojan war, Dares and the *Ilias latina*, (4) Sidonius and the earlier Christian poets, Alain's *Anticlaudianus*, and Matthew's *Tobias;* (5) a group of works on style, i. e., Geoffrey's *Poetria;* the *Doctrinale* and *Græcismus*, Matthew's *Ars versificatoria*, Martianus Capella, and Bernard Silvester.[24]

The section on metric (687–834) exemplifies the leonine verses repudiated by Matthew,[25] the handling of phrases and clauses—even to such ingenuities as reversible lines, several patterns of internal rime in the hexameter,[26] and

[21] For this medieval textbook see Hamilton (G. L.) in Modern Philol. VII (1909), 169–185. The work, which is of the middle of the ninth century, is assigned by Manitius (I. 570) to Godescalc, as the name suggests. It is called an eclogue because of the matching of pagan with Christian instances between Pseustis and Alethia, with final appeal to Phronesis. John of Salisbury alludes to it, *Metalogicus*, 859 C.

[22] These items appear also in the later schoolbooks known as *Auctores* (*Autores, Actores*) *octo*. The one used at Troyes in 1436 contained: a Cathonet, a Théodolet, a Facet (*Facetus*), *Carmen de contemptu mundi*, Matthew's *Tobias*, Alain's *Parabolæ*, an Ysopet, and a Fleuret (*Floretus*), and added Sulpicius of Veroli's *De moribus puerorum* (Carré, *L'enseignement secondaire à Troyes* . . Paris, 1888, page 20). Cf. Paetow's ed. of Henri d'Andeli, 16, 37, 53. The same contents, with some variations of order, appear in two sixteenth-century *Autores* printed at Lyon. See also Haskins, 131.

[23] For the three styles of ancient rhetoric, see ARP 56, 57–59, 228; for St Augustine's application, above, page 68; for the transfer to poetic, Geoffrey's prose treatise II. 145 (F 312), John's *Rota Virgili* below, page 192, and Walter of Speier above, page 144.

[24] Bernard Silvester is one more reminder of *dictamen*.

[25] *Ars versificatoria* II. 43 (F 166).

[26] For instance, the pattern of the *Hora novissima*, below, page 199.

typical faults. After lamenting a schoolmaster's hardships (835–990), Évrard concludes (991–end) with classified specimens of *rhythmi*. There is a noticeable preponderance of trochaic measures.[27] The final group of quatrains in a measure common both in hymns and in Goliardic use is clearly a school exercise in framing a stanza to end upon a familiar quotation.

#### 4. Johannes de Garlandia, *Poetria* (probably before mid-Thirteenth Century)

John's work differs from the other three in specific application to *dictamen*.[28] The inclusion of *poetria* and *dictamen* in one treatise, though ill managed, is a practical adjustment to the teaching of the time. As taught, both were *rhetorica*, and both were confined within the single department anciently called *elocutio*. John begins, indeed, as Geoffrey does, with *inventio;* but his treatment of it [29] shows how faint in his time were even the echoes of its ancient function. Invoking for it simultaneously the "Ars poetica" and the *Rhetorica ad Herennium*, he first misapplies it to adaptation of style to person, occasion, etc., as in a letter—and as in the "three styles" of which Vergil is again made the exemplar! Then he perverts it to the search for appropriate proverbs, of which he provides a classified list for use in *dictamen*. His further applications show that *inventio* in his practise is purely verbal and leads, as fatally as all other approaches, to the lists of figures. "Nor should it be for-

[27] I am unable to follow always the classification in F.

[28] *Dictamen*, however (for which see below, Chapter VIII), is in the background of all these manuals. The title is *Poetria magistri Johannis anglici de arte prosayca metrica et rithmica*.

[29] Chapter I.

gotten," he adds (897),[30] "that any theme (*materia*) can be expressed in six ways according to the six cases of the noun." As if uneasy at the ancient application of the term, he appends a final section *De arte inveniendi materiam*, as a separate device for "boys wishing to amplify and vary a theme." For example, in writing about a book they might find occasion for praise or blame in the efficient cause, i. e., in the writer; in the material cause, i. e., in parchment, ink, etc. This can hardly be the mere dotage of John the Englishman. It is a sharp reminder of the educational level of these manuals; and it shows that the old *inventio* had departed from *rhetorica*.[31]

Otherwise he could hardly go on (Chapter II): "After *inventio* . . follows *electio*. Tully after *inventio* puts *dispositio*, then the art of memorizing, and finally delivery; but, for writers of poetry or *dictamen*, after *inventio* the useful art is that of choosing"! The choosing that he means is of the right style, "brief for affairs of the Curia (i. e., *dictamen*), diffuse for poetry" (897). Again he exemplifies by a specimen letter. *Memoria* is considered merely as mnemonic; and the cardinal mnemonic is a diagram of the "three styles" (900), each with its proper furniture of persons and things occupying a segment of a circle, the *Rota Virgili*.[32] As in the other manuals, the "art of beginning" (905), though divided into several modes, has little to do with composition. A letter (907) may begin with a proverb, an example, a comparison, with *si*, or *cum*, or *dum*, or an ablative

[30] The numbers refer to the pages of Mari's edition in *Romanische Forschungen* XIII.

[31] Matthew begins with the same topics, but without the perverted ancient terms.

[32] Reproduced in F. 87. Vergil exemplifies *genus tenue* in the *Bucolics*, *medium* in the *Georgics*, *grande* in the *Æneid*.

absolute. The "six parts of a discourse" (911) are summarily defined as by the ancients, but thereupon exemplified in seventy-eight elegiacs. As in the other
manuals also, the art of concision (913) is mentioned;
but the art of dilation (914) by figures is dilated.

Such clumsy handling makes obvious the misapplica-
tions of rhetoric to poetic that are current among John's
contemporaries. Another perversion equally general
is that of the *narratio* [33] of a speech to narrative. After
exhibiting quite properly the statement of facts in a letter as an application of *narratio*, John deviates as follows:

> But since *narratio* is common to prose and meter, we must
> enumerate its kinds [the three kinds of poetry taken by Bede
> from Diomedes [34]]. . Under the second falls the *narratio*
> which is distinguished by Tully thus: there is a kind of *nar-
> ratio* remote from legal pleading . . *fabula, historia, ar-
> gumentum* (926).

Brunetto Latini shows not only the same deviation,[35]
but also that "natural order and artificial order" which
John (905) and the other pedagogues had perverted
from Martianus Capella's *narratio* to narrative, and,
behind both, the general misconception of the ancient
*dispositio*.[36] Terms traditional in ancient rhetoric for
the processes of composition are deviated at once to
poetic and to style because the consideration never extends beyond figures, feet, or clauses.

[33] For the ancient *narratio* see the index to ARP.

[34] See above, page 131.

[35] *Trésor* III, part I. ii and xxxvii; Chabaille 471 and 518.

[36] See the section on Brunetto Latini, D. 4 of the preceding chapter.
It is noticeable that he too is preoccupied with *dictamen*. For the elementary exercises *fabula, historia, argumentum*, see the tabular view of
Quintilian in ARP 64, compare the section on Hermogenes in Chapter I above, and consult the index to this volume.

Thus John is able to add (928) to the "three poetic styles . . four other styles in modern use: (1) the Gregorian, (2) the Tullian, (3) the Hilarian, (4) the Isidorian. By the first he means the Roman style in *dictamen*.[37] The second he distinguishes not by rhythm, but by *colores*, and as "used both by poets when they write prose and by teachers in school exercises." The third, defined metrically, is exemplified both by an ancient hymn[38] and (929) by a letter. The fourth, that of Augustine's *Soliloquies*, marks the balance of clauses not by equality of length, but by chiming cadences. To the usual list of figures are added the ten commonplaces (939) for the description of a person;[39] to a lust-and-blood plot (*tragedia*), further specimens of *dictamen*. Rhetoric and poetic are merged in one scheme of style. The scheme is confused; but the intention is single.

The final section, *ars ritmica*, is significant, as Évrard's is, by its very presence in a schoolbook. It shows (56)[40] the same school assignment of a stanza framed to end on a familiar quotation. Its classification of examples, though not illuminating, is much clearer than the subdivisions of the chapters preceding. *Rhythmus*, the verse of the hymns, distinguished from *metrum* though discussed in some of the ancient metrical terms, is pre-

---

[37] Utuntur notarii domini pape, 928. Fierville, in the study mentioned above, note 2, finds: (1) stilus gallicus seu Aurelianensis, based on stress (i. e., rhythmic), (2) stilus Tullianus, based on quantities, (3) stilus romane curie. See below, Chapter VIII, B and C.

[38] Primo dierum, AH 51: 24.

[39] As in Matthew; see note 12 above.

[40] The references are to the pages of Mari's *Trattati*. One of John's own poems (AH 50: 554) ends each stanza with a hexameter taken from Vergil, Ovid, or Lucan.

sented for study and practise. For the schoolboys who
used it, as for the modern explorer, this section must have
offered the relief of an active poetic after the drill of deviated rhetoric.[41]

## 5. Common Traits

The pedantic subdivision of these manuals shows
that their aim was not to organize the study of poetic,
but to cover its elements by as many exercises as possible.
Imitative writing of Latin verse, long part of the study
of *grammatica*, has been combined with the theory of
*rhetorica* through exercises in figures, and with its practise through exercises in *dictamen*. Doubtless the re-
sulting aggregation was called *poetria* both because the
exercises were still connected with the traditional *prælectio* and were oftenest in verse, and because, whether
in verse or in *dictamen*, they were focused on that heightening by ornament and by dilation which was conventionally regarded as poetic. *Poetria*, then, meant generally the study of style, and specifically the study of
stylistic decoration. The lore for this was rhetoric,[42]
partly indeed by misapplication, partly from the vagueness of the boundary in Latin tradition. The "colors
of rhetoric," not always clearly distinguished, sometimes strangely spelled, were faithfully recited as a sort
of Greek ritual of poetic. The confusion went to its

[41] As a document also it is interesting both for its examples and, if
the text may be trusted, for some of its terms: "a rithmo qui constat
ex duabus *percussionibus*" (35); "in *prosis* que cantantur in ecclesia"
(42, the regular twelfth-century use, as for the hymns of Adam of St
Victor); "frequenter contigit in gallicis consonantiis" (59); "sed in toto
ymnario quo nos utimur nonnisi tres diversitates metri autentice sunt"
(60).

[42] For the common derivation of the *colores* from the *Rhetorica ad
Herennium* see the valuable tables in F 52–54.

bitter end in that stock perversion by which Vergil's poetic was broken on the wheel into three pieces of rhetoric.

The vital difference between rhetoric and poetic in composition, probably beyond the ken of these writers, was certainly beyond the intention of these manuals. Composition for them goes no further than the adjustment of a sentence. The ancient *inventio* and *dispositio*, sometimes dragged in by misapplication, are generally ignored. The distinction of "natural" from "artificial" order provides a pattern, not to promote composition, but to obviate its necessity. So the "methods of beginning" are presented as verbal devices. The scope of these manuals suggests that rhetoric, whether in its own name or as *poetria*, did not teach composition. What had once been part of rhetoric was now left to logic and the debates of the schools. As for poetic composition, the active progress of vernacular verse narrative would hardly be represented in a schoolbook. What is represented, what appears alike in school Latin and in professional vernacular,[43] is surviving conventional pattern, the passive voice of poetic, not its active. Marie had found another poetic. Chrétien, though he had accepted some of the same conventions of style, had learned otherwise what he knew of narrative movement. Even Latin narrative had been otherwise studied by Walter Map. To poetic in this larger composing activity the *poetria* of the schools offers no clue. At the turn of the next century Dante, who knew all its poetic conventions, ignored them in a supreme composition; and within that century Chaucer, who knew them too, laughed them away.

[43] F presents many interesting correspondences, with indications for further study.

## C. Hymns

### 1. Progress of Rimed Stress Verse

The ancient quantitative metric learned in school was often practised in such occasional verse as Baudry de Bourgeuil's.[44] Both his elegiacs and his partially rimed verses are literary exercises. More significant is the tentative use of rime in the same eleventh century by Fulbert.

> Verbum Dei Spiritumque legifer in Genesi,
> Rex David secundo psalmo post tricenum cecin*it;*
> Sic uterque Trinitatem unitatis prodid*it.*
>
> Sapiens cum genitore sancto suo Salomon
> Plane verbo declaravit esse Deo Fili*um,*
> Verbum scilicet æternum corde ejus genit*um:*
>
> PL 141: 342.[45]

Heribert, Bishop of Eichstätt in 1021, rimed more confidently, but still without insistence.

> Salve, crux sancta,        salve mundi gloria,
> Vera spes nostra,          vera ferens gaudia,
> Signum salutis,            salus in periculis,
> Vitale lignum,             vitam portans omnium. . .
>
> AH 50: 291.

The danger of insistence in rimed stress verse was already evident in many accentual hexameters riming the end of the verse with the middle. How easily the combination lapses into doggerel appears in a common seven-stress verse with marked cæsura (4+3).

---

[44] See above, Chapter V, footnote 31.
[45] Part of the interesting collection of Fulbert's verse in PL 141 is printed as prose.

> Gratiæ millesimo ducentesimoque
> Anno sexagesimo quarto quarta quoque
> Feria Pancratii post sollempnitatem
> Valde gravis prelii tulit tempestatem
> Anglorum turbatio castroque Lewensi,
> Nam furori ratio, vita cessit ensi. . .
> *The Battle of Lewes* (in Wright's *Political Songs,*
> Camden Society, 1839, page 72).

Such mechanical versifying merely makes obvious that stress rhythm was the established habit.[46]   By the twelfth century anything else was merely literary exercise, quite out of the literary current; and the danger of obtruding the stress pattern of failing to fuse it with the other means of suggestion, was more and more expertly avoided.

How far even a very marked pattern of stress and rime could be carried was demonstrated in the famous *De contemptu mundi* of Bernard of Cluny.[47]   Though its arraignment of his age soon faded, its detail of doom and redemption, its realization of eternal life, showed poetic vitality.   Bernard's failure in organizing the movement of the whole is thus forgotten in the striking success of these parts.[48]

[46] The ignoring of the quantity of an unstressed syllable appears in such rimes as *chóris* with *salvatóris, vitā* with *levítā*.  Every dissyllable stresses the penult (Alexander de Villedieu, *Doctrinale,* 2299); and the disregard of quantity is even more marked in calling it indifferently a spondee.  See below, Chapter VIII, note 44.

[47] Called also Bernard of Morlaix or Morlas.  The poem, some 3000 lines, is of 1140.  It is printed in Wright's *Anglo-Latin Satirical Poets and Epigrammatists of the Twelfth Century,* vol. II, London, 1872 (Rolls Series).  A considerable portion, including the familiar parts, is in Harrington's *Medieval Latin,* Boston, 1925, pages 315–322.  Bernard's rime is no less insistent in his *Mariale,* AH 50: 426.

[48] The modern revival of these parts is due largely to John Mason Neale.  His *Rhythm of Bernard de Morlaix, monk of Cluny, on the celestial country* gives verse renderings beginning: "The world is very evil," "Brief life is here our portion," "There Jesus shall embrace us," "For

> Nescio, nescio quæ jubilatio, lux tibi qualis,
> Quam socialia gaudia, gloria quam specialis.
> Laude studens ea tollere, mens mea victa fatiscit.
> O bona gloria, vincor; in omnia laus tua vicit.
> Stant Sion atria conjubilantia, martyre plena,
> Cive micantia, Principe stantia, luce serena.

The heavenly Jerusalem has never been contrasted with
the cities of the perverted present more eloquently.
For Bernard's achievement of style is rather in the ample
realizations of eloquence than in poetic compression.
The poetic distinction is in the verse. The sheer technical mastery of insistently rimed stress rhythm shows
the possibilities of the verse habit of his time.

> Hora novissima, tempora pessima sunt; vigilemus.
> Ecce minaciter imminet arbiter, ille supremus.

Thus the poem begins; and the cento made from it is
often entitled [49] *Hora novissima*. Accentual hexameters
rimed within—the Leonine system carried a step further—
are rimed together as couplets. They are entirely dactylic except in the last foot; the typical ancient variation by spondee within the line is never used. Finally
they are divided into three staves of two beats each, thus
foregoing another ancient variation, the shift of cæsura.
The first two staves of each line rime together; the last
rimes with the last stave of the next line. The pattern could
hardly be more marked. Yet the drumming dactyls, the
insistent rime, are kept in movement; they do not stall
even when the weaving of the line becomes sheer virtuosity.

> Pax ea pax rata, pax superis data, danda modestis.

thee O dear, dear country," "Jerusalem the golden," with the corresponding Latin text (first ed. 1858; seventh, 1865). *Britt* (170–173)
quotes large portions.

[49] As in the musical setting of Horatio Parker.

Bernard demonstrated that even insistently rimed stress rhythm could be kept from jar and jingle by attending constantly to movement. For this he exhibited further the capacity of accentual dactyls. More generally he displayed with great technical skill the range and flexibility of rhythm always chiming with word-accent, that is always answering the habit of speech.

The currency of rimed stress verse is obvious in student songs and other jocular and satirical poems known generically as Goliardic.[50] A little satire on masters and bachelors of arts, assigned to the eleventh century, is typical of the ease with which such verse could be turned.

| | |
|---|---|
| Jam fit magister artium | Jam fiunt baccalaurii |
| Qui nescit quotas partium | Pro munere denarii |
| De vero fundamento. | Quamplures idiotæ. |
| Habere nomen appetit, | In artibus ab aliis |
| Rem vero nec curat nec scit, | Egregiis scientiis |
| Examine contento. | Sunt bestiæ promotæ. |

E. du Méril, *Poésies populaires du moyen âge*, Paris, 1847, page 153.

Of the numerous twelfth- and thirteenth-century poems of this sort, many of which have been repeated ever since, none is more famous than the drinking song once attributed to Walter Map.

> Mihi est propositum in taberna mori.
> Vinum sit appositum morientis ori,
> Ut dicant cum venerint angelorum chori:
> Deus sit propitius huic potatori. . . .

Du Méril, 205.

[50] For an introduction to the Goliardic poetry see the article *Goliard* in Encyclopedia Britannica, with its bibliography.

## 2. Variations in Trochaic Stanza

Rime no longer incidental, but integral and composing, opened to medieval poetic wide artistic possibilities of stanza. The austere requiem sequence of Thomas of Celano, *Dies iræ*, is cast in three-line trochaic stanzas of a single rime.

Dies iræ, dies illa,       Quantus tremor est futurus
Solvet sæclum in favilla,   Quando Judex est venturus,
Teste David cum Sibylla.    Cuncta stricte discussurus! . . .
Britt, 87.

That forty of the forty-five hymns assigned by Misset-Aubry to Adam of St Victor are trochaic shows the strong preference of the time. The commonest of these trochaic stanzas, the favorite hymn measure of the twelfth and thirteenth centuries, expands *Corde natus* into a six-line stanza by doubling the first stave in a riming couplet twice and using the second stave between the two couplets and at the riming end.

In natale Salvatoris       Felix dies hodiernus,
angelorum nostra choris    in quo Patri coeternus
  succinat conditio.          nascitur ex virgine;
Armonia diversorum      felix dies et iocundus!
sed in unum redactorum    illustrari gaudet mundus
  dulcis est connexio.        veri solis lumine. . . .
Adam of St Victor, In die Natali Domini.

Using this scheme oftener than any other, Adam rarely holds to it throughout a hymn. His way is rather to vary it in one or two stanzas; and in some of his hymns he even interpolates a stanza of a different measure. For example, the ninth stanza of this Christmas hymn

departs entirely from the pattern except in the middle
and end lines.

> Quam subtile Dei consilium,
> quam sublime rei misterium!
> virga florem,
> vellus rorem,
> virgo profert filium.
> Nec pudorem lesit conceptio,
> nec virorem floris emissio:
> concipiens
> et pariens
> comparatur lilio.

This is the only variation; all the other stanzas are regular. The *Lauda Sion* sequence of St Thomas Aquinas
varies the measure but slightly; and the *Stabat Mater*
keeps it strictly—even reinforces it with additional
rimes.

Adam's harmonizing of rimed rhythmic, conspicuous
above, has great range and variety. The range appears
in the following contrast:

> Suggestor sceleris
> pulsus a superis
> per huius aeris
> oberrat spacia,
> dolis invigilat,
> virus insibilat;
> sed hunc adnichilat
> presens custodia.
> *St Michael*, v
> (Misset-Aubry 214)

> Salve dies dierum gloria,
> dies felix Christi victoria,
> dies digna iugi leticia,
> dies prima!
> Lux divina cecis irradiat
> in qua Christus infernum spoliat,
> mortem vincit et reconciliat
> summis ima.
> *Feria IV* [*Pasche*], i
> (Misset-Aubry 185)

Within a hymn the variations are delicate adjustments.
The hymn on the Cross strikes the familiar measure,
swerves from it, returns to it, varies it.

Laudes crucis attollamus,
nos qui crucis exultamus
   speciali gloria.

   Dulce melos
   tangat celos,
   dulce lignum
   dulci dignum
credimus melodia.
Voce vita non discordet;
cum vox vitam non remordet,
   dulcis est simphonia.

Servi crucis crucem laudent
qui per crucem sibi gaudent
   vite dari munera.
Dicant omnes et dicant singuli:
Ave, salus totius seculi,
   arbor salutifera.

O quam felix, quam preclara
hec salutis fuit ara,
   rubens agni sanguine,
   agni sine macula
   qui mundavit secula
   ab antiquo crimine!

*De cruce,* i–iv (Misset-Aubry 189)

## 3. Symbolism

Quite as widely Adam realized the poetic possibilities of symbolism. Imagination in the middle age was stirred habitually by types. As these spoke in sculpture and glass they spoke in the hymns. Medieval symbolism sought to induce mood, to stir emotion, not by individualizing concrete details, but by familiar typical associations: lamb, vine, star of the sea. Such symbols, long ago drawn from Messianic prophecy,[51] had become both numerous and familiar. They differ essentially from the figures of the *poetriæ* in being not decoration, not epithets or periphrases used instead of proper names, but immediate lyrical approaches. *Light* is used, not instead of the sacred name, or of some such title as Redeemer or Savior, but to focus attention on the Light of the World. So *Cornerstone,*[52] or *Lamb,* or *Bread,* suggests

[51] See the *Hymnum dicat turba fratrum* above, page 120; the seven Advent antiphons (*O Sapientia,* etc.) known as the seven O's, and *symbolism* in the index.

[52] Lapis, petra, fundamentum, silex, etc., and further, mel de petra, oleum de saxo, etc.

redemption immediately in one aspect.  So the Redeemer is seen to be foreshadowed in Isaac,[53] Joseph, or David; for medieval art sees history as the progress of the redemption of mankind.

In this aspect the symbols of the Virgin Mother are lyric not merely in warmth of emotion, but in visions of human progress as divine.  In turn *Bush* burning but unburnt, *Flower, Fleece* bedewed, *Star* immemorially guiding sailors, she embodies personally hope after hope. This habitual symbolism of stone and glass and hymn is less sentimental than intellectual.  While it appeals to childhood memories, it opens vistas.  The surcharging of the Corpus Christi hymns does not cloud their scholastic precision.

Ecce, panis angelorum,
Factus cibus viatorum,
Vere panis filiorum,
　Non mittendus canibus.
In figuris præsignatur,
Cum Isaac immolatur,
Agnus Paschæ deputatur,
　Datur manna patribus.
*Lauda Sion*, x; AH 50: 584.

Panis angelicus fit panis ho-
　minum,
　Dat panis cælicus figuris ter-
　minum;
O　res mirabilis!　Manducat
　Dominum
　Servus pauper et humilis.
*Sacris sollemniis*, vi; AH 50:
　587.

Keeping much of the tradition of its earliest centuries, hymnody has nevertheless widened its range; keeping communal devotion, it has risen in contemplation.  This is the character of the poetry written for the new feast by the Angelic Doctor.[54]  The enthusiasm of the popular

[53] This is one of the suggestions that Adam seems to have taken from Hugh of the same community.

Adam's most frequently recurring symbols are grouped conveniently in relation to medieval habit by Misset-Aubry, pages 56–110.

[54] The doctrine of transubstantiation was promulgated by Innocent III at the Fourth Lateran Council in 1215; the feast of Corpus Christi,

processions is answered, but it is also brought to its goal. The greatest medieval hymns obliterate the crude distinction between "reason" and "feeling," between "thought" and "emotion." They remind us of that ancient saying about the sublime, that it springs from intellectual vigor of conception.[55] That is why, of all medieval poetry, they are the best approach to the *Divina Commedia*.

by Urban IV in 1264, for the Thursday after Trinity Sunday. The proper hymns were written by St Thomas Aquinas: *Lauda, Sion* for the sequence of the Mass; *Pange, lingua* (containing *Tantum ergo*), *Sacris sollemniis, Verbum supernum* (containing *O salutaris*), for the office; *Adoro te devote,* for adoration. See AH 50: 583–591; *Britt,* pages 173–192.

[55] ARP 123, 124.

# CHAPTER VIII

## *DICTAMEN*

### REFERENCES AND ABBREVIATIONS

Bornecque    Bornecque (H.), *Les clausules métriques latines*, Lille, 1907, Travaux et mémoires de l'Université de Lille (for the ancient tradition, but including late Latin).

Butow    Butow (A.), *Die Entwicklung der mittelalt. Briefsteller*, Greifswald (dissertation), 1908.

Clark    Clark (A. C.), *The cursus in medieval and vulgar Latin*, Oxford, 1910. See also his *Fontes prosæ numerosæ*, Oxford, 1909.

Clerval    (as in headnote to Chapter VI).

Croll    Croll (M. W.), *The cadence of English oratorical prose*, Studies in philology, 16 (1919): 1–55.

Fierville    Fierville (C.), *Une grammaire latine inédite du xiiie siècle*, Paris, 1886.

Gaudenzi    Gaudenzi (A.), *Sulla cronologia delle opere dei dettatori bolognesi da Buoncompagno a Bene di Lucca*, Bulletino del' istituto storico italiano, 14 (1895): 85. See also in Bibliotheca iuridica medii ævi, vol. II, Bologna, 1892, his *Rainerii de Perusia ars notaria* (page 25) and *Boncompagni rhetorica novissima* (page 240).

Hahn    Hahn (S. F.), *Collectio monumentorum . . .*, Braunschweig, 1724.

Harmon    Harmon (A. M.), *The clausula in Ammianus Marcellinus*, New Haven, 1910, Conn. Acad. of Arts and Sciences.

Havet    Havet (L.), *La prose métrique de Symmache . . .* Paris, 1892.

Langlois — Langlois (C. V.), *Formulaires de lettres* . . ., six articles in NE, 34 (parts 1 and 2), 35 (part 2).

Manacorda — (as in headnote to Chapter VI).

MGH — *Monumenta Germaniæ Historica.*

NE — *Notices et extraits des manuscrits de la Bibliothèque Nationale* . . .

Paetow — Paetow (L. J.), *The arts course at medieval universities with special reference to grammar and rhetoric*, University of Illinois Studies, vol. 3, No. 7, Jan., 1910. See also the bibliography in his *Guide to the study of medieval history*, University of California Press, 1917.

PL — *Patrologia latina* (Migne) cited by volume and column.

Polheim — Polheim (K.), Die lateinische Reimprosa, Berlin, 1925.

Poole — Poole (R. L.), *Lectures on the history of the Papal chancery* . . ., Cambridge (University Press), 1915.

Rockinger — Rockinger (L.), *Briefsteller und Formelbücher* . . ., 2 vols., Munich, 1863–1864, Quellen zur bayerisch. u. deutsch. gesch.

Thurot — Thurot (C.), *Notices et extraits* . . . *pour servir à l'histoire des doctrines grammaticales au moyen âge*, Paris, 1868, in NE 22, part 2 (entire).

Toynbee — Toynbee (P.), *Dantis Alagherii epistolæ* . . . with introduction, translation, notes, and indices, and appendix on the *cursus*, Oxford, 1920.

Vacandard — Vacandard (E.), *Le cursus, son origine, son histoire, son emploi dans la liturgie*, Revue des questions historiques, n. s., 34 (1905): 59–102.

Valois — Valois (N.), *De arte scribendi epistolas apud gallicos medii ævi scriptores rhetoresve*, Paris, 1880, in Bibl. de l'École des Chartes, 22: 161, 257.

The art of letter-writing, especially the composition of official and other ceremonious letters, was of cardinal importance in the middle age. Even to-day, when letters of affairs are facilitated and multiplied by devices for dictation and despatch, it has a field smaller than the medieval in proportion to the other means of communication. Since these conditions lasted into modern times, letter-writing kept its importance throughout the Renaissance; but its art, developed in Latin antiquity and keeping for all affairs of moment the Latin language, became in the middle age a necessary ally alike to law and to diplomacy. *Dictamen* was a recognized profession and an habitual means of education. The model for the official correspondence of the western world was the Papal Chancery. The chief center of teaching was Bologna.[1] Though there was rivalry at Orléans, there was a recognized primacy of *stilus Romanus*.

No medieval form of writing has come down to us more abundantly in manuscripts; and none is more abundantly available in print. In addition to the collections of letters by famous men, or included with them, are many form-letters preserved as models.[2] Medieval epistolary habits are thus amply exemplified as the most widespread applications of the study of style. As a fine art medieval diplomatic correspondence is seen at its finest in the letters of John of Salisbury. The expertness that illuminated even routine affairs and determined the direction

[1] Thurot, 91, 114 (note 2), 483 (note 1). Thurot finds Orléans more in touch with Italy than with its own part of France.

[2] Several of the collection by Pierre de Blois in PL 207 seem to be form-letters; and this is the main intention in the tenth-century *Collectio Sangallensis*, MHG, Legum Sectio V, Formulæ, pages 390–433. See Clerval, 114, on the letters of Fulbert in Bibl. Nat. MS 14167; 311–313, on Pierre de Blois, Étienne de Tournay, and John of Salisbury.

of great ones was recognized in his own day. The Archbishop of Rheims, writing to the Pope concerning the
exile of the Archbishop of Canterbury, leaves the form of
his letter to John.[3] At an earlier crisis of that exile, when
Becket cried out against Henry's influence at Rome, the
indignation of the great prelate was submitted to the
great secretary; and he was too faithful a friend to forget
his art.

> On reading the letter that you have decided to send to the
> lord William of Pavia, though I dare not judge its intention,
> I cannot approve its literary conception. . . . If the items
> of your letter are thus brought up one by one, your reply will
> seem to have proceeded rather from bitterness and rancor than
> from the singleness of charity. *Ep.* 220; PL 199: 246.

Having shown a list of grievances to be ineffective as
composition, he adds immediately that accusations are
dangerous as style. But not stopping with criticism, he
took the great hazard upon himself in the following letter
to the same Cardinal.

> Popular rumor reports to us that you and the lord Otto,
> Cardinal Deacon of the Holy Roman Church, invited by our
> illustrious lord the King of the English, and commissioned by
> Papal mandate, are come down to the Aquitanian country,
> with the help of God by your best endeavor to restore to the
> English Church its inalienable freedom, and to renew peace
> and concord between the king and the archbishop. By princes,
> yea, and even by prelates, it has been heard that our afore-
> said lord the king so trusts your devotion that his acceptance
> of your advice in every particular is a foregone conclusion:
> in my exceeding joy whereat, I have decided that I too should
> ask advice of you and assistance, ready in all things to obey

[3] Scribit Remensis archiepiscopus pro causa nostra domino Papæ,
præcipiens litteras suas ad meum formari arbitrium. *Ep.* 286; PL,
199: 326.

you, saving my freedom of conscience and my personal honor. For I trust in the Lord that with you consideration of personages and of rewards will not be so influential that by any of your actions the Church shall be injured, scandal be engendered in lay folk, or your bright reputation be darkened. These, indeed, are the works of men by whom either the law is unknown or its Author is disregarded.  Not such are you, whose good faith and whose prudence the Lord has so honored with his approval that you are set before the world upon the golden candlestick of seven lamps as a lantern and as a beacon, that yours may be the light for all men that enter.  On you, therefore, all men are fixing their observation; and many fear lest the temptation of Lucifer should end in extinction and in ruin, lest the intimacy with the king, which they say you have lately been cementing, be to you beginning of dereliction. And indeed.

> Sin will be judged by intent; but its crime becomes
>      greater and greater
> Strictly with every degree of the criminal's office
>      and station.

(Juvenal, III. viii. 140.)

But in the meantime I am hopeful that this intimacy between you and the king, which to many is so suspect, will be fruitful to the Church, necessary to us, salutary to him, to you a further glory.  For if he gives you obedience where even legal necessity binds him, and where any evasion would be at the risk of his salvation, without doubt he will be repentant, will confess his transgression, and humbly giving the Church satisfaction, will restore to us all peace and freedom with our stolen integrity, and will tear quite out of his heart the hate of his brethren.  Otherwise what power is able to save him from the snare of the devil?

I am most certain, since it is indubitably true and even most obvious, that not even Peter himself received of the Lord such plenitude of commission that he could absolve the impenitent; and it no less certainly follows that if stolen goods can be restored and are not restored, the move is not penitence, but stratagem.  Where, therefore, the prince of the apostles has restricted authority, no argument will convince me that power can be validly exercised by any man whatsoever. I admit, for it is true, that our lord the king, as a prince among the most glorious, is most highly to be considered, but with the condition that God be never offended. Otherwise arises a form of idolatry, when on whatsoever pretext of expediency the creature is put above the Creator, as we are taught by Paul the apostle. Wrongs are not to be done that good things may issue; nor may any right of dispensation counter the Lord's commandment, which in law or in gospel has always the final ruling.

As for me, that you may the more conveniently advise me, that the cry of the poor man may be admitted to have its hearing, exile for me has now passed its fourth year; notwithstanding my lord the king, by me and through others, has often been notified that, though at the bar of my conscience I have not deserved his anger, yet to regain his favor I would gladly perform whatever might please him, saving my conscience and the integrity of my honor. Certain intermediaries, indeed, have approached me, suggesting that I withdraw my fidelity and devotion from the lord Archbishop of Canterbury, and swear fidelity to the king and observance of the laws of the kingdom. Because I cannot do this, and will not, for it is against my conscience and my honor, proscribed as an exile, I shall be gladly an exile till God shall deliver me. Am I to break my obligation of obedience when the Church is in danger, and God in the trial? Father and suzerain deserted, am I to swear to laws disapproved by the canons, when our lord the Pope in council at Sens with the brethren, with yourselves, I imagine, in audience, has denounced them? Nay, I would not swear that I had kept all the canons, or even all the gospel, since, as the apostle sadly reminds us, in much we have all been offenders. A lesser wickedness is simple prevarication than prevarication that is loaded with perjury. Well I know that perjury, disobedience, or any other baseness whatsoever, no one dare impute to your Lordships.

But since I fear you may weary of my wordiness, my words shall reach their conclusion, a fervent prayer that you may be zealous to end the misery of a Church too long in danger of foundering, and to defend us from the assaults of unremitting injustices.

May my lord fare well, and upon the proscripts of Christ may he have mercy. For I am interceding in the name of all my fellows in exile; and if I fail of my consolation, none the less I shall hold myself paid by whatever I know the other proscripts of Christ to have through your offices. *Ep.* 221; PL 199: 247.[4]

Medieval letters, long studied for history, should be better known as literature.

Less available, though for our purposes more directly important, are the manuals. Called generically *ars dictaminis* (or *dictandi*), or *summa dictaminis*, they are sometimes brief introductions to the formularies, sometimes substantial and detailed separate works. The latter have much less often than the formularies been printed. The ampler manuals apply to letter-writing a review of both grammar and rhetoric. This is instructive in Conrad's *Summa de arte prosandi*.[5] The *Boncompagnus*,[6] so widely used that Boncompagno's name, like Donatus, became a common noun, is amplified rather by diffuseness and by abundance of specimens. The *Rhetorica novissima* [7] of the same author is at once over-divided and ill-digested. Equally diffuse and equally relying on specimens, it appeals to students of law by deliberate and often inept variations from the traditional lore of rhetoric. The vogue of Thomas of Capua is hardly explained by the

---

[4] *Ep.* 223, page 389, in the collection of the letters of Gerbert, John of Salisbury, and Stephen of Tournay printed by Ruette, Paris, 1611. Both texts, omitting the *salutatio*, have the simple heading *Guillelmo Papiensi*. PL dates the letter 1167.

[5] Rockinger, I. 405–482.

[6] See Gaudenzi, who also edits it in *Bibliotheca iuridica*, I. It is printed in part by Rockinger, I. 121–174.

[7] Edited by Gaudenzi in *Bibliotheca iuridica*, II.

meager printed text of his *Dictator*.[8]  None of these is at
once so ample and so specific as a work by a Florentine
of the Bolognese school, perhaps Bene of Florence, entitled *Candelabrum*.[9]

## A. THE RHETORIC OF *DICTAMEN*

The international affairs of the Roman Curia demanded
and developed professional *notarii*.[10]  Their first and
abiding concern was precision.  Legal correctness of
language, exactitude, systematic verification and record,
precaution against tampering and forgery, all demanded
an elaborate technical skill.  This was *ars notaria* in the
stricter sense, an important branch of the practise of law,
especially of canon law.[11]  Beyond legal correctness and
dignity it developed style befitting Rome.  Privileges,[12]
decrees, mandates, dispensations, commissions, and other

[8] Hahn, I. 279–385; composed mainly of specimens.  For Guido Fava
and Bene di Lucca, see Gaudenzi.

[9] Described from MS Bibl. Nat. fonds St Victor, 906, and several
times quoted, by Thurot, 414, 415, 483, 484, 485; mentioned by Clark.
Manacorda, II. 266, citing Gaudenzi, says it is by Bene of Florence.
The *Candelabrum* is digested below, section B. 1.

[10] The term was more special than *dictator*, which meant more generally
a master in the art of prose; but Boncompagno, perhaps because of his
legal bent, uses the two side by side in his *Rhetorica novissima:* "Dictator,
prout hodie sumitur, est ille qui oratorum dicta legit et repetit, et repetita
variat et componit. . Dictatoris officium est materias sibi exhibitas
vel a se aliquando inventas congruo latino et appositione ornare: tales
namque interdum notarii appellantur."  Bibl. iurid. II. 257.

[11] Under the title *Rhetorica ecclesiastica* this is studied for the twelfth
century by Emil Ott in Sitzungsberichte der K. Akad. der Wissenschaf-
ten, philosophisch-historische Klasse 125 (1891–1892), Abhandl. 8:
pages 1–118, Vienna, 1892; and in the series edited by Dr. Ludwig
Wahrmund with the sub-title Quellen zur Geschichte des römisch-
canonistischen Processes im Mittelalter, Innsbruck, vol. I, 1906.

[12] E. g., the *privilegia* of Urban III (1185) and of Gregory VIII (1187)
in PL 202.

forms observed exact appropriateness and rhythms that were at once marks of authenticity and models. The same care extended to diplomatic correspondence. The documents in both fields, a mine for students of medieval history, amply attest the importance of *dictamen* as a profession.[13]

So wide a demand would of itself have maintained schools of professional technic. But since the technic demanded preliminary general training, it became a development of *rhetorica*. Not only so; it divided with preaching the whole field of daily prose composition. In current application oral composition was preaching, written composition was *dictamen*. The two were the typical medieval fields for the ancient lore of persuasion. The manuals of *dictamen* often begin by defining it in the general sense of writing.[14] Dividing all writing into (1) *metricum*, the ancient quantitative verse still taught as a branch of *grammatica*, (2) *rithmicum*, the accentual rimed verse of the hymns, and (3) *prosaicum*, they confine themselves to the third, and make it equivalent to letter-writing (*prosaicum vel epistolare*). To this they apply the current ancient authorities, *De inventione* and *Ad Herennium*, adding for its maxims of aptness *Ars poetica*. The ampler manuals include the sacred list of figures obligatory in the *poetriæ*.[15] Otherwise the application of the ancient rhetoric is practical and pointed.

For in fact the ancient lore was immediately and practically applicable. It did not, as in the *poetriæ*, have to

[13] Poole provides the best English introduction to this study.

[14] E. g., Alberic in Rockinger, I. 9. Ermini finds it used in the tenth century to mean *devoir*, or theme, "specimen eruditionis," "lavoro scolastico," *Poeti epici latini del secolo x*, 70, 109.

[15] E. g., *Candelabrum*, as also Conrad in Rockinger, I. 442. For the *poetriæ*, see above, Chapter VII. B.

be perverted. Of the traditional five parts of ancient rhetoric, *inventio, dispositio,* and *elocutio,* though not *pronuntiatio* and *memoria,* bear directly on letters, whereas the first two have nothing properly to do with verse-writing. *Elocutio* is applied practically by being focused on the cardinal ancient virtue of appropriateness; artistically, by elaborating *compositio* as prose rhythm. Immediately adaptable were the five parts of a speech. The *exordium* is always cardinal in a letter as *benevolentiæ captatio. Narratio* applies exactly in its proper sense of statement of the facts. *Petitio,* though it has less scope, is quite pertinent. *Conclusio,* though varying most from its ancient function, has some general correspondence. In a word, the classical doctrine for the parts of a speech applied to a letter by mere reduction of scale.

*Dictamen* was equally practical in actual teaching. Besides giving exercises in correctness, it compelled attention to elegance. Its study of appropriateness was readily extended by such imaginary adaptations as were inculcated in the ancient *prosopopœia,* and thus provided in writing the kind of practise sought orally in the ancient *controversiæ.*[16] John of Garlandia's confused combination of verse and prose in a single manual [17] is insufficient to prove that the two were often taught concurrently; and the higher tone of the *artes dictandi* suggests that they were addressed to older pupils.

[16] For *prosopopœia* and *controversia* see the index to ARP.
[17] See above, page 191.

## B. DIGEST OF *CANDELABRUM* I–V [18]

## Book I.  Choice of Words, Rhythmical Composition of Sentences

*Dictamen* is defined with the usual inclusiveness as apt and elegant writing, inseparable from subject matter, depending on native ability, teaching, and practise, using to some extent all five traditional parts of rhetoric, but mainly style (*elocutio*).

Exercising in all three styles (*humilis, mediocris, sublimis*),[19] it must beware of the corresponding vices: aridity, looseness, inflation. Its three requisites are choiceness of diction (*elegantia*), sentence skill (*compositio*), and dignity (*dignitas, ornatus*). Choiceness, or elegance, includes both purity (*latinitas*, the avoidance of barbarisms and solecisms, and, more widely, exactness of syntax) and lucidity (*explanatio*, including such figures as are illustrative).

All the rest of Book I is devoted to *compositio* as rhythm.

"*Compositio* is order polished smooth (*ordinatio verborum equabiliter perpolita*). If, therefore, we wish to give discourse this charm, we must so change the natural order that speech may have a *cursus* [20] charming and smooth and that we may not seem to talk vulgarly. *Compositio* seems to be threefold: natural, casual (*fortuita*), and apt [i. e., adjusted, called below artistic]. The natural, proper to expositors, reduces the artistry of discourse to the natural order. Even in this the *dictator* must give most careful attention to elegance. . . . If following the natural order does not give elegance, that

[18] Made from the Plimpton MS.

[19] For the three styles, see the indexes to ARP and to this volume.

[20] *Cursus* is used in this general sense by the thirteenth-century grammar edited by Fierville (119), which also applies to *compositio* the phrase *equabiliter perpolita* (116). *Rhet. ad Heren.* has *æqualiter perpolita*.

For *cursus* in its special sense, see below, section C.

superficial *compositio* is inadmissible. Casual may be called
that which, regarding only elegance, arranges words not
artistically, but with simple freedom. It is observed in manuals and in the Scriptures, and commended by holy men;
for, as says the apostle, 'the kingdom of God consists not in
word, but in work and power' [1 Cor. 4. 20]. Further a certain sage says: 'the simple word is the guardian of our faith'.
That *compositio* is artistic (*artificialis*) which gives the sentence charm by harmonizing its words in equable arrangement.
But this is observed in one way at Orléans, in another by the
fount of Latinity, Cicero, in another by the Apostolic See.
For the Orléans arrangement is by imaginary dactyls and
spondees; the Ciceronian tradition, by the artistry of the
several feet—a style therefore absolutely dependent on the
laws of metric. We, however, shall proceed according to the
authority of the Roman Curia, because every one finds its
style simpler."

Considering the positions of nominatives and of oblique
cases, of relative clauses, of infinitives, of locutions fixed
in certain places by usage, the author quotes Geoffroi
de Vinsauf: "A noble gravity comes from order itself
when what is joined by syntax is separated by order." [21]
A word ending in a consonant should be followed by one
beginning with a vowel, and *vice versa*. The *cursus* should
not be continuously swift or slow but varied:

> E. g., neither *animo simplici colitur dominus*, nor *simplicitate
> cordiali dominator summus perfecte veneratur*, but *simplicitate
> animi perfecte dominus veneratur*.

So the *dictator* will add, subtract, or transpose.

> E. g., *Vestra amicitia presentium tenore cognoscat* is relieved
> by transposing the first two words.

[21] *Poetria nova* 1051–1060 is quoted here with some variations from
Faral's text. The *Candelabrum* is therefore posterior to 1208–1213.

He will consider the rhythms of terminations: [22]

> of adjectives in *-ivus, -aris, -alis, -osus, -orus, -ensis, -atus*
> [stressed on the penult], against those in *-icus* and *-eus* [stressed
> on the antepenult]; of verbs, e. g., *nobilitat et coronat*, noticing
> that participles are available oftener than gerunds.

The rule for cadences (*de finibus distinctionum*) is that
they must satisfy.

> "The *cursus* must not be held up by a crowded or stinted
> close.   Clauses (*distinctiones*) should therefore end on polysyl-
> lables, that the whole *cursus* may be forwarded by the sentence-
> closes.   For style limps and is involved in delay if the end is
> suffocated by the crowding of contracted speech. . . .   Neither
> monosyllables nor words of more than four syllables are in
> place at the end."   The rule is then exemplified in detail.

These considerations open the large principle, fundamental in ancient rhetoric and clearly discerned by this
writer, that sentence skill consists in composing rhythmical units in a total movement, i. e., in composing by
heard clauses.

> "We have spoken often of *distinctiones* since no discourse
> can please that is indistinct. . .   A *distinctio*, then, is an
> integral member of one sentence,[23] weaving its words in apt
> order and releasing its thoughts from any tangle of doubt. . . .
> There are three kinds: . . . [1] *dependens* [later styled by its
> ancient name *comma*, or *cæsum*, [2] *constans* [a statement com-
> plete in itself, but carrying on, *colum, membrum*, also called

---

[22] Cf. Matthieu de Vendôme, II., section 13 seq.; Faral, 155 seq.

[23] "*Unius clausule integrum membrum.*"   *Clausula* is consistently used
to mean what we now call a sentence.   It is so defined below (folio 6):
"De clausulis quoque sequitur ut agamus, quoniam ex distinctionibus
clausule compinguntur.   Clausula igitur est plurium distinctionum
continuatio ambitum perfectum sententie comprehendens."   The
author adds that it is otherwise used *abusive*.   His definition agrees with
Fierville, 119.

*distinctio media*], [3] *finitiva*, that *distinctio* in which the whole
sentence is finished (*totalis clausula terminatur*), called by the
Greeks *periodus*, i. e., *circuitus*, or *finalis*." [24]

In punctuation the author prefers the simple and spar-
ing Roman use, and deprecates applying to *dictamen* the
rules followed in pointing the religious offices.[25]

The final consideration of this section is of sentence
length. Book I closes with general advice.

> "Let the *dictator* be so attentive in weaving his series of
> sentences as not to obstruct his auditor's ears with burden-
> some words, nor to induce prolixity; but by aptness, as well of
> words as of thought, let all seem to proceed so easily (*expedite*)
> that each has its place as chosen fitly."

## Book II. Figures

The second book, on stylistic ornament (*ornatus, dignitas*) is devoted to the traditional figures. These are the
same list from the *Rhetorica ad Herennium* as serves for
the *poetriæ*, and are rehearsed in the same order.

> The author even excuses himself for not providing new ex-
> amples. The book closes with three lists of vices in sense or
> sound: (1) *achirologia*, etc., as in Alexandre de Villedieu; (2)
> *repetitio*, etc., as in *ad Herennium;* (3) six derived from *Ars
> poetica.*

[24] Alberic (Rockinger, I. 25) has the same threefold division, but calls
[1] *suspensiva*, and says that it ends *acuto accentu*. Conrad (Rockinger,
I. 443) follows Alberic's terms, and quotes (444–445) Alexander de
Villedieu's *Doctrinale*, 2348–2358. The *Candelabrum* grasps clearly the
ancient conception of a period as a sentence rhythmically composed and
rhythmically completed.

[25] The technical significances of this section cannot safely be suggested
by translation. The available terms of modern English, if not misleading,
would be at least prejudicial to an interesting inquiry. A considerable
part of the original is printed by Thurot, 415: "De punctis . . . et
modo punctandi," etc.

## Book III. *Salutatio*

The three kinds of *dictamen* are: (1) prose, i. e., free composition (*sermo communis*, or *solutus*); (2) metrical; (3) rhythmical (*genus rithmicum*), which observes syllabic equality and rime.[26] "Since we have nothing, however, to do with the two others, . . let us now proceed to the prose *dictamen*, the *dictamen* of letters; for that is demanded of all and recognized as of great utility. It increases eloquence, promotes favor, enlarges honors, and often enriches the needy." The typical parts of a letter—there may be more, or fewer—are *salutatio, exordium, petitio, conclusio*. This whole book is devoted to prescriptions for the first. The *salutatio* must always be in the third person. Its order is determined by the relation of the rank or dignity of the sender to that of the recipient, though this in certain cases is waived. It is careful of titles and of their appropriate modifiers.

The use of *Dei gratia* with a title is determined specifically. "The main consideration, however, in any *salutatio* is who is writing to whom; for there must always be made an adjustment of the one to the other (*collatio personarum*). The Pope thus salutes the Emperor: '*dilecto filio F. romanorum imperatori et semper augusto*'. . . The Emperor calls the Pope '*sanctissimum in Christo patrem.*'" So on down the list of dignities and occupations [27] the author specifies what is

[26] "Quod paritatem sillabarum et similem consonantiam sine ulla temporis consideratione observat." The example is the hymn *Ave, Maria, salvatoris.* There is added, by way of caveat, the different ancient definition of *rhythmus;* but the medieval use is vindicated "ad delectationem et quandam mollitiem; quoque ad dignitatem . ." So Conrad: "Rithmicum observat tantummodo certum numerum sillabarum, distinguendo clausulas versiculorum in quadam finali concinnantia." Rockinger, I. 419.

[27] Cf. Conrad's list headed *Diversitas personarum.* Rockinger, I. 425 seq.

correct, or suggests what is appropriate, in noun and modifier, and answers certain questions of syntax.

The book closes with a protest. Merely to consult a formulary is a poor substitute for studying the art of *salutatio*. It is like swimming with corks. "The ideal (*forma*) of *salutatio* which we have here worked out, well grasped and held, will save writers both from borrowed plumage and from deficiency."

## Book IV. *Exordium, Narratio, Petitio, Conclusio*

The *exordium* is such a prelude to the statement of the facts as will make the hearer [28] open-minded, well disposed, and attentive.

The reader's sympathy is engaged by the writer's reference to himself, to his opponent,[29] to his reader, or to the occasion. According to the nature of the subject, the *exordium* may be either direct (*principium*) or indirect (*insinuatio*). Its diction must be fluent, correct, unstudied, i. e., it must avoid harshness, deviation from recognized usage, and pomp.[30] Especially must the writer avoid any language that can be turned against him. To begin with a proverb, though this is advised by some authors,[31] is to deviate the *exordium* from its proper function.

[28] The ancient term *auditor* is kept, as well as the traditional three functions. The second function being cardinal in a letter, *benevolentiæ captatio* in some manuals, e. g., Alberic's (Rockinger, I. 18), is used as the heading, instead of *exordium*. In others, as, here, it is a subheading. The doctrine here is from *Rhet. ad Herennium* I.

[29] Reference to the opponent is kept from ancient rhetoric, though often inapplicable in a letter. But see the opening of John of Salisbury's letter at the beginning of this Chapter.

[30] The ancient counsel against pomp in the *exordium*, though repeated, seems to have been less regarded than the others.

[31] E. g., by Geoffroi de Vinsauf, *Poetria nova*, 126–133 (Faral, 201); Guido Fava (Rockinger, I. 185; Gaudenzi, 129).

*Narratio*, statement of the facts,[32] should be concise, transparently clear, and plausible (*brevis, dilucida, verisimilis*). The application of the ancient maxim is to the connection of *narratio* with *exordium* by proper conjunctions and in several possible cases. Similarly are set forth the ways of connecting it with the following *petitio*, which is summarily defined. *Conclusio* in a letter is not, as in a speech, the logical result of proof. Rather it is the satisfaction of whatever expectations have been aroused. It may be affirmative, negative, or conditional, so long as it is a satisfying close. Modes of connecting it with the rest of the letter again have most space.

## Book V. Summary Review of the Preceding Books

The fifth book, reviewing all these items in the same order, constitutes a summary manual, a *summa dictaminis*.

"Since I know that some will find the multiplicity of the preceding burdensome, let the multiplicity be reduced in this book to paucity in consideration for the unlettered (*rudium*). Thus, as for those who rejoice in abundance I have displayed letters both various and adequate, so for the many of weaker stomach who wish to be fed on light diet I ought to set forth food at once moderate and proper (*honestum*)." The author then proceeds seriatim with a digest.

[32] The term is said to be more inclusive. "Narrationum genera tria sunt: oratorium, digressorium, et poeticum." *Digressorium* probably refers to the *digressio* for which a place in the speech was provided by ancient rhetoric after the division (see ARP, 65). *Poeticum* is of course divided into *historia, fabula, argumentum* (for which see the index). The author makes no use of this, or of the whole division, which indeed is inapplicable to a letter; but it seems to have troubled him, as it troubled the *poetriæ* (see above, page 193). Quintilian's clear distinction seems to have escaped them: "Et historiæ, quæ currere debet ac ferri, minus convenissent insistentes clausulæ," etc., IX. iv.

This book by itself provides about the same quantity of precept as suffices in other manuals to introduce collections of specimens; but it is exceptionally systematic.[33]

## C. *Cursus*

In the twelfth and thirteenth centuries the practise of *cursus* became more technical, and the use of the term more special. The Chancellor appointed by Pope Urban II was John of Gaetà (Giovanni Gaetano), who had learned *dictamen* from Alberic of Monte Cassino,[34] and who was specifically commissioned to "reform the style of ancient grace and elegance in the Apostolic See" and to "restore the Leonine rhythm with its lucid rapidity." [35] The dominant chancery style, thus reformed, embodied the principle of rhythmical close in three types of prose cadence:

(1) *cursus planus*, víncla perfrégit;
(2) *cursus tardus*, víncla perfrégerat;
(3) *cursus velox*, vínculum frègerámus.[36]

[33] At this point the author turns from Roman use to French, beginning Book VI with a new set of definitions.

[34] Alberic's *Rationes dictandi* are printed in Rockinger, I. 9–28, and are followed by *Albericus de dictamine*, 29–46.

[35] *Liber pontificalis*, 162, vol. II. 311, as translated by Poole (84) in context. The Chancellor was afterward (1118–1119) Pope Gelasius II.

[36] The key phrases are Clark's (10), repeated by Poole (90). The grave accent in the last indicates that at this point there is often a secondary, lighter stress.

*Tardus* is called *ecclesiasticus* in a thirteenth-century work quoted by Thurot, 482.

A fourth form, *trispondiacus* (Vacandard, 72, 89), is regarded by Croll (2) as a modification of *velox*.

For correctness of cadence as a mark of authenticity see the passage from Pierre de Blois quoted by Langlois, NE 34, part 2:26.

The best English summary of the technic of *cursus* is Poole, Chapter IV, which also reviews Valois, Havet, W. Meyer, and Clark. The best

The first sentence of a mandate of Innocent III shows all three.

> Inter omnes munitiónes et cástra (*planus*)
> quæ Romana ténet ecclésia (*tardus*)
> munitionem et castrum Montis Fiasconis non solum inténdit
>   sed cúpit (*planus*)
> et providéntius gùbernári (*velox*)
> et studiósius cùstodíri (*velox*).[37]

The indignant closing paragraph of Dante's letter to the Florentines begins:

> O miserrima Fæsulanórum propágo (*planus*),
> et iterum iam puníta barbáries (*tardus*)!
> An parum timoris prælibáta incútiunt (*tardus*)?
> Omnino vos tremere árbitror vìgilántes (*velox*),
> Quamquam spem simuletis in facie verbóque mendáci (*planus*),
> atque in somniis expergísci plerúmque (*planus*),
> sive pavescentes infúsa præságia (*tardus*),
> sive diurna consília rècoléntes (*velox*).[38]

indication of the significance of *cursus* is Croll; for though this essay is directed to a later period, it reviews medieval habit and through English examples exhibits the influence of *cursus* in the development of vernacular prose rhythm.

[37] *Reg.* VI. 105, June 30, 1203, as quoted and pointed by Poole (97), who thus prints the whole mandate.

[38] *Ep.* VI, 6; Toynbee, 75; pointed by Clark, 20. Both record W. Meyer's emendation for *cursus, puníta* (for *Púnica*, a former corrupt reading). The *cursus* in John of Salisbury's *Ep.* 221 are followed in the translation above, page 209. The text begins as follows: "Fáma vulgánte (*plan.*) didicimus vos et dominum Ottonem sanctæ Romanæ Ecclesiæ diáconum càrdinálem (*vel.*) ad preces illustris domini nostri régis Anglórum (*plan.*) ex mandato dómini pápæ (*plan.*) in partes Aquitániæ dèscendísse (*vel.*) ut auctore Deo, si fieri potest, Anglicanæ Ecclesiæ debitam reddatis libertatem (not conformed) et inter dominum regem et Cantuariensem archiepiscopum pacem et concórdiam rèformétis (*vel.*). A magnis etiam et a venerabilibus víris audítum est (*tard.*) quod præfatus dominus noster rex adeo de amore véstro confídit (*plan.*) ut consilio vestro in omnibus obtemperáre decréverit" (*tard.*).

The fixing of these three cadences in Roman use would of itself have given them a vogue beyond letter-writing. Moreover they were chosen not at random, but as typical fulfilments of rhythmical expectation. For they appear also, though not exclusively, in the collects of the liturgy and in the daily offices.[39] The collect for the fourth Sunday after the Epiphany has all three.

Deus qui nos in tantis perículis cònstitútos (*vel.*) pro humana scis fragilitate non pósse subsístere (*tard.*) da nóbis salútem (*plan.*) méntis et córporis (*tard.*) ut ea quæ pro peccatis nostris patimur (not conformed) te adjuvánte vincámus (*plan.*).[40]

The longer measures of the collect composed in 1264 by St Thomas Aquinas for Corpus Christi fall upon *velox*.

Deus, qui nobis sub sacramento mirabili passionis tuæ memóriam rèliquísti, tribue, quæsumus, ita nos corporis et sanguinis tui sacra mystéria vènerári ut redemptionis tuæ fructum in nobis júgiter sèntiámus.

The English translation, following this cadence in the first measure and the third, departs in the second.

O God, who in this wonderful sacrament hast left us a memórial of thy pássion, grant us, we beseech thee, so to venerate the sacred mysteries of thy body and blood [not conformed] that we may ever perceive within ourselves the frúit of thy redémption.[41]

Hearing these cadences over and over, preachers of course used them often in Latin sermons. Thus the cadences that were obligatory in ceremonious letters, and habitual

[39] For this see Vacandard's historical review.
[40] Pointed by Croll (27), who compares the English versions of this and of other collects in the Book of Common Prayer.
[41] If the second measure could have ended on *mýsteries of thy bódy*, it would have conformed.

in other use, confirmed the conception and practise of Latin prose as rhythmical.

The rhythmical conception of prose, as the middle age knew well, had been dominant in classical antiquity. But medieval Latin prose, though its tradition came through the schools of Gaul, had had its own development. As in verse,[42] so in prose, the shift of rhythmical control to stress opened, not a breach, but a new artistic life. Medieval Latin ran as a living language with the movement of living speech. This was recognized even by the grammarians.[43] So the thirteenth-century manuals of *dictamen* kept the terminology of ancient metric to describe accentual rhythms [44] because Latin to them was present as well as past, and seemed to reach indefinitely into the future. The future, by the time of the Renaissance, was seen to be with the vernacular for poetry. More slowly it was seen to be there also for prose. Meantime Latin poetic and rhetoric came to be studied by revival of antiquity. Revival translates Renaissance exactly. Italian

[42] See above, Chapter IV. C.

[43] See above, pages 111, 184.

[44] *Candelabrum,* describing French interpretation of prose rhythms by metrical terms, says: "Nor do they consider those feet according to shortness or length, but according to number of syllables and word-habit." The whole passage is quoted by Thurot (484), who notes its correspondence to Maître Guillaume (quoted at 481): "The feet used in verse are three, dactyl, spondee, trochee. In *dictamen,* however, we use two, spondee and dactyl. Nor are the feet to be measured by length and shortness, but by the run (*cursus*) of the words. For every dissyllable, whether long or short, is a spondee; and a trisyllable with a short penult is a dactyl." Ponce (quoted also at 481) lays down the same principle. The *cursus,* that is, was determined by the number of unstressed syllables between word-accents. The old terminology of quantitative metric was kept, partly because it was conveniently familiar, partly because the new rhythms were legitimate descendants of the old. But the abeyance of quantity could not be more clearly indicated than by the dictators' habit of calling every dissyllable a spondee.

scholars, and after them French and English, sought to turn Latin prose back to Cicero. Though they thus accomplished some most worthy ends, their theory and their practise interrupted Latin prose composition. Their contemptuous rejection of medieval rhythms hastened the processes by which Latin became a "dead" language. In the middle age it was living. A conspicuous evidence of its vitality, not merely a legal technic, but the formulation of a rhythmical habit, was the *cursus*.

# CHAPTER IX

## PREACHING

### REFERENCES AND ABBREVIATIONS

Bourgain   Bourgain (l'Abbé L.), *La chaire française au xiie siècle* d'après les manuscrits, Paris, 1879.

Clerval    (see the list for Chapter VI).

Cruel      Cruel (R.), *Geschichte der deutschen Predigt im Mittelalter*, Detmold, 1879.

Douais     Douais (C.), *Essai sur l'organisation des études dans l'Ordre des Frères Prêcheurs au xiiie et au xive siècle* (1216–1342). Prèmiere province de Provence. Province de Toulouse, avec de nombreux textes inédits. Toulouse & Paris, 1884.

LM         Lecoy de la Marche (A.), *La chaire française au moyen âge*, spécialement au xiiie siècle, d'après les manuscrits contemporains, Paris, 1886 (2nd edition).

Owst       Owst (G. R.), *Preaching in medieval England*, an introduction to sermon manuscripts of the period c. 1350–1450, Cambridge, 1926.

PL         *Patrologia latina* (Migne), cited by volume and column.

Perdrizet  Perdrizet (Paul), *Étude sur le Speculum humanæ salvationis*, Paris (thèse), 1908.

Polheim    Polheim (Karl), *Die lateinische Reimprosa*, Berlin, 1925.

The historian of twelfth-century preaching finds the "prodigious success"[1] of St Anselm's sermon on the Assumption not even faintly echoed in the flat record. The same disappointment awaits any one who shall turn from the fame of John Bunyan's preaching to his printed sermons. In both cases the reputation is more convincing than the record. The testimony leaves no doubt that the preacher was eloquent; but his eloquence has not been preserved. The seventeenth-century record and the medieval, though in different directions, are alike insufficient.[2] Even when we have on the page before us the very sentences—and often we have something less, or even something different, we lack something of the eloquence. For the difficulty of transmission is so fundamental that it thwarts even the records of our own day. Oratory is typically the energizing of a message by a speaker for a specific audience. Its style depends on all three. In varying degrees all three enter into its composition. The occasion becomes part of the message. Between speaker and audience there is mutual response. Therefore of all the arts oratory is the most perishable.

But the history of oratory, though often baffling, is not hopeless. So perishable that it can never be quite recaptured, oratory may be so charged that even through imperfect record much often transpires. For any given

[1] Bourgain, 31. The sermon is in PL 158.

[2] "The lord Abbot preached in chapter on the Epiphany a magnificent sermon. I have rendered it rapidly, as well as I could from memory, to send to you." Odo, quoted by Bourgain, 16.

"Les sermons d'Hildebert n'ont donc pas été prononcés tels qu'ils sont écrits." Bourgain, 41.

Cf. LM 120–121 on the manuscript sermons of St Thomas Aquinas. For the text of St Bernard's, see Mabillon's introduction to PL 183.

period its records not only reveal much of the habit of the time, but conversely can often be so interpreted by that habit as to become really significant. Medieval sermons can thus be related not only to the medieval pedagogy of rhetoric, but to actual habits of composition and of style. In a form of oratory continuous for nearly two thousand years they will show at least what in preparation, composition, utterance, record is typically medieval.

For the middle age preaching is the characteristic form of oratory. Political oratory being in abeyance, legal oratory having little scope, preaching practically monopolizes the third field distinguished by Aristotle, occasional oratory, the oratory of here and now. Teaching, clearly of course a sermon function, sometimes becomes the main object; but even so it is not incompatible with other oratorical use of the occasion. Indeed, a sermon hardly succeeds as teaching except through the typical means of occasional oratory. For a sermon is different from a lesson, and even more different from an essay. As a form of oral composition it has opportunities and methods distinct from those of the bar or the senate. Occasional oratory, always beset by temptations toward sophistic,[3] has always opened on the other hand the highest ranges. In preaching, the safeguard against sophistic is in the distinctive use of the occasion to move men to action. Always emotional, occasional oratory becomes in preaching a distinct form of persuasion. Relying less than political oratory on argument, reasoning less and pleading more, it is even more urgent toward a goal. This character, achievement alike and misuse, is vivid in the medieval preaching of the friars.

[3] See Chapter II above.

Medieval preaching is occasional oratory not only in

the ancient application to special solemnity, but more

significantly in using the familiar recurrences of the

The whole western world kept not only

Christmas, but Candlemas, Michaelmas, and the rest.

Nothing is more characteristic than the focus of popular

emotion upon Corpus Christi.

The calendar of feasts

and fasts was the actual calendar. A medieval auditory

had a great common fund of conscious and subconscious

The surrounding symbolism of stone and

glass was familiar from land to land. The pulpit was

beside the altar. The regular sermon on a Sunday or

a feast was at Mass after the gospel, which furnished its

text.[4] The atmosphere of prayer was intensified by

specific petition preceding and following. "Let us there-

fore ask our Lord to give me good words for you" ended

the exordium, or "Pray that we may be illuminated,"

or "Pray the Lord, therefore, that by the power of

spiritual teaching to-day your hearts may be uplifted"; [5]

and the congregation united in *Pater* and *Ave*. So the

sermon ended with prayer, and was immediately fol-

lowed by common intercessions. Though some of these

conditions are constant throughout the history of Chris-

tendom, never before or since have they combined at

once so amply and so widely to constitute the conditions

of preaching. In this special sense medieval preaching

was the oratory of occasion. At no other time has oratory

had at command so large and constant a fund of common

emotional associations.

[4] Special sermons, panegyrics for instance, might be preached after
Mass. Both were called *sermones in mane* in distinction from the af-
ternoon *collatio*, which, however, might continue or confirm them.
See LM, 223–226.

[5] Quoted by LM, 289.

## A. Vernacular to the People, Latin to the Clergy

The appeal of medieval preaching to this common emotional fund, though it cannot often be measured, can be analyzed often as to style and composition, oftener as to habit of thought, in abundant documents. Even in print hardly any medieval material is more abundant— and there are further stores in manuscript—than collections of sermons. In order to interpret these, we must constantly remember how they were made and why. First, medieval sermons are habitually gauged to one of the two typical audiences. Either they are for the lay folk in parish church or cathedral (*sermones ad populum*), and were preached in the vernacular; or they are for the clergy (*sermones ad clerum*), i. e., before synods, councils, schools, oftenest of all in monastery chapels, and were preached in Latin.[6] In either case, until the late middle age, the record was always in Latin; in either case the preparation also, the notes and outline and more or less of the further composition, was usually in Latin. In the former case of a sermon preached to a lay congregation the record gives at most only a translation.[7] In the latter case of a sermon preached to a monastic community the record is at least nearer to the spoken word. We can press further, therefore, the analysis of sermons preserved

---

[6] The evidence is so ample as to leave no further dispute, though there were naturally exceptions, as in the case of lay brothers in monasteries. See the review in either Bourgain or LM, and for the sermons of St Bernard Mabillon's introduction to PL 183.

[7] E. g., Pierre de Blois (PL 207: 750) sends by request a written (Latin) version of a sermon preached in French, remarking that the Latin naturally has more amplitude.

by such communities as the Cistercians and the Victorines.[8]

Though popular preaching is no less worthy of study, less of it has been transferred to the written page.[9] But translation, though it could convey little of the spoken vernacular style, must not be thought of as involving the difficulties of to-day. In the middle age every cleric was bilingual; and every preacher of distinction enough to be recorded not only read and wrote Latin habitually, but spoke it fluently.[10] His schooling having been in Latin, both written and oral, his daily offices, his reading, and whatever writing he did being still in Latin, he used Latin easily and naturally in thinking out and ordering a sermon or in giving another's sermon, or his own afterward, the permanence of writing. Since he would not be embarrassed, as young preachers sometimes are to-day, by trying to recall phrases and sentences, preaching in the vernacular from Latin notes might even leave oral composition the more free.

## B. COLLECTIONS

The other process, the final rendering in Latin, was by no means always of the sermon as preached. It might

[8] As was suggested by Langlois, L'éloquence sacrée au moyen âge, Revue des deux mondes, 115 (Jan., 1893): 177.

[9] Cruel, 338, has some racy bits from the Dominican Frater Peregrinus.

[10] Samson, famous twelfth-century Abbot of St Edmund's, preached in two vernaculars, as well as in Latin. This, doubtless, and his Norfolk accent, seemed worthy of record. His command of Latin and one vernacular would hardly be mentioned. "Homo erat eloquens gallice et latine magis rationi dicendorum quam ornatui verborum innitens. Scripturam anglice scriptam legere novit elegantissime, et anglice sermonicari solebat populo, sed secundum linguam Norfolchie, ubi natus et nutritus erat; unde et pulpitum jussit fieri in ecclesia et ad utilitatem audiencium et ad decorem ecclesie." Cronica Jocelini de Brakelonda, Camden Soc., London, 1840, page 30; "Rolls Series," 96, vol. I, page 244.

be merely a digest, or more expansive, or the whole sermon. All three degrees seem to be exemplified among the printed sermons of Fulbert.[11] The compilers of Odo of Morimond say: "he was very eloquent; but in writing his sermons we have ignored the form for the substance." [12] Collections often show distinctly less concern for record, for commemoration of achievement, than for guidance. Some even of the more important collections have evidently this practical aim. They propose not only inspiration, but practical suggestion and direction for future sermons on recurrent themes. They are less anthologies than repertories. Maurice de Sully, Bishop of Paris, thus designed his widespread collection primarily for the pastors of his diocese.[13] The study of preaching, not merely the preservation of notable sermons preached in his time (*sermones reportati de auditu*), seems to have been the object of the collections of Pierre de Limoges. Clearly the best known of these, his *Distinctiones*,[14] arranging not only whole sermons, but outlines and suggestive passages alphabetically by subjects, is meant for reference. That the collections commonly had in view the practical use of successful sermons as models is suggested again and again, and sometimes indicated.[15]

The great thesaurus of Jacques de Vitry[16] is systematically practical, a collection not primarily *of* sermons, but *for* sermons. Models, outlines, suggestions, intended

[11] *Sermones ad populum*, PL 141.
[12] Bourgain, 86.
[13] Bourgain, 48; LM, 45.
[14] About 1273. See LM, 107–10ʳ
[15] See, e. g., Polheim, 390, on St Anthony of Padua; Cruel, 337, on Frater Peregrinus.
[16] Cardinal, bishop, historian, famous preacher; died 1240.

for adaptation in the vernacular [17] are arranged according
to the Church calendar: four books for the seasons, a
fifth for the saints, with three expositions for each day,
the first of the introit, the second of the epistle, the
third of the gospel. The sixth book is classified for
adaptations to typical social groups. What has naturally
most attracted modern historians in this storehouse is
the abundance of illustrative descriptions and stories,
the *exempla*. A resource prized in all times for popular
address, the *exemplum* was so cultivated in medieval
preaching as to call forth many collections. [18] It looms
unduly large to modern readers because the *exempla*
have now an extraneous interest in reflecting medieval
life, and because they were taken not only, as now, from
contemporary life, from history, from legend, but also
from the bestiaries.

The basilisk, they tell us, bears in his eye his poison, vilest
of animals, beyond others to be execrated. Wilt thou know

[17] This, as well as their derivation from his own *sermones ad populum*,
explains the title *sermones vulgares*. The scheme by books is:
 I. Advent to Septuagesima, tempus deviationis;
 II. Septuagesima to Easter, tempus revocationis;
III. Easter to Pentecost, tempus reconciliationis;
IV. Pentecost to Advent, tempus peregrinationis.
 V. Sancti Maiores, Commune Sanctorum.
VI. Secundum Diversitatem Personarum.
 See LM, 55–58.

[18] E. g., Étienne de Bourbon's *Tractatus de diversis materiis prædi-
cabilibus*, for which see LM, 113. See also Little (A. G.), *Liber exem-
plorum ad usum prædicantium sæculo xiii compositus a quodam fratre
minore anglico de provincia hiberniæ secundum codicem dunelmensem
ed.*, Aberdeen, British Society of Franciscan Studies, 1908.

For Jacques de Vitry see Crane (T. F.). *The exempla . . . from the
sermones vulgares of J. de V.*, ed. with introduction, analysis, and notes
[of sources and parallels], London, 1890 (Pub. Folk-lore Soc. XXVI)

See also Mosher (J. A.). *The exemplum in the early religious and didactic
literature of England*, New York (Columbia University Press), 1911.

the eye that is empoisoned, eye of evil, eye that has fascina-
tion?  Then think thou upon envy.
St Bernard on the Psalm *Qui habitat*, xiii. 4; PL 183: 237.

The mythical zoölogy is now often too diverting to
keep its effectiveness as illustration.  But to recover this,
and to realize that the bestiaries do not convict the middle age of credulity, we need not go back of St Francis
de Sales.  *Exempla*, after all, are a commonplace of preaching because they are a necessity.

The general thesaurus and the special [19] alike confirm
the impression of wide use of a common fund of topics
and illustrations.  But sermon helps are not peculiar to
the middle age.  Every age has offered to its preachers
something equivalent to the medieval handy manuals.[20]
Not only preaching, but all occasional oratory, has always
been beset by the temptation to rely on pattern and
stock.[21]  That the middle age had many conventional
sermons is less significant than that it had St Bernard
and the early Dominicans.

## C. Manuals

Medieval manuals of preaching are no more specific
than modern manuals as to their rhetoric.  That is
typically generalized, or even taken for granted.  For
instance, Guibert de Nogent's *Liber quo ordine sermo
fieri debeat*,[22] concerned entirely with interpretation, has

[19] For Guillaume d'Auvergne's *De faciebus mundi*, a thesaurus of
figures, see LM, 70.

[20] One of these was called from its first text, the Advent "Let us cast
away the works of darkness," *Abjiciamus*.

[21] See above, Chapter I.  As in sophistic, encomium was most readily
formalized.  See Bourgain, 198, on stock panegyrics.

[22] PL 156: 22.  See Bourgain, 67.  Guibert died in 1124.

no rhetoric at all. The anonymous Chartres work on
popular preaching quoted in part by Clerval [23] gives,
besides the usual procedure and advice, a practical
counsel for preparation and one for delivery. The first
is to fix meditation on the specific object of that sermon
and on the specific means most likely to bring it home,
not on the words. The words will come if the matter is
surely ordered. The second is to increase urgency from
quotations of texts through *exempla* uttered with loud
appeal until the congregation shows emotional response,
then to moderate the tone so as to lead quietly to the
final benediction.

Another anonymous manual [24] sets forth eight methods
of expansion (*De dilatatione sermonum*): (1) definition
and exposition of terms, especially of their "moral" significance; (2) division, not to be so minute in a sermon
as in a treatise; (3) proof, by contraries, enthymemes,
examples, again to be guarded from subtlety; (4) cita-
tion of confirmatory texts; (5) degrees, i. e., positive-
comparative-superlative, as in exhibiting one of the
virtues; (6) metaphors, not to be multiplied nor mixed;
(7) symbolism, i. e., allegory, tropology, anagogy; (8)
cause and effect. Most of these are commonplaces of
rhetoric. Some of them, and their use for dilation, suggest the same preoccupations as the *poetriæ*. [25]

The Dominicans, devoted to preaching, maintaining
a long and severe discipline of studies, provided systematically for oral composition. "*Legendo, studendo,
disputando*" [26]—the last tallies not only with Dominican

[23] 314, from MS Bib. Nat. fonds latin 9376, folio 89.
[24] MS latin 16530, as summarized in LM 295–296.
[25] See above, Chapter VII. B.
[26] Quoted and discussed in Douais, 65–67. See also LM 131. LM

fame, but with the focus, and the increasing emphasis, of oral training on logic.[27]   Otherwise the manual of the fifth Dominican General, the *De eruditione prædicatorum* of Humbert de Romans, says little of rhetoric.   Rather it is practical psychology, as are the second book of Aristotle's *Rhetoric* and the sixth book of Jacques de Vitry.

Practical by another method is the manual of Alain de Lille, *Summa magistri Alani doctoris universalis de arte prædicatoria*.[28]   "First we must see," he says at the end of his preface, " *what* preaching is, its distinguishing qualities of expression and of thought, and its typical species; secondly, *who* should preach; thirdly, *to whom;* fourthly, *why;* fifthly, *where*."   His first chapter, after brief consideration of preaching as public speaking, sets forth the special sanction for sermons of the gospels, the Psalms, the Pauline epistles, and the "books of Solomon" as offering instruction in morals.   Winning his audience by his own humility and by the practical import of his message,[29] not by appeals to applause, the preacher proceeds to the twofold exposition of the text.   "Let his words be sometimes emotional (*commotiva*), to soften the minds of his hearers and bring tears.   But let the sermon be concise, lest prolixity bring instead boredom. . . Finally he should use *exempla*."

Chapter ii proposes for a theme the scorning of the world (*De mundi contemptu*), and for its text, "Vanity

notes (27) that in 1273 half of the principal sermons at Paris were by Dominicans, a large proportion of the remainder being by Franciscans. Humbert de Romans died in 1277.

[27] See above, Chapter VI.

[28] PL 210: 110–198.   For Alain's *Anticlaudianus*, see above, Chapter VI. D. 1.

[29] The phrase *captare benevolentiam* and the two ways are traditional and oft-repeated.

of vanities; all is vanity." Distinguishing the vanity of this world as thus typically threefold, Alain quotes *Romans* and the Psalms and adds Persius. "Thus the preacher should confirm each division of his text. His next step is to show where is vanity, where vanity of vanities, where all is vanity. . . The scorning of the world, thus established by the way of the world itself, should be established also by consideration of man's end (*a causa finali*)." The peroration apostrophizes human blindness (*O homo, si mundana,* etc.).

In a word, Alain furnishes a specimen order and procedure. Succeeding chapters thus present other usual topics: scorning of oneself, gluttony, the other deadly sins, the heavenly hope, spiritual grief and joy, patience and each of the other virtues, love of God and of one's neighbor, etc. The remaining headings of his prefatory division are taken up at chapter xxxviii; and his consideration of different types in congregations has the humor to include the sleepy. The title *Summa*, then, implies a preacher's book of reference, with advice and direction subordinated to classified material. The distinction of this *Summa* is its systematic conciseness.

## D. SYMBOLISM

Much more distinctive than any provision of collection or manual for ordinary use of a common fund is the prevalence of symbolism. The "moral" exposition that followed the literal commonly had this direction. For medieval symbolism was not merely a habit of exposition; it was seen as well as heard because it was a habit of conception. The cathedrals still exhibit in sculpture and glass what came in words from their pulpits. The Psalms, especially those recurring in the daily offices,

thus conveyed from generation to generation the eternal
word of God.   For every psalm was the lyric cry of
David, or of some other ancient Hebrew, only in the
first instance (*litteralis expositio*).   It always meant more;
and its further meaning (*moralis expositio*), as cumulat-
ing progressive experience of God, was more important.
It always meant not only David, but every other soul
thus answering God, the "poor man" of every time and
of every clime, every individual then and there focusing
and enlarging by those words his own experience.

So far the "moral" interpretation treats the psalm
as an extreme case of literary inspiration, appropriates
it as having the universal validity of every lyric that has
survived the centuries.   A religious classic, more widely
and intensely spiritual than any other body of lyrics, the
psalter is still only a classic.   But medieval interpretation always took a third step.   Every psalm meant not
only David, and further not only every "poor man"
making it his own, but also "the man," the Lord incarnate
to share all humanity and to give men "power to become
the sons of God."   Thus the Psalms spanned the centuries, connected the New Testament with the Old in-
divisibly, and were the voice of man in every age answering God in the Church.   The habitual use of the Old
Testament, and even of secular history, as prefiguring
is here focused in its simplest form.[30]   Simplest and

---

[30] Quatuor sunt regulæ scripturarum quibus quasi quibusdam rotis
volvitur omnis sacra pagina: hoc est historia, quæ res gestas loquitur;
allegoria, in qua ex alio aliud intelligitur; tropologia, id est moralis
locutio, in qua de moribus componendis ordinandisque tractatur; anagoge, spiritualis scilicet intellectus, per quem de summis et cœlestibus
tractaturi ad superiora ducimur.   Guibert, *Liber quo ordine sermo fieri
debeat*, PL 156: 25 D.

In the Victorine thesaurus *Sermones centum* (PL 179) the 39th opens

commonest instance of symbolism, the interpretation
of the Psalms is characteristic. Though not, indeed,
peculiar to the middle age, it opens a widespread medieval habit.

The habitual use of the *Song of Songs* as symbolic of
the Christ and his Church reminds us that symbolism is
essentially poetic. It was the usual poetic of medieval
preaching in interpreting not only the Scriptures, but
all human experience. As behind the word lay spiritual
meaning, so behind the veil of the senses lay the realities
of life. The so-called "otherworldliness" of medieval
preaching is no ignoring of physical facts; it is a sustained and consistent call to see through them. What
medieval philosophy defined as seeing "in the aspect of
eternity" (*sub specie æternitatis*) medieval preaching
inculcated as a habit of vision. The habit might, indeed,
degenerate, as in that popular manual of the fourteenth
century, the *Speculum humanæ salvationis*,[31] into extravagance or minute formalism; but even so it kept
some view of history as a providential progress. It
might rise, on the other hand, to express the immediate
apprehension of the mystic, the vision of spiritual genius.

according to this scheme as follows. *Jerusalem civitas sancta* (Apoc.
21) et *civitas sancti* (Isa. 52). Secundum historiam civitas est terrena,
secundum allegoriam sancta est Ecclesia; secundum tropologiam vita
spiritualis, secundum anagogen patria cœlestis. PL 179: 999.

See also Hugh of St. Victor's *De triplici intelligentia sacræ scripturæ*,
chapter iii of his *De scripturis et scriptoribus sacris*, PL 175: 11–12.

[31] For this and for its relations to symbolistic habit see Perdrizet.
For one of the many earlier examples of minuteness see the Advent
sermon of Pierre de Celles on Isaiah xvi. 1, "Send the lamb" (*Emitte
agnum tuum*), PL 202: 637, which draws significance from every part
of the lamb: the four feet, the belly, the back, etc. Alain's chariot
(above, VI. D. 1), remote and artificial to us, was a familiar allegory.
Cf. his theological application of *grammatica* and *rhetorica* in the verses
*De incarnatione Christi*, PL 210: 577, and Bourgain, 256.

But the distinction of the medieval mystic is rather in degree than in kind. The whole age is characteristically habituated to mysticism. No other poetic vision is equal to Dante's; but no other form of poetry in his age, whether in verse or in sermon, is commoner than the vision. Not only to the rapt was the visible world eloquent of the unseen eternal.

> Full, indeed, is everything of supernal mysteries, abounding each in its special sweetness if the eye that beholds be but attentive, as of him who knows how to suck honey from the stone and oil from the hardest rock.
>
> St Bernard, *De Laudibus Virginis Matris*, I. 1; PL 183: 56.

In the following sermon of this series St Bernard refers seriatim to the accepted prefigurations of the Blessed Virgin. She is the perennial antagonist of the serpent (Genesis iii. 15), the *mulier fortis* of Solomon (Proverbs xxxi. 10), the burning bush (Exodus iii. 2), Aaron's budding rod (Numbers xvii. 8), Isaiah's rod from the root of Jesse (xi. 1), the rod that smote the rock (Exodus xvii. 6) and divided the sea (Exodus xiv. 16), Gideon's fleece (Judges vi. 37–40), the woman who is the Lord's new creation (Jeremiah xxxi. 22). The prefigurations of this list had an obvious appeal in sermons through being familiar in hymns, in sculpture, in glass. Evidently St Bernard loved them for their poetry; but he is also convinced of their sanction. He even formulates the theory of symbolic prefiguration.

> These words ["To-day ye shall know that the Lord will come"], indeed, have in Holy Writ their [historical] location in place and time; but not incongruously have they been adapted to the vigil of the Lord's Nativity by mother Church —the Church, I say, she who has with her the counsel and spirit of her Spouse and God. . . When, therefore, she

changes or shifts words in Holy Writ, her combination (*compositio*) has more weight than the passage in its original place, the more, perhaps, the greater the distance between figure and fact, between light and shadow, between mistress and handmaid.

St Bernard, *In Vigilia Nativitatis Domini*, III. 1; PL 183: 94.

His second sermon for Advent carries out the prefiguration of the rod, or stem (*virga*).[32]

From these passages I think it now manifest what is the stem proceeding from the root of Jesse, and what is the flower on which reposeth the Holy Spirit. For the Virgin Mother of God is the stem, her son is the flower, flower indeed the son of the Virgin, flower white at once and ruddy, the chosen from thousands (Cantic. v. 10), flower that angels desire in their visions, flower at whose fragrance the dead have revival, and, as he himself beareth witness, flower of the field (Cantic. ii. 1), not of the garden. Flowereth the field without human ministry, not by sowing of any one, not upturned by spading, not from without made fertile. So entirely, so the Virgin's womb hath flowered; so inviolate, unimpaired, and chaste the body of Mary as the pasture of the eternal vigor hath burgeoned its flower, whose is a beauty beyond corruption, whose a glory unfading forever. O Virgin! stem of the highest, to what a summit thou liftest on high thy holiness! even to him that sitteth on the throne, even to the Lord in his majesty. Nor is that a great marvel, since thou has sent so deep the roots of thy meekness. O truly celestial plant, that art precious above all and holy above mankind! O true tree of life, which alone was worthy to bear the fruit of salvation!

*De Adventu Domini*, II. 4; PL 183: 42.

The symbolism of his sermon in the Epiphany octave on the marriage at Cana is specifically moralized.

[32] The following translations from St Bernard in this chapter attempt to suggest his characteristic rhythms. Though these cannot, of course be imitated exactly, even partial or approximate rendering may make him sound the more like himself.

Now, methinks, ye have fathomed to what my words are tending. To-day ye have been hearing the wonder performed at the marriage, beginning indeed of the Lord's tokens, even as a story sufficiently wonderful, and in significance still richer in gladness. Great indeed was the sign of the heavenly power, that water turned into wine at the Lord's bidding; but far better that other changing at the right hand of the Highest which in this one is prefigured. We are bidden every one to the spiritual marriage at which of a truth the bridegroom is Christ our Lord. Wherefore we sing in the Psalter: *And he as a bridegroom coming forth from his chamber* [Psalm xviii. 6]. Spouse indeed are we to him, if this seem not to you incredible, both all together one spouse and every soul by itself a spouse singly. But when can this be conceived of its God by human weakness, that we should be his beloved as a bride is beloved by her bridegroom? Far enough is this bride below her bridegroom in origin, below in her nature, below in her dignity. Nevertheless for that ancient Æthiop woman the son of the eternal king from far made his advent, and that for his own he might espouse her, feared not even to die for her. Moses, indeed, took to wife an Æthiop woman, but his marriage availed not to change the Æthiop's color: Christ will present his bride, whom he loved in her baseness and all her foulness, glorious with his own glory, his Church without spot or wrinkle. Aaron may murmur; Miriam (Maria) may murmur, not the new, but the old, not the Lord's mother, but Moses' sister; not, I say, our Mary, she who shows her solicitude if some lack perchance is found at the marriage. Ye, therefore, as is meet, amid the murmurs of the priests, amid the murmurs of the synagogue, give your entire devotion to these our common acts of praise and thanksgiving. *Dominica Prima post Octavam Epiphaniæ*, II. 2; PL 183: 158.

Such preaching shows the same preoccupation as the symbolic windows of the cathedrals, their carved capitals, above all the thronged but harmonized groups of their great porches. It is not merely conventional illustration; it is a constant and consistent reminder of the history of mankind as a scheme of redemption.

## E. COMPOSITION

## 1. Imaginative Method

The most conventional form of symbolism is allegory. This may be no more than what Lowell calls "personification by capital letters," as in the Vice and Virtue, the Reason, Feeling, or Nature, of the eighteenth century. Even so it has more point when the convention is as instantly recognizable as the seven deadly sins of medieval capitals and poems, or the four cardinal and the three theological virtues, or even the seven liberal arts, each with appropriate costume, attitude, gesture, or action. How pleasant allegory may be in verse is evident in the wide popularity of the *Roman de la Rose*.

But no less evidently such pictorial aggregation offers little to preaching, since it has no vigor of composition. To be moving, allegory as well as higher symbolism must be narrative. The classic demonstration of this, the *Pilgrim's Progress*, was written by a preacher. The art has never been more widely or more expertly pursued than in the middle age. The fourteenth-century English *Piers Plowman* suggests even more vividly, with its strongly oral manner, how allegory might move in preaching. A sermon might be not only enlivened by passages of easily recognizable description; it might further be vivified by making the figures individuals and by putting them into speech and action. A complete demonstration is furnished in the interlude, prologue, and tale of Chaucer's Pardoner. That accomplished rascal is made to display the whole art of oral narrative, from its vulgar drama to its high ranges of symbolic suggestion. The case is extreme; but the method has been a resource of popular preaching from the days of Nathan's rebuke to

David down to the present. Oral narrative, often with dramatic dialogue, has been heard again and again, both in such base uses as the Pardoner's and in such urgency of message as Bunyan's, because it has been found surely persuasive.

Here is the high art of the *exemplum*. Often the medieval record puts us off with a summary; sometimes the manuals give a mere note, "Tell the story of so-and-so"; but sometimes there are clear clues to such narrative art as makes the Pardoner's tale breathless. An *exemplum* of Walter Map's lets us divine how dramatic the tale might be in the pulpit.

> But for other men the monastic life turns out otherwise. Far more pitiable was the fate of a noble and eloquent man who, likewise a monk of the same community, was in the same case recalled to arms. [After winning great fame as a warrior, he had in penitence become a monk, vowing never again to shed blood. But when the countryside was harried, his old comrades dragged him forth, in spite of his protests, and made him lead them once more.] Enduring many reverses of battle with a noble fortitude, he was always reanimated by defeat to fight again, and, inflamed as it were with new ardor, would fly at the enemy the more fiercely, and whether they fled or held their ground, would indefatigably stick to them like glue. When the enemy sought to crush him by the size of their company, they found that victory goes to bravery, not to numbers. Burning with wrath, therefore, and increasing their force many fold, they surprised him in a valley hemmed between two cliffs, and had him almost trapped. No hope, for he was caught; no issue, for he was held; they went to work the more leisurely because the more securely. But he, bursting into their midst like a tempest, scatters them like dust in a whirlwind, and so stupefies them by his daring that they see nothing to do but run. Promptly he hangs on their rear with his band, small enough in comparison with theirs; and the throng of the enemy, in the effort to save their

lords from him, becomes the prize of a single monk. But one leader of that attack, after escaping, makes a detour ahead and, mingling unrecognized with the monk's men, works back steadily toward the monk, risking his own life to take his. The monk, almost stifled with toil and sun, calls his page, enters a vineyard, doffs his armor, and, while his band passes on, stretches himself half-stripped to the air under the shade of a tall vine. Then the skulker, leaving the line of march and slipping up stealthily step by step, pierces the monk with a deadly dart and escapes. The monk, knowing himself near death, confesses his sins to the page, the only person within reach, bidding him impose penance. He, being a layman, swears he knows not how. But the monk, extreme in his penitence as in everything, says: "Impose upon me by the mercy of God, dearest son, that in the name of Jesus Christ my soul may be in hell doing penance up to the day of judgment; so that then the Lord may have mercy upon me, lest with the wicked I behold the countenance of his wrath and anger." Then replies the boy with tears, "My lord, I impose upon thee for penance that which here before the Lord thy lips have uttered." And he, accepting with word and look, devoutly received the penance and died.

Here let us remember the words of mercy, In whatsoever hour a sinner shall repent, he shall be saved. Wherein he might have repented and did not, whether he omitted anything possible, we may discuss; and God have mercy on his soul.

Walter Map, De nugis curialium, I. xiv.

## 2. Logical Method

Composition as a progress of thought, logical sequence, ordering by paragraphs, shows on the other hand little that is distinctively medieval. As in other times, differences here are rather individual. Bourgain does not establish his assertion of a general weakness of order;[33]

---

[33] Bourgain, 261. Clerval makes the same criticism (313) of Pierre de Celles. Cruel gives some means of testing it as a generalization by his abundant analyses and digests.

and his addition that even St Bernard proceeds by leaps [34] is extravagant.  Lecoy de la Marche has more warrant for asserting that medieval sermons generally lack such sustained progress [35] as Bossuet's.  For often the course of a medieval sermon is not only shorter; [36] it is less sustained by a progress of paragraphs than forwarded by stages of emotion.  The latter method may be for its audience no less valid.  Indeed, preaching must learn poetic as well as rhetoric.  Its composition, ideally embracing both, will be bent toward the one or the other by the particular preacher and audience.  The medieval abeyance of sustained logical progress, if in fact it was general, may have been due to preoccupation with those poetic methods which were effective with some of the greatest preachers.

The school lore of rhetoric, however, was weak in the inculcation of logical progress.  Busy with style, confusing in this study rhetoric with poetic, it offered too little practical guidance for preaching as composition.  Doubtless the lack was filled in some cases by the teacher; [37] but the shift of pedagogy to logic implies, among other things, dissatisfaction with rhetoric.[38]  What medieval rhetoric lacked, medieval logic, for all its triumphs in other directions, could not quite supply for preaching.  The disputations of the schools, excellent for general training in oral fluency, in precision, in detecting and

[34] "St Bernard lui-même ne marche que par soubresauts."  Bourgain, 261.

[35] "On ne trouvera point au treizième siècle le grand art, l'éloquence de longue haleine."  LM, 17.

[36] But here too the record may sometimes be misleading.  See above, page 234.

[37] For the Dominicans, see above, page 237.

[38] For this implication in John of Salisbury, see above, page 171.

meeting error, could not reach the specific skill of continuously instructing, winning, and moving a silent
congregation. They might even lead a vain or unwary
preacher astray. Medieval preaching has been accused
of habitual over-division, of tedious minuteness in headings and subheadings. Unfortunately such sermon divisions are not peculiar to any period. They seem no less
common, for instance, in printed English sermons of the
seventeenth century. But the medieval record, at least,
does not always reproduce the actual preaching method.[39]
Sometimes it gives little beyond the outline, which thus
seems the more barren. Sometimes it uses a sermon as
the occasion for further development, rather providing
for future than following actual exposition of the text.
Where the record seems to follow, there is evidence
enough to make probable that the dominance of logic did
deviate many late medieval sermons into over-analysis.

Analysis, the very function of logic, can never suffice,
as Aristotle makes clear, for presentation. In preaching, its value is not for organizing, but for preliminary
study. It is rather for the preacher than for his audience.
It belongs rather in his notes than in his sermon. But
though doctors analyzing daily in the schools might rely
unduly on their habitual method when they preached,
they preached oftenest to the schools themselves, that is
to special audiences habituated to logical method. The
popular preaching of the Franciscans can hardly have
had that bent. The Dominicans, severely trained in
logic, were also trained specifically to preach. St Bernard, preaching both to monastic communities and to
the people, will not be accused of over-division. Neither
St Anthony of Padua nor St Bernardine of Siena can

[39] See above, page 229.

have set Italy on fire with elaborate analysis. These considerations, though largely *a priori*, are at least as weighty as contrary inferences from the sermon record. They permit the belief that medieval preachers realized as generally as preachers of other times the apothegm of St Ambrose: *Non in dialectica complacuit Deo salvum facere populum suum.*

## F. STYLE

Medieval sermons, for all the defects of transmission, offer ample and various demonstration of the force and beauty of medieval Latin. In contrast to the archaistic composition of the Renaissance, medieval sermon Latin moves at its best with ready variety and even in ordinary use with easy fluency.

## 1. Rhythm

Pierre de Celles,[40] fairly typical of ordinary expertness, is clearly rhythmical. St Bernard's ardor and winsomeness, the oral immediacy of his expression, appear in no resource of his style more strikingly than in his very pace.[41]

> We have heard with our ears what is full of grace and worthy of acceptance: "Jesus Christ the Son of God is born in Bethlehem of Judah." My soul hath been melted at this announcement; but my spirit in my breast is surging in haste to utter this joy and this exultation of your desire at the time appointed. Jesus is interpreted Savior. What so necessary to the fallen, what so desirable to the wretched, what so use-

[40] PL 202: 637 seq.

[41] St Bernard's dactylic pace is more marked at the opening of the first sermon of this series: "Laborat affectio mellifluæ dulcedinis copiam latius effundere gestiens, nec inveniens verba. Tanta siquidem est gratia sermonis hujus ut continuo incipiat minus sapere si unum iota mutavero." PL 183: 87.

ful to the hopeless? Nay, elsewhere whence is salvation, whence even some slight hope of salvation, in the law of sin and the body of our death, in the evil of the present day and the place of our affliction, unless it were born to us anew and unlooked for? Thou perhaps desirest salvation; but the bitterness of the remedy, when thou thinkest alike of thy weakness and of thy illness, affrighteth thee. Fear thou not. Christ is very gentle, mild and of great mercy, anointed with the oil of gladness above his fellows, who receive, though not his very fulness, yet some of the fulness of his anointing. But lest thou, hearing his gentleness, shouldst undervalue the might of thy Savior, cometh his title, the Son of God.

*In Vigilia Nativitatis Domini*, VI. 1; PL 183: 109.

Now let us return unto Bethlehem, and let us see this word which is wrought, which the Lord hath wrought and hath shown to his people. House of bread it is by old rendering; good for us there to tarry. Where hath been the word of the Lord, naught shall fail of the bread which shall strengthen the heart, as saith the prophet: "Comfort thou me according unto thy word" (Psalm cxviii. 28). In every word from the mouth of God proceeding mankind liveth, liveth in Christ as Christ in him is living. *Ibid.* 10; PL 183: 114.

Happy then forever are these our brethren, who now have been freed from the snare of those that hunted them, who from the tents (*tabernaculis*) of our campaigning to the halls where we shall be resting have made their passage, their fear of evil lifted, their hope singly and fully now established. This is the faithful, all the faithful body, greeted in "There shall no evil happen unto thee; neither shall any plague come nigh thy dwelling" (*tabernaculo:* Psalm xc. 10).

*In Psal. Qui habitat*, XI. 2; PL 183: 225.

## 2. Balance and Rime

Balance, beloved of occasional orators from Gorgias down,[42] is useful in sharpening the iterations and contrasts of preaching.

[42] See Chapter I above, page 42.

Human weakness must realize its limitation. . . . The counsel of preaching, rather the counsel of the truth itself and of the divine reason, calls on man to yield his own reason. Let him fear not to yield himself entirely, following God entirely, and boasting in the Lord entirely, knowing him in whom he believes as able to keep the deposit of oneself and to give it increase (2 Tim. i. 12). He will restore thyself to thee, and with interest. He takes it as earthly, to restore it in heaven. He takes it in humility, to restore it exalted. He takes it as diminished, to restore it perfected. He takes it as empty, to restore it face to face with God in contemplation. He takes it corrupted, to render it incorruptible. He takes it in wretchedness, to render it happy, transferring a creature of time to the eternal, man unto the godlike.

Achard of St Victor, *De septem desertis* [43] (peroration).

Such balance often leads, through mere inflectional correspondence, to rime. That rime of clause with clause was avoided as a vice even in classical Latin is an exaggeration of Renaissance scrupulosity.[44] The middle age, following rather Augustine and the tradition of the schools of Gaul,[45] found rime desirable, and often

[43] Modum suum agnoscat humana imbecillitas. . . . Consilio meo, immo consilio ipsius veritatis et rationis divinæ suam deserat homo rationem. Non timeat se totum deserere, totus Deum sequens, et se totum jactans in Domino, Sciat cui credit quia potens est depositum ipsius reservare sed et augmentare. Ipsum tibi restituet, et cum usura. Accipit in terra et restituet in cælo. Accipit humilem et restituet sublimem. Accipit diminutum et restituet perfectum. Accipit vacuum et restituet facie ad faciem Deum contemplantem. Accipit corruptum et reddet incorruptibilem. Accipit miserum et reddet beatum, temporalem transferens in æternum, hominem in Deum. Quoted by Hauréau, *Histoire littéraire du Maine*, I. 19. Achard was Abbot of St Victor 1155.

Cf. St Bernard's "Neque sine salute Jesus, neque sine unctione Christus, nec sine gloria venit Dei Filius: siquidem ipse salus, ipse unctio, ipse gloria." *In Vigil. Nativ. Dom.* I. 2; PL 183: 87.

[44] For the history of Latin prose rime, with ample documentation, see Polheim; for concise summary, Perdrizet.

[45] See above, Chapter III. A.

sought it to mark parallel or contrast. Simple, ordinary use of it is heard again and again in a sermon by Hilduin.[46]

> Porro bruttis animalibus paleam littere relinquamus, et de medulla tritici panem vite confestim filiis porrigamus.

Elinand uses it to point an epigram.[47]

> Quæsivit me diabolus, et invenit, et circumvenit; quæsivit me Christus, invenit et subvenit.

Richard of St Victor's rime often marks insistently exact balances.

> Hic flos factus est nobis medicina, ex illo mel et cera, in ipso potus et esca; medicina in redemptione, potus et esca in justificatione, mel et cera in glorificatione.

| Ex hac medicina | sanitas sempiternæ | incorruptibilitatis; |
|---|---|---|
| ex ejus esca | refectio internæ | satietatis; |
| ex ejusmodi potu | ebrietas æternæ | securitatis; |
| de illius cera | splendor summæ | claritatis; |
| in ejus melle | dulcor indeficientis | felicitatis. |

PL 196: 1032.

It may mark a progressive iteration. Repeating *florida* and *transeamus* from what he has just said, he goes on:

> Sternamus itaque viam nostram floribus talibus, et per florida virtutum transeamus, munde et honeste procedamus, ut processionem nostram pulchram et gratam faciamus, et pascha floridum digna celebritate perficiamus.

*In Ramis Palmarum*, PL 196:1059.

Even such insistence remains within the limits of rimed prose; it is only extreme use of a widespread habit.

---

[46] *In Fest. S. Dionisi,* last sentence of the exordium. The sermon is quoted in full by Bourgain, 384 seq.

[47] *In Ascens. Dom.,* quoted in context by LM 312 from Tissier VII. 252.

Exceptional, on the other hand, since it repeatedly verges toward verse, is St Anselm's Lament of the Magdalen at the tomb.[48]

> Audivimus, fratres, Mariam
> ad monumentum foris stantem;
> audivimus Mariam
> foris plorantem.

The device was so easily abused as to call forth more than one warning;[49] but it was so obvious a means of emphasis as to be widely prevalent.

## 3. Refrain

St Bernard, though he does not avoid rime, shows habitually no need of it to strengthen his iterations. With him iteration often advances from rhetorical cumulation to poetical refrain.

> "Therefore the Lord himself shall give you a sign. Behold a virgin shall conceive, and bear a son, and shall call his name Immanuel," which by interpretation is God with us. Flee not, fallen Adam; for God is with us. Fear not, mankind, nor hearing the name of God be affrighted; for God is with us: with us likened by incarnation, with us by unification.

[48] MS latin 2622, ff. 12–18 (Incipit omelia Beati Anselmi super Johannem de planctu Magdalene.), as printed in Bourgain, 373–383. Bourgain's comment, 225–227, does not clearly distinguish between such passages and the rimed prose of most of this *Planctus*.

For a discreet use of rimed prose, deliberate but relieved from insistence, compare the passage from Alain de Lille quoted in Bourgain 88: "Fenum et stipule sunt", etc.

[49] E. g., the one quoted in Bourgain, 235, against "rimorum melodias vel metrorum consonantias que potius fuerunt ad aures audientium demulcendas quam ad animum informandum" (MS latin 15005, folio 193).

All for us his coming, though he be one of us, like unto us
in our suffering.

*De Adventu Domini*, II. 1 (end); PL 183: 41.

His fifth sermon for the vigil of Christmas uses incremental iteration to contrast *to-day* and *to-morrow*.

This our task to-day; for to-morrow's shall be neither in
sanctification nor in preparation, but in the very vision of
majesty. "To-morrow," saith the word, "ye shall see the
majesty of God in you." This is the meaning of the patriarch
Jacob: "To-morrow unto me shall my justice make answer"
(Genesis xxx. 33). To-day, indeed, justice is in observance;
to-morrow it will answer: to-day it is practised; fruit cometh
to-morrow. But that which man hath not planted neither
shall he harvest. For neither shall he then behold the majesty
who hath meantime made light of the holiness, nor shall the
sun of glory rise for him to whom the sun of justice has not
arisen, nor shall he see the light of to-morrow who has not
been enlightened by to-day. Nay even he himself, who to-day
for us is made justice by God the Father, shall appear as our
life to-morrow, that we also may appear with him in glory.
For to-day he is come to us in childhood, that man may not
have wherewith to magnify himself, but that we may be
rather converted and become as children. To-morrow shall be
shown how great is God, how worthy of praises, that even we
ourselves may be magnified in praises, since every man shall
have his praise of God. Nay, those whom to-day he has
justified, to-morrow he shall magnify; and to the achievement
of holiness shall succeed the majesty of vision. No empty
vision this, consisting only in similitude. We shall be like
him, for we shall see him as he is. Therefore here also the
words are not simply "Ye shall see the majesty of God";
but significantly is added "in you". To-day, indeed, as in a
mirror, we see ourselves in him as he taketh our nature; to-
morrow we shall see him in us, when he giveth of his nature,
since he will show us himself and take us up to himself. This
is what he promised to minister at his coming; and meantime
we have received of his fulness, not indeed glory for glory,

but grace for grace, as it is written 'The Lord will give grace
and worship' (Psalm lxxxiii. 12). Despise not, then, the
gifts preceding, if thou yearnest for those that follow.
*In Vigilia Nativitatis Domini*, V. 3; PL 183:107.

Refrain reinforces other incremental iteration in an
ardent sermon on the *Magnificat*.[50] The very insistence
exhibits strikingly the value of cumulative progress for
charging exposition with emotion.

1. *Magnificat anima mea Dominum.* Magnificat voce,
magnificat opere, magnificat affectu. Magnificat laudando,
amando, prædicando. Magnificat, laudandi, amandi et
magnificandi formam simul et materiam dando. *Magnificat
anima mea Dominum:* quia magnifice a magnifico Domino
magnifica est. In primis ad imaginem et similitudinem Dei
anima mea mirabiliter a Domino creata est; sed postea in
Adam miserabiliter deformata, nunc mirabilius, gloriosius
et magnificentius a Domino renovata est. *Magnificat anima
mea Dominum.* Magnificat omnis creatura Dominum, sed
amplius super omnem creaturam anima mea Dominum
magnificat. In omni enim creatura nihil tam magnifice fecit
Dominus sicut animam meam. Sed Dominus est: sicut
voluit, sic factum est. *Magnificat anima mea Dominum.*
Dominum magnifica, non temetipsum. Qui semetipsum
magnificavit, quantum in ipso fuit, Deum exhonoravit: et
ideo non se exaltavit, sed præcipitavit. Tuum est te ipsum
humiliare, Domini exaltare.

2. *Et exsultavit spiritus meus in Deo salutari meo.* Vide
qualis ordo. Prius citharam, postea psalterium tetigit: prius
animam, postea spiritum posuit: non enim prius quod spirituale, sed quod animale; deinde quod spirituale. *Et exsultavit*

[50] *In Canticum Beatæ Virginis Mariæ*, placed by Mabillon among the
sermons attributed to St Bernard doubtfully or erroneously (PL 184:
1121).
Imitative translation is practically precluded by the intractable
rhythm of the familiar English "My soul doth magnify the Lord."
For an exposition of this text different even in the handling of iteration see Hugh of St Victor in PL 175:416.

*spiritus meus*, extra omnem creaturam, extra seipsum etiam
præ immensitate gaudii saltavit. In quo? Non in me; sed
*in Deo* creatore meo, cognitione et amore ejus fervendo: et
hoc non per me, sed mediante et salvante me *Salutari meo*
Jesu filio meo, singulariter meo. Meus est Deus, meus Salutaris, meus est filius, Omnium quidem et mei conditor est,
sed mei solius filius est: et me mediante omnium salus est.

# CHAPTER X

## POETIC ACHIEVEMENT IN VERNACULAR

NOTE. This chapter indicates the poetic animating certain typical or outstanding literary developments in the vernaculars. Its intention is both historical review in this single aspect and suggestion of further study. Since it is thus selective and suggestive, not attempting the impossible appraisal of vernacular poetic as a whole, it offers no general list of references. Particular references will be found in place.

### A. LYRIC AND EPIC

Lyric, earliest medieval poetic achievement in Latin, shows full development in the vernaculars. On this the widest Latin influence was of course the hymns. The most distinct and conspicuous vernacular poetic, that of the Provençal troubadours, is mainly a minute and elaborate stanza technic. The fame of troubadour virtuosity gave vogue in other vernaculars to metrical skill. This is its historical significance in the development of medieval lyric. Lyric in any time, however, has a short history. As in Greece, so again and again, having perfected its diction and its metric, it comes to its own and abides. For more than any other form of poetic it is timeless; not ancient, nor medieval, nor modern, but perennial.

Germanic epic,[1] surviving as a strong influence in medieval English romance, persisted as a distinct poetic among the Scandinavians. In remote Iceland they

---

[1] For Anglo-Saxon epic see above, Chapter V. E.

developed an elaborate technic of verse epic, and later a distinct art of prose epic. Not even the troubadour poetic in the south is more detailed and elaborate than the epic doctrine of the *Skáldskaparmál*.[2] No medieval stories have more force of narrative directness than the prose sagas; and few have as much. In narrative stripped and stark the chief medieval author, perhaps, is Snorri Sturlasson. But in spite of Viking travels the Old Norse poetic of verse and of prose remained apart from medieval habit. Bounded by its own civilization, it was so little appropriated in the general medieval development of narrative that its recovery in modern times was as startling as that of the Etruscan sculpture at Perugia.

French epic, flowering later than Germanic, is already in the eleventh century tinged with romance. The French *chansons de geste* reflect a society distinctly feudal; their communal sense is of a larger community; and they constitute a first chapter in European vernacular poetic. Epic still in characterization and in the youthful zest of their combats against odds, they are swayed by new literary currents. The physical environment is less sharply detailed than in Germanic epic, perhaps because a kindlier nature was more taken for granted. A sharper difference is in style. They have none of that Germanic conventional elaboration which made epic diction a language apart. Much simpler,[3] they are also more

[2] For the Prose Edda as "a textbook for apprentice poets" see A. G. Brodeur's introduction to his translation (New York, 1916), which includes the *Skáldskaparmál* entire, and Gustav Necker's introduction to his German translation (Jena, 1925, vol. 20 of the series *Thule*). Parts of the *Skáldskaparmál* are included in R. B. Anderson's translation, *The Younger Edda*, Chicago, 1880.

[3] "Nulle intention littéraire, nul souci de l'effet ne gâtent l'absolue simplicité du récit. Le style, tel quel, purement déclaratif, ne s'interpose pas entre l'action et les vers." Lanson, *Histoire de la littérature française*, 25.

diffuse, in both respects nearer to common speech.  The
movement in detail is of ten-syllable verses gathered
into irregular stanzas (*laisses*) by assonance.  A more
significant distinction is the habit of narrative.  *Roland*
presents substantially the same situation as *Maldon*.
In Anglo-Saxon it is focused by concentration; in French
it is approached as the culmination of a series.  Habitually French epic is more extended and fluent, expansive
not descriptively but historically, running through more
events in a single composition.  Whereas Anglo-Saxon
epic typically selects and intensifies a crisis, French
epic tells the whole story.

## B. Experiment and Convention in Romance

### 1. Romance in Latin and in Vernacular

Medieval story-tellers in turning to the vernacular
found wider opportunity.  The Latin poetic that they
all studied in school, practised in *historia, fabula, argumentum*, and at greater length in saint's legend, was too
much absorbed in descriptive elaboration to teach them
much of narrative.  Outside the cloister, at the regular
stations of the pilgrimage routes, waited audiences of
increasing size and diversity; and the development of
feudalism established the castle hall as a social center.
The development of vernacular narrative answered with
the more social art of romance.  The narrative future was
increasingly for the vernacular.  Meantime Latin narrative continued not only for its more special audience,
but in various interplay.  *Exempla*, sketched or summed
in Latin, were preached in vernacular.  An ugly old legend of folklore, moralized in Latin for an *exemplum*,
Chaucer gave back to the wider audience in the ex-

quisite art of his Prioress. Romances and legends of saints interpenetrated. The complicated development of the Grail legend must be followed in both Latin and vernacular. Nevertheless poetic was beckoned into new narrative paths mainly by the wider appeal through the vernacular.

Something, of course, was carried over from the *poetriæ*,[4] oftenest the conventional lore of style. By contrast we are made the more sharply aware of the escape and adventure of individual bent and native inspiration. *Aucassin et Nicolete* has another appeal by another method. Its style, in spite of occasional conformity, is not in the tradition of the *poetriæ*. Chrétien, though conforming more, draws his psychology rather from observation of social habits and even of individual character than from the classified lore of appropriateness to type. Dante not only commits the most serious enterprise of medieval poetic to the vernacular; he utterly ignores the Latin school lore. At the end of the middle age, the Renaissance already tinging his thought, Chaucer passes through a whole course of Latin conventions, adapting critically as he goes, and ranges beyond.

## 2. Walter Map and Marie

In the twelfth century Walter Map's Latin notebook *De nugis Curialium* [5] shows both the persistence of old forms and the stirring of new in rendering new material. Some of his stories are clearly oriental. His-

---

[4] For this see Faral, *Les arts poétiques du xiie et du xiiie siècle*, 93–97.

[5] Edited for the Camden Society by Thomas Wright, London, 1850; reëdited by Montague Rhodes James in Anecdota Oxoniensia, Oxford, 1914; translated and edited by James, Lloyd, and Hartland, London, 1923; by Tupper and Ogle, London, 1924. See Hinton in *Studies in Philology*, 20: 448 (Oct., 1923).

torical anecdotes and *exempla*, often given in mere lucid summary, occasionally indicate narrative composition.[6] He tries a story in the way of Ovid, or again in the Petronian way of the "Matron of Ephesus." Two longer tales show not only a firmer conciseness, a sharper vividness, but what is more significant, grasp of narrative movement. The Friendship of Sadius and Galo (III. ii) [7] and Sceva and Ollo (IV. xvi) are enlivened in scene and furthered in plot by dialogue. Both are carried through progressively to an issue. The former skilfully combines the Orestes-Pylades motive of friendship with the Joseph-Zuleika motive of the scorned queen. The latter turns the cynicism of its oriental source to brisk social satire. Here in Latin are narrative experiments full of promise. Looking over Walter's shoulder, we can divine a new literary stir.

More suggestive of response to a new interest of his audience is the abundance of Celtic folklore. There are banshees, wandering dead, a nicker, a pact with a demon. King Herla (I. xi), like Rip Van Winkle, stays too long in fairyland. The fairy mistress appears four times. Once (II. xi) the old tale is hardly more than notes. In Edric the Wild (II. xii) the moonlight dance (*chorea feminarum*) keeps its ancient spell. Meridiana (IV. xi) associates a different and longer version quite disconcertingly with the great Gerbert. Though none of these brings the tale to the sequence of Sadius and Galo, we feel an artist at work. Some of these shorter tales may be Latin summaries, like the *exempla* of the collections, for telling in French. Whether he worked out his nar-

---

[6] See the *exemplum* quoted above, page 246.

[7] References are to the books and *distinctiones* into which the collection was grouped by some compiler, evidently not by Walter himself.

rative art in the vernacular we do not know. Though some critics have inferred for him a considerable part in the development of the Grail legend, the only surviving work that is certainly his is this artist's sketchbook.

There are fewer suggestions of narrative experiment in the contemporary French *lais* of Marie.[8] Her *Yonec* is satisfied with the rapid summary of Latin tradition. Her charming *Honeysuckle* is an episode of the Tristram story. Iseult, finding a peeled wand by her way through the wood, knew that Tristram was near. As much lyric as narrative, such episodic poems suggest what the *lai* may have been in its earliest use of Celtic fairy adventure. *Lanval* and *Eliduc* handle with more narrative progress what we now call a situation. Another rendering of the former situation, the anonymous *Graalent*, shows by contrast Marie's discernment either in choosing a version narratively superior or in herself reshaping. Generally her art is less of composition than of style. Her habit with a situation is not the fluent onwardness of *Aucassin et Nicolete*,[9] nor the intensive and progressive sequence of the later *Chastelaine de Vergi*.[10] The technic of the latter, though distinctly realized in the middle age, remained exceptional. It receives little attention even in the *Decameron;* and it stands out among the *Canterbury Tales*.

[8] The charm of Marie's *lais* as poetry is suggested by the metrical versions of F. B. Luquiens, New York, 1911, which has a bibliography and a valuable introduction. There are several prose translations.

[9] The appendix of adventures in *Aucassin et Nicolete* seems to be a later addition, not part of the original composition. Among the translations, Andrew Lang's keeps its distinction.

[10] Translation by Alice Kemp-Welch, London, 1903, with the French text.

## 3. Chrétien de Troyes

A romance of five or six thousand lines, but still selective, was developed by Chrétien de Troyes.[11] His *Erec* tells the tale which Lady Charlotte Guest translated in her *Mabinogion* as *Geraint the Son of Erbin* from a later Welsh version. Enid is stricken with shame that Geraint's love of her should run to ignoble fondness. Her lament, overheard and mistaken by Geraint, rouses his jealous pride to prove her long and cruelly. This moment the Welsh writer sees in its setting.

> And one morning in the summer time they were upon their couch, and Geraint lay upon the edge of it. And Enid was without sleep in the apartment, which had windows of glass. And the sun shone upon the couch. And the clothes had slipped from off his arms and his breast, and he was asleep. Then she gazed upon the marvellous beauty of his appearance, and she said, "Alas! and am I the cause that these arms and this breast have lost their glory and the warlike fame which they once so richly enjoyed?" And as she said this, the tears dropped from her eyes, and they fell upon his breast.[12]

At such a point the Welsh writer's abundance of description is not merely pretty; it is fitting. What he thus dwells upon until we must feel it because we can see it, is an important moment in the story. But in general he blurs his story by spending equal elaboration on what is quite subordinate, or even irrelevant. His incidents claim attention equally in succession; Chrétien's

---

[11] Prose translation of *Erec, Cligés, Yvain,* and *Lancelot* by W. W. Comfort, Everyman's Library, 1914, with introduction, notes, and bibliography. The fourteenth-century English translation of *Yvain* (*Ywain and Gawain*) has been edited by G. Schleich with study of its relation to the original, Oppeln and Leipzig, 1887.

[12] Lady Charlotte Guest, *The Mabinogion* (1877), 162.

are lengthened or shortened with a sense of their narrative values.  For Chrétien, relying less on the traditional picturesque description, has the better narrative.  Using descriptive detail less for itself, he uses it more to bring out character or give to important moments salience. Instead of merely accumulating adventures and telling each for what it is worth by itself, as is the habit of the longer romances, he has selective art enough to bring out those that will keep attention on the conquest of the proud, selfish devotion of the husband by the nobler devotion of the wife.  And at the end he impresses the significance of the whole course of adventures, the meaning of the story as a whole.  He discerns, though he does not always achieve, the narrative force of unified progress.

How far the art of such romances was studied in the middle age appears again on comparison of the fourteenth-century *Ywain and Gawain* with its original, Chrétien's *Chevalier au Lion*.  The Englishman, without losing anything of the plot, reduces the length one-third by compressing, modifying, or even omitting Chrétien's detail.  And since Chrétien's detail is not merely added for richness, but spent to bring out character or mood, a change here is a change in the total effect, a shifting of interest from the persons to the events.  Thus to Chrétien the central situation is this.  A widow forced to marry again, as medieval widows were if they had property, accepts the slayer of her husband.  How would she feel?  Might she not, from making a virtue of necessity, come to love her second husband if he were young and brave?  If, tiring of her riches and ease, he would be off to his wars again, would she forgive him for breaking his promise to return on a day?  And might he not then, learning from the loss of her to value her truly, devote himself to winning her back by proving his better manhood? The situation is almost the reverse of that in *Erec*. Such questions of character and feeling lead Chrétien to dwell upon the scenes between Ywain and Alundyne, and even to comment satirically now and then on their mental attitudes. Most of this the English translator omits.

But that the omissions were deliberate appears in his throwing emphasis upon what directly furthers the movement of the story. What makes a story quick and strong he understands so well that he even quickens and varies Chrétien's pace by turning some of the indirect discourse into direct dialogue. Nor was he insensible to Chrétien's suggestions of character or mood. At the final revelation, where Chrétien says simply that Alundyne started (*la dame tresaut*), he renders:

> Then went the lady far aback,
> And long she stood ere that she spake (3983–3984).

This is exactly in Chrétien's habitual manner. Rendering with discernment and spirit, then, keeping the plan and transitions that hold the tale together, he bends the story in the direction of his own interest and skill. He too knows something of narrative art. His simpler, more onward version throws into relief Chrétien's superiority not only in delicacy of verse and style, but in those ampler and finer suggestions of character which bring out of a situation its deeper narrative values.

The increasing audience for romance invited much mere retelling, many versions inartistic or even unintelligent. But the scientific study of sources, while it defines the diffusion of current tales and carries their history back to folklore and myth, should not blur the history of medieval narrative art. In the midst of almost impersonal transmission were both artistic experiment and artistic achievement. Chrétien de Troyes and a few others have survived by name. Nameless, but no less convincing, is the narrative art of *Aucassin et Nicolete*, of the *Chastelaine de Vergi*, of *Gawain and the Green Knight*.

## 4. Conventional Composition

Generally the artist is less clear, the impersonal processes of transmission and the conventions of telling clearer, in the long romances. Adventure, when fairyland was no longer new, was sometimes supplied by mere aggregation. Love, presented mainly as wooing, crystallized into the code of *amour courtois*. Chivalry, a motive even more clearly ideal, could be no less presented as a code. Adventure, love, chivalry, established as the three habitual motives of romance, were readily combined in stock forms. Better artists vitalized them by characterization; but since romance can be composed acceptably without characterization, its journeywork, medieval or modern, tends to content itself with types. The hero is "a very perfect gentle knight"; and his action consists in having many adventures. The heroine is a beautiful young lady, and needs no action at all. Both may be described at length without being individualized. Even on these terms, much as they have always amused satirists, romance may have charm of style and some of the perennial appeal of youth. But it has no properly narrative vigor. Its composition tends so easily to repeat that the stock adventures can be assigned as well to one knight as to another.

In fact, the middle age saw adventures transferred from one hero to another who had meantime become more popular. Thus Gawain, coming straight out of fairyland, gradually lost more and more of his glory; and the process is one of the ways in which there grew up cycles of romance. The longer Lancelot stories are aggregations of many separate adventures. One of the best remembered feats in Malory's, compilation is the three-days' tournament. Not only is this told of other knights in other romances; it is found also by itself, as in the tale of Ipomedon. Some medieval rewriter added it to his Lancelot; and there it stayed. The Lancelot story was further swelled by adventures formerly ascribed to Gawain, who had already lost some of his feats to Percival. Even the winning of the Grail quest, which had early been transferred from Gawain to Percival, went to Lancelot's son Galahad. Finally the Lancelot aggregation was attached to the cycle of Arthur.

Whether or not it was attached to one of the cycles, a conventional long romance could thus aggregate. *Bevis of Hampton* or *Guy of Warwick* might be longer or shorter without the slightest narrative difference. It is long because it is interminable. Even in better hands the medieval long romance prevails part by part, as it was read. It was not composed as a single narrative. Such singleness as the middle age cultivated in romance must be sought in the parts considered as separate stories, and will be found oftener in the shorter romances that remained by themselves. For lack of it the most conventional long romances become series of typical descriptions. The typical hero, typically equipped without and within, has one typical encounter after another.

The difference between such aggregative transmission

and narrative progress can be discerned among the many versions of the Grail. A magic talisman from folklore had been transmuted by the popular emotion focused at Corpus Christi;[13] but it became a narrative goal only for those with art enough to conceive the great quest as something more than a series of adventures. Meeting an earlier form of it in his Balin and Balan, Malory brought it into no distinct relation to that tragedy. Its recurrence in his later books is similarly unharmonized and inconclusive. Wolfram von Eschenbach, also using more than one version, had focused his *Parzival* sufficiently to give a long romance some movement onward.

## C. The Poetic Composition of the *Divina Commedia*

The solitary eminence of Dante is a perpetual reminder of the limits of any lore of poetic. As for medieval lore, its approach to the *Divina Commedia* is hopelessly short. The ultimate reason, of course, for its inadequacy is that the greatest poetic achievement of the middle age is far more than medieval. It is for all time even more clearly than the *Œdipus Rex* or the *Æneid* or *Othello;* and like them it derives its greatness from something beyond poetic.

Nevertheless it is also medieval and also a great achievement of poetic composition. So to consider it is to discern both more of its greatness and more of medieval habit. In the current medieval lore the main lack is seen by contrast to be in the larger movement of composition. Medieval poetic carries us so short a distance

---

[13] See note 52 to Chapter VII, and Lizette A. Fisher, *The Mystic vision in the Grail legend and in the Divine Comedy*, New York, 1917 (Columbia University Press).

toward the *Divina Commedia* because it is preoccupied
with style. Vergil is currently cited and quoted, but
usually as an exemplar of the three styles.[14] Medieval
romances carried nationalism back to Troy for centuries
without discerning the larger art of the *Æneid* in composition. For Dante Vergil was guide not only in a
deeper sense, but also in poetic.

This makes clearer why Dante turned his back on
current lore. He knew that lore, not only the elaborate
technic of the troubadours, but the Latin *poetria*. His
ignoring of it is tantamount to an arraignment of its
cardinal weakness. It had too little technic for his
main poetic concern, the movement of the whole. It
had too much schoolmasterly fiddling with words to carry
orchestration beyond a few conventional modes. No
one can study the history of poetic without finding this
deficiency exceptional only in degree. In kind it is historic. Here, again and again, appears the gap between
pedagogically formulated poetic and poetry.

In Dante's style the medieval *poetria* is not merely
outdistanced; it is repudiated. Matthieu de Vendôme,
Geoffroi de Vinsauf, John the Englishman, might have
tolerated figures of wrestlers and dogs in hell, but hardly
broth, cooks, oxen, and swine. They would have challenged bellows in purgatory; they would have been

[14] Book II of Dante's unfinished *De vulgari eloquentia* has several
passages suggestive of the preoccupations of his time and of his own
bent: "Si poesim recte consideremus: quæ nihil aliud est quam fictio
rethorica musicaque composita" (III, page 393 of the Oxford 1 vol. text
of the Works); "magister noster Horatius" (*ibid.*); "grandiosa modo
vocabula sub prælato stilo digna consistere . ." (VII. 395); "ornativa
vero dicimus omnia polysyllaba . ." (VII. 396); "tota igitur ars can-
tionis circa tria videtur consistere: . . cantus divisionem . . partium
habitudinem . . numerum carminum et syllabarum" (IX. 397).

For the three styles, see the indexes to ARP and to this volume.

shocked at rooks and a fish-pool in heaven. The decorative descriptions of a rhetoricated poetic seem nowhere else quite so futile as beside Dante's figures of precise geography.

As seems beetling Carisenda, when a cloud goes over it so as to make it hang the other way, so seemed Antæus to me as I stood watching to see him bend.

I. xxxi. 136.[15]

As that stream which has its own path first from Monte Veso toward the east on the left coast of Apennine, which is called Acquaqueta above before it descends to its low bed, and at Forlì has lost that name, reëchoes there over San Benedetto from the alp, because its fall has a single leap where for a thousand should be room, so down an abrupt bank we heard resounding that turbid water. I. xvi. 94.

As for Paolo and Francesca, Ugolino, and a hundred other passages, with those single lines that enrich memory,[16] no better praise can be compassed than Matthew Arnold's word "touchstones." They tell us, better than any definition, what poetry is. But the mere historical significance of Dante's luminous precision is its vindication of that true theory of poetic diction which was formulated in the *De sublimitate*.[17] The essential character of poetic style is not dilation, which belongs to rhetoric; it is sublimation. Dante's extraordinary con-

---

[15] The references are to book, canto, and line. I refers to *Inferno;* II, to *Purgatorio;* III, to *Paradiso*. The translations are adapted from the convenient and familiar edition in Temple Classics.

[16] Tanto vilmente nel eterno esilio. I. xxiii. 125.

La concreata e perpetua sete. III. ii. 19.

E la sua volontate è nostra pace. III. iii. 85.

Non fu dal vel del cor giammai disciolta. III. iii. 117.

[17] See ARP, 128.

ciseness, austere, ascetic, is never bare; it is surcharged. For style too, as well as for composition, he must have discerned that ancient critic's fine distinction: rhetoric and poetic must never be confused; but at high temperatures they can be welded together.

Poetry conveyed vision oftener, perhaps, in the middle age than in any other period. *Piers Plowman* and *Pearl* carry on in the next century a persistent medieval preoccupation. The *Divina Commedia*, fulfilling this aspiration, reveals man's need, his quest, his attainment, of vision. "Blessed are the pure in heart; for they shall see God." Purity remains negative to those who have no desire to see God. But Dante answers those for whom it is positive and constructive.

> Ye other few, who have lifted up your necks betimes to the bread of angels, by which men live here, but with which none cometh away sated. III. ii. 10.

The poetry of this "concreate and perpetual thirst" (III. ii. 19) animates for all time a whole cosmogony antiquated merely as science, and communicates the great philosophy of the middle age to the heart. The *Divina Commedia* achieved the high quest of the Grail romances. It is *the* vision poem.

The heaven of Dante's vision transcends time and space.

> And I was with him; but of my mounting I was no more aware than is a man, ere his first thought, aware that it is coming. Beatrice is she who thus discloses from good to better so instantly that her act has no extent in time. III. x. 34.

> Brother, thy high desire shall be fulfilled in the last sphere, where all the rest are fulfilled, and mine. . . For it is not in space, nor hath it poles, and our ladder attains even so far. III. xxii. 61.

But it is not reserved for rapt contemplatives.

> Of the seraphim he who is most rapt, Moses, Samuel, or
> that John whom thou choosest to take, nay, even Mary has
> not a seat in another heaven than these spirits who but now
> appeared to thee; nor have they to their being more or fewer
> years; but all make beauteous the first circle, and have sweet
> life differently as they feel more or less the eternal breath.
> III. iv. 28.

For the *Divina Commedia* ranges beyond the lyric
exaltation of the individual poet. It is suffused with
social sense, as constantly aware as the *Piers Plowman*
of the "fair field full of folk," of the world of striving
men and women. Its vision begins with society gone
bad and frustrating itself; it arrives at society perfectly
realized as immediate intercommunion and interaction.
So the Church, the heavenly society, recurs constantly
in communal echoes of hymns and canticles: *Ave, Agnus
Dei, Benedictus qui venit, Salve Regina.* In the same
spirit Cynewulf had composed his *Christ* upon the seven
great antiphons of Advent.[18] Familiar gospels are recalled. Most frequent echoes, as of symbols most suggestive of common human experience, are of the Psalms.[19]
The artistic harmony is based upon the medieval conception of social history as the redemption of mankind.

The word allegory has come to suggest vagueness, or
conventionalization, or fancy. None of these has any
place in the *Divina Commedia.* Allegorical, indeed, it
may be called in a sense large enough to include *Piers
Plowman,* the *Faerie Queene,* and the *Pilgrim's Progress;*
but no other allegory is so large in scope, so consistent
and complete in composition. For such details as the

[18] See the introduction to Cook's edition, Boston, 1900.
[19] See above, page 240.

sacred chariot, the eagle, wolf, and dragon (II. xxxii) we search the carved capitals and the windows; but including all these and ranging beyond them is the constant interpretation of the whole sensible, transitory world as typical of the eternal. Ephemeral matters, politics, even quarrels and grudges (I. xvi. 73), are interpreted permanently. The intensely specific realism is made constantly to serve idealization. Human life is revealed *sub specie æternitatis*.

For life beyond is seen as the prolongation of the line that we give to life here and now. Its motive power throughout is love radiating from God and leading men back to him. The disturbance of life is sin. The horror of the *Inferno* is of sin as perversion. The warpings of life there tormenting Italians or ancients are typical to the fearsome degree of revealing our own. Thus the course of the *Divina Commedia* is of ideas and principles of action so embodied as to lead emotion on. What is familiar in lyric is here carried through a whole conception of life. Theology is translated through vision into emotion and will, as if lyric were carried through into drama.

Thus the persons are typical, not merely as wearing recognizable costumes and uttering appropriate sentiments, but more intensely as acting in our drama. The thieves transformed into serpents, which in turn absorb them (I. xxv), are thus akin artistically to the sculpture of medieval capitals. They are not pictorial imitation of the other arts, as are the conventional descriptive pauses of the *Roman de la Rose* and the *poetriæ;* for they are narrated. There is no ecphrasis.[20] The method is never static. The speaking flames move.

[20] For ecphrasis, see the index.

> As a little cloud ascends, so moved each flame along the throat of the chasm, none showing its theft, each stealing away a sinner. I. xxvi. 39.

Such narrative progress in detail is integral with the progress of the total symbolism toward culmination. The famous ascent in Paradise moves both in and by itself and with the movement of the whole.

> Now were my eyes fixed again on the face
> of my lady, and my mind with them,
> and from every other thought were removed.
>
> And she smiled not; but " Were I to smile",
> she began, "thou wouldst fare
> as Semele when she turned to ashes;
>
> For my beauty, which up the stair
> of the eternal palace kindleth more and more,
> as thou hast seen, the higher it ascends,
>
> Were it not tempered, is so radiant
> that thy mortal power at its flash
> would be foliage shriveled by thunderbolt." III. xxi. 1.

In method, as in degree, this is the individual achievement of a great poet; in kind the symbolism is characteristically medieval. For in detail and in total conception the *Divina Commedia* starts not with the individual event or person, not with Beatrice Portinari,[21] but with the idea. Whether Dante recalls a youthful love is a question so subordinate as to be artistically immaterial.

---

[21] For the demonstration of this see Gratia Eaton Baldwin, *The new Beatrice, or the virtue that counsels*, New York, Columbia University Press, 1928.

Neglect of this medieval habit has hindered the interpretation of *Pearl*. See the study of it by Sister M. Madaleva, New York, 1925.

He has not sublimated earthly passion into heavenly. His conception is heavenly from the beginning, and progressively throughout.   He carries a single, controlling idea forward imaginatively, stage by stage. Each stage is vivid with intensely specific realism; but this realism, as that of the carved capitals, is neither the object nor the occasion; it is only the imaginative means to impress the idea.   The idea is constant; it is beginning and end.   The final vision is not transformation; it is conclusion.

Such grasp of poetic movement doubtless owed much to Vergil.   Dante's homage to the "courteous soul of Mantua" (I. ii. 58) is more than conventional tribute.

> Art thou then that Vergil and that spring which spreads so large a stream of speech? . . . O poet's honor and light, may the long zeal avail me and the great love which made me search thy volume.   Thou art my master and my author, thou alone he from whom I took the fair style that hath brought me honor.   I. i. 79.[22]

The larger narrative movement of the *Æneia*, which quite escaped the average medieval romancer, was not lost on so great a composer.   Of all the ancient art available in his time this alone could give him that instruction. But if the *Æneid* inspired him with its poetic scope and reach, and gave him a sense of the poetic energy of on-

[22] The passage refers specifically, though not in the usual medieval terms, to Vergil's diction.   So do I. ii. 67, "la tua parola ornata"; and II. vii. 16, "O gloria de' Latin . . per cui mostrò ciò che potea la lingua nostra."

There are many references and allusions to specific passages; e. g., to the fourth Eclogue, often interpreted symbolically in the middle age, in II. xxii. 70; to Dido's "Agnosco veteris vestigia flammæ" (*Æn.* IV. 23), in II. xxx. 48.

Justinian's vision of Rome in III. vi may be said to carry out the idea of the *Æneid* in having the same Romanism.

wardness, it did not prescribe his method. The *Divina Commedia* is not an imitation of the *Æneid*. Its movement is both different and more compelling.

For the movement of the *Divina Commedia* is at once logical and imaginative, an extraordinary fusion of rhetoric and poetic. The first canto closes with a forecast of the whole progress.

> Lead me where thou hast said, that I may see the gate of St Peter. I. i. 134.

Throughout, the progress is so reasoned that it can be mapped and briefed. None the less the *Divina Commedia* is a great exemplar of poetic movement. It arrives not at a demonstration, but at a catharsis. Its conception, at once constant and widening, is carried forward imaginatively. We move not from proposition to proposition, but from scene to scene. The *Faerie Queene*, no less imaginative in detail, has none of this force of imaginative composition. The *Christ* in the earliest middle age, the *Pearl* in the latest, have far less scope. The *Divina Commedia* reveals the whole capacity of medieval symbolism by sustained poetic movement.

So sustained a movement has no time for the conventional descriptive pause. In spite of the abundance of its illustrations, the *Divina Commedia* is never merely pictorial.[23] Nor is the steady movement monotonous. The transitions are beautifully various. *Purgatorio* does not repeat the plan of *Inferno;* and it has more interaction. As the action advances through *Purgatorio* into *Paradiso*, there is increasing exposition of ideas.

---

[23] See above, page 271. The sculptured reliefs in II. x, though doubtless reminiscent, as many a medieval ecphrasis, of the wall-pictures in Dido's palace, are *exempla*, not decoration.

There is even the Gothic variety that enlivens the cathedrals. The grotesque devils of the twenty-second canto of *Inferno* are brothers to those on the capitals of Vézelay. At the other pole of sentiment, the eleventh canto of *Purgatorio* opens with a poetic amplification of the Paternoster. The fifth canto of *Paradiso* is Justinian's summary of the history of Rome. But the variety is never merely picturesque. Never merely aggregative, the variations of the *Divina Commedia* are more like those of Bourges than like those of Chartres. They are still more like the variations in a symphony.

The logical order fused with this poetic movement is: *Inferno*, the punishment of self-enslavement; *Purgatorio*, the progress of self-mastery; *Paradiso*, the rapture of self-expression. From perversion and frustration we pass through discipline to the liberation of personality.

> Then said my lady, "Let out the heat of thy desire, so that thy utterance bear the print of the press within; not that our knowledge may increase by thy speaking, but that thou mayst learn how to tell thy thirst, that drink be given thee." III. xvii, 7.

It is through this liberation of personality that the human drama becomes divine. "I am come that they might have life, and that they might have it more abundantly." For the *Divina Commedia* is far more than a vindication of free will; it is a vision of the progressive freeing of the will. After the terrible revelation of hell as self-enslavement, free will is asserted from purgatory as essential to divine justice.

> Ye who are living refer every occasion only up to heaven, as if all moved of itself by necessity. Were it so, in you would be destroyed free will; and it would not be justice to have joy for good, mourning for evil. II. xvi. 67.

But this liberty is not innate merely as are the physical impulses. God's gift of free will is a progressive ener-gizing of man's struggle to will higher and higher till he attains perfect freedom.

> Now in order that to this [will] every other may be reunited, innate in you is the virtue that giveth counsel.[24] and ought to guard the threshold of assent. This is the principle whence is derived the scheme of desert in you according as it collects and winnows good loves and guilty. Those whose scheme of life went to the foundation became aware of this innate liberty, and so left ethics to the world. III. xviii. 61.

So developed by the mutual response of God and man, free will becomes the greatest gift ("lo maggior don," III. v. 19). Heaven is the final release and achievement of personality.

The culmination is quite beyond what is usually meant by self-satisfaction. As personality can be progressively released and achieved only through giving, so the self-expressive joy of *Paradiso* contributes to the common joy. It is simultaneously giving and receiving, utterance and response. No longer, as the poet of *Pearl* discerned again in the parable of the laborers, is giving and receiving frustrated by competition. Immediately every joy is the joy of all, every expression of personality is a gift and a response, in the creative activity of love.

> As in a fish-pond that is still and clear the fishes draw to what so comes from without that they deem it their food, so saw I more than a thousand radiances draw toward us, and in each was heard: "Lo! one who will increase our loves." III. v. 100.
>
> I saw more radiances, living and conquering, make of us a center and of themselves a corona, sweeter in voice than lucent to behold. III. x. 64.

[24] See note 21 above. I owe to this book the interpretation of Dante's intention as the progressive freeing of the will.

The amazing figures in which this triumph is symbolized sum up also Dante's poetic: vividness of charged simplicity in expression carried forward in a composition of progressive movement.

No other single work of medieval art conveys so much of the middle age; for no other concedes so little to medieval convention. The centuries of St Bernard, Adam of St Victor, and St Thomas Aquinas, of Chrétien and the *Roman de la Rose*, of Vézelay and Bourges, like other centuries, had their artistic conventions. These, as too often in other centuries, seemed to the makers of manuals to comprise the theory of art. Such theory needs both correction and expansion from great artists.

## D. The History of Medieval Verse Narrative in Chaucer

Chaucer, more clearly than most poets, shows the whole artistic progress from expert verse translation through convention accepted and convention modified to creation. From the *Roman de la Rose* through his study of Boccaccio to the *Canterbury Tales* his work comprehends in itself much of the history of medieval poetic. He was ahead of his time; that is, he was artist enough to feel new currents of thought and new ventures in expression, to bend toward these the received modes, and finally to enlarge the scope and perfect the technic of medieval narrative. The Renaissance movement, which he was quick to feel in Italy, he could not communicate to England. It had to be brought again, and in different ways. But the art of narrative, most popular of medieval arts, he led from accepted poetic habits in new directions and to new achievements. Consummate metrist, he knew what to do in English with the richer couplet, the more fluent stanza, of Boccaccio. Composition in the larger sense he learned more slowly. The road is long from the leisurely conventions of the *Book of the Duchesse* to the intensity of the Pardoner and the sustained poetic progress of the *Troilus and Criseyde*. All the more clearly he illuminates the significance of previous experiments by revealing what was vital in their technic. For since he was a studious artist, and even a critic, as well as a genius, his career epitomizes the progress of medieval verse narrative. Medieval poetic may fairly be said to end with his death in 1400.

## 1. Poetic Conventions in the Earlier Poems

The first part of the *Roman de la Rose*, Chaucer's literary point of departure, represents the conventions and the mood of the fashionable fiction of courtly love. Its allegory is simple personification carried out by costume and attitude, less by speech and action, appropriate to type. It is less narrative than descriptive. Relying mainly on style, it has so little vigor of composition that in spite of its great medieval vogue it has been long dead. Chaucer's translation shows no small command of diction and of verse. Though the French octosyllabic and the English line of four stresses differed less then than later, translation had much to teach a bilingual poet not only reading, but constantly hearing and speaking two rhythms. It made him early aware both of the difference between the two and of the directions of development for the English of his choice. He has already found variations to evade the tendency of this short couplet toward jingling monotony; and still more verse control is evident in his catching one of the chief charms of the original, its easy fluency.

His own *Book of the Duchesse* uses the same magazine
of courtly love: rehearsal of a tale of Ovid, May-morning
dream-vision, "love's servant" in "complaint," praise
of the lady, tapestry description, couplet of facile fluency.
How much poetry could still be conveyed through these
symbols he showed later in the pageant prologue to the
*Legend of Good Women*. Kittredge [25] finds the conventional dream manipulated in the *Book of the Duchesse* to
give some sense of actual dreaming. Every attentive
reader has been relieved by the realism of the half-grown,
unbroken dog,

> A whelp that fauned me as I stood,
> That hadde y-folowed, and coude no good.
> Hit com and creep to me as lowe,
> Right as hit hadde me y-knowe,
> Hild doun his heed and joyned his eres,
> And leyde al smothe doun his heres. 389–394.[26]

The touch of individualizing stands out, indeed, because
most of the description is conventionally generalized and
decorative; but it may be significant as forecasting Chaucer's later use of gesture, and as a means of transition.
There is an attempt at variety in the punctuation of the
long praise of the lady by dialogue; and the closing dialogue is really rapid. An expert metrist in conventional
modes, with originality enough for pleasing variations—
we can hardly read more of Chaucer into the *Book of the
Duchesse*. The Ovidian thin lucidity of narrative, the

[25] *Chaucer and his poetry*, Cambridge, 1915, page 58.
[26] A similar touch is added in the English *Ywain and Gawain*.
> He bad his lyoun go to rest;
> And he laid him sone onane
> Doun byfore tham everilkane.
> Bitwene his legges he layd his tail,
> And so biheld to the batayl. 2592–2596.

usual aggregation, the involution, above all the stalling for description, show that he was not yet giving his mind to narrative composition.

He was spurred to explore narrative by the timely stimulus of Italy. First of English artists to learn there, he was among the most responsive. The *Parlement of Foules* shows immediate artistic development and promises more. The verse is enriched. The five-stress line, so near the beginning of its long English history, is realized not only for variety, but for flexibility to the mood of speech. Most of its typical variations, shift of cæsura, syncope, doubling of the unstress as in anapest or dactyl, close on stress or on unstress, are here. Though there is not yet that narrative fluency which makes the verse constantly further the story, there is narrative stanza. Stanza, of course, was no innovation. Such set lyric forms as *balade* and *rondel*, which were to hold their popularity into the sixteenth century, were exploring the technic of refrain. Linking refrain, used simply in verse narrative,[27] was carried in *Pearl* to intricate harmonies. In French and in English, stanza

[27] Lecoy de la Marche quotes from a versified morality on the Blessed Virgin a passage exemplifying simple use of linking refrain.

> Ne trova pas l'angeles vostre cuer vain ne vole,
> Quand il semma an vos la saintisme parole;
> Ne li fiz Deu meismes ne vos tint pas a fole,
> Quant il sor totes femmes vos retint a s'escole.

> A sor vos retint li verais gloriox . . .
>> *La chaire française au moyen âge*, 284.

Thus it is used in the stanzaic *Morte Arthur*.

> . . . . . . .
> Lancelot sayd: "yiff I sayd nay,
> I were wele worthy to be brent.

> Brent to bene worthy I were"
> . . . . . . . 3696–3698.

was an assured technic.   But its narrative development owes much to Chaucer.   His adaptation of the Italian stanza in the *Parlement of Foules* opened the way toward that technical mastery which is one of the characteristic achievements of his narrative.

The *Parlement of Foules* shows development thus in detail.   The total composition, the movement of the whole, is still to seek.   Here again are conventional allegory, this time mainly from Alain de Lille,[28] rehearsal from the medieval treasury, dream-vision, decorative description, without any narrative progress.   But the allegory is vivified as in *Piers Plowman*.   The classes are differentiated by the lively speech of their representatives.   The interaction, though elementary, is more than mere *débat*.   There is even approach to individual character in distinguishing the second tercel from the first. In these modifications there is promise [29] of a still more characteristic achievement, the interludes of the *Canterbury Tales*.

## 2. Poetic Innovation in *Troilus aud Criseyde*

The narrative stanza of *Troilus and Criseyde* is a technical triumph.   Even the rich harmonies of *The Faerie Queene* hardly dispute its eminence; for they are adjusted rather to description.   Chaucer's stanza is narrative in sure and fluent onwardness.   It so furthers the movement of the story as rarely to invite separate attention, so deftly merges with the other means of nar-

---

[28] *De planctu naturæ*, translated by D. M. Moffat, New York, 1908 (Yale Studies in English).

[29] "We have already here some of that variety of tone, that dramatic briskness, that air of gaiety mingled with romance." Legouis, *Chaucer*, 85.

rative suggestion that its values transpire not from quoting this stanza or that, but from reading on and on. No other verse narrative is more satisfying to read aloud. The subtle harmonies of *Pearl* are adapted to lyric reflection. The easy movement of *Childe Harold* pauses again and again on picturesqueness. A fairer comparison is Byron's triumph of fluency, *Don Juan*. Those stanzas have the same achievement of onwardness where Byron gives himself to the story. Chaucer's story, deeper, more consistent, more progressive, is always his main concern. His distinction is in making his stanza constantly serve this.

For *Troilus and Criseyde* carries verse narrative beyond Boccaccio's scope and beyond his own habit.[30] Perhaps the challenge of the *Filostrato* was the more provocative because he already suspected the ways of romance. Here was the perennial situation of romance with a new emphasis. Passion, so little realized in French, was presented convincingly; and the lover's complaint was not the conventional tribute of devotion, but the anguish of disillusionment. Passion, then, left dust and ashes. The French literary lover had been forever wooing a literary goddess; the Italian lover, smitten with the beauty of flesh and blood, won it easily, held it in ecstasy, and could not recover from its loss. As if divining here something truer, which yet was not the whole truth, Chaucer planned one of the few great love-stories. What the romances generally left out of Tristram and Iseult, what only the best of them saw in Lancelot and Guene-

[30] "From Italy, and primarily I think from Dante, came the inspiration to tell the story of Troilus in the *bel stilo alto*, to write in the vernacular with the dignity and elevation which mark the great ancients." Root, *The book of Troilus and Criseyde* . . Princeton University Press, 1926, page xlv.

vere as motive, was the effect of illicit love on character. Passion, stronger than *amour courtois*, was it stronger than the whole social code? And what then? Chaucer lived to present love in other aspects and in other ways; but first Boccaccio's story moved him to carry the passion of the noble and beautiful through to its bitter end. He composed not at all a French romance, not the lyric Italian story, but a verse narrative at once so realistic and so dramatic that we naturally call it a novel.

*Amour courtois*, both conventional and feeble as plot, he relegated to the setting as one of the fictions of high society. Troilus languishes appropriately and writes a complaint. Cressid keeps a proper distance. Pandarus makes allowance for moonshine. What Chrêtien had found surely appealing in social romance, the habit of society itself, is appropriated as amply as in *Gawain and the Green Knight*. Medieval rendering of all stories in contemporary terms is here carried into realism. Pandarus, visiting Criseyde,

> . . fond two othere ladyes sete and she
> Withinne a paved parlour; and they three
> Herden a mayden reden hem the geste
> Of the Sege of Thebes whyl hem leste.
>
> Quod Pandarus, "Madame, god you see,
> With al your book and al the companye."
> "Ey! uncle myn, welcome ywis ", quod she;
> And up she roos and by the hond in hye
> She took him faste, and seyde, "This night thrye—
> To goode mote it turne—of yow I mette."
> And with that word she doun on bench him sette.   II. 81–91.

The dialogue is more than realistic; it gives leads for the story.

Quod tho Criseyde, "Lat me som wight calle."
"Ey! God forbede that it sholde falle ",
Quod Pandarus, "that ye swich foly wroughte!
They mighte deme thing they never er thoughte." III. 760–763.

Description, too, is made to serve the narrative economy.
The garden setting (II. 813) combines with the song of
Antigone to turn Criseyde's mood, which is then revealed
in their brief dialogue. Setting in *Gawain and the Green
Knight*, equally distinct as social background, oftener
picturesque as scenery, is less forwarding, less woven
into the texture of the story. The clue to this advance
in poetic is in Chaucer's accompaniment of significant
speech by significant gesture. He often indicates the
stage "business."

With this he stente and caste adoun the heed;
And she bigan to breste awepe anoon. II. 407–408.

Finally dialogue is used to bring a scene to an issue.
*Stage business, scene, issue,* the terms are not too dramatic for the method of the passage between Pandarus
and Criseyde over the first love-letter.

" But for al that ever I may deserve,
Refuse it nought," quod he, and hent hir faste,
And in hir bosom the lettre doun he thraste,

And seyde hir, "now cast it away anoon,
That folk may seen and gauren on us tweye."
Quod she, "I can abyde til they be goon."
And gan to smyle, and seyde him, "eem, I preye,
Swich answere as yow list yourself purveye;
For trewely I nil no lettre wryte."
"No? than wol I," quod he, "so ye endyte."

Therwith she lough, and seyde, "go we dyne." II. 1153–1163.

The scene becomes a situation.  The eleven lines are dramatic not only in presenting the situation as spoken and acted, but in developing by interaction both character and plot.  Chaucer has found how to tell the whole story of illicit love progressively by revealing in speech and action not merely type, not merely situation, which had rarely been so used to its full significance, but character moving to its issue.  In this larger movement, sustained and advanced by progressive characterization, *Troilus and Criseyde* is the great medieval love story.

The achievement of creation becomes the more conspicuous on review of what the story had been.[31]  Mere unrelated episodes of the older sources, mere scattered incidents in Benoît's huge *Roman de Troie*, had kindled Boccaccio's *Filostrato*.  Of its 5512 lines Chaucer used 2730, or about half, but carried his own story to 8239. His addition, most of the first half of his story, is devoted to the gradual yielding of Cressid.  Boccaccio has no such approach because he has no such person.  His story is of Troilus; and his Cressid, remaining the typical fair inconstant that he found in Benoît, falls as readily into the arms of her first lover as into those of her second. Chaucer's Cressid is the first great character of English fiction.  The characterization, delicate enough to keep her graciousness even in ruin, and to give the unashamed materialism of Pandarus engaging frankness and humor, is dynamic.  It gives the story motive.  Cressid is always dominant, not in having more space, but in bringing about before our eyes alike the heartbreak of Troilus and her own degradation.  This is Chaucer's achieve-

[31] For Chaucer's sources see the critical summary in the introduction to Root's edition (Princeton University Press, 1926) and the bibliography, pages 567–569.

ment of narrative progress. Cressid, we say to ourselves, *would* yield to Diomed. But though dominated by Cressid, the movement is of all three characters interacting, of characterization advancing by stages.[32] Thus Chaucer's refocusing is neither modification of Boccaccio's story nor such variation as had been already achieved; it is progressive motivation toward a significant issue.

## 3. Criticism of the *Poetriæ*

The dramatic interaction effective in *Troilus and Criseyde* is less continuous, though no less striking, in the Canterbury interludes. It is not drama, it remains subordinate to narrative, partly because the time for drama was not ripe, more because Chaucer knew verse narrative for his own art. The bent of his genius he followed in both experiment and study. One of his first technical achievements, the weaving of description into the action, appears not only in progressive mastery, but also as distinct theory. Here evidently he discerned as a critic the deviation and the insufficiency of the poetic that he had learned at school.[33]

> Thise olde gentil Britons in hir dayes
> Of diverse adventures maden layes
> Rymeyed in hir firste Briton tonge,

[32] Price finds the movement typically dramatic: rising action with suspense and complication to the climax in Book III, peripety in the exchange of prisoners, falling action in the yielding to Diomed, conclusion on the despair and death of Troilus. PMLA 11 (1896): 307–322.

[33] For Chaucer's knowledge of the *poetriæ* see J. M. Manly, *Chaucer and the rhetoricians*, Warton Lecture on English Poetry XVII (read June 2, 1926), printed in Proceedings of the British Academy.

The following pages on Chaucer's criticism of the *poetriæ* are adapted from my *Cicero on Parnassus*, PMLA 42: 106–112 (March, 1927).

For the *poetriæ* see above, Chapter VII. B.

Which layes with hir instruments they songe,
Or elles redden hem for hir plesaunce;
And oon of hem have I in remembraunce,
Which I shal seyn with good wil as I can.
But, sires, bycause I am a burel man,
At my biginning first I yow biseche
Have me excused of my rude speche.
I lerned never rethoryk certayn;
Thing that I speke, it moot be bare and pleyn.
I sleep never on the mount of Pernaso,
Ne lerned Marcus Tullius Cithero.
Colours ne knowe I none, withouten drede,
But swiche colours as growen in the mede,
Or elles swiche as men dye or peynte.
Colours of rethoryk ben to me queynte.
My spirit feleth noght of swich matere;
But if yow list, my tale shul ye here.

*Franklin's Prologue*, F. 709–728.

Let me tell an old British tale in my own plain way; for
I am unversed in ornaments of style.   This is all that the
Franklin's prologue means on its surface.   The connotation beneath is inviting.   Are "aventures," "layes,"
"rymeyed," "instruments" intended precisely?   How
much grasp they suggest of early medieval poetic is
perhaps beyond our determination.[34]   But the term
"colours of rethoryk" occurs also in the *Hous of Fame.*
The interlude before the Clerk's Tale has a sarcasm of
the Host against these same "colours" in the same con-

---

[34] It is advanced, however, by Tatlock's interpretation of the evidence
as suggesting rather Chaucer's adoption of the "lay" as a literary form
than his use of a particular "lay" as a source (*The Scene of the Franklin's
Tale Visited*, London, Chaucer Society, 1914).

Skeat notes the reminiscence of the prologue (appearing in better
manuscripts as an epilogue) to the *Satires* of Persius.

Nec fonte labra prolui caballino,
nec in bicipiti somniasse Parnaso
memini, ut repente sic poeta prodirem.

nection. The Squire's disclaimer has the same significant terms as the Franklin's, and the same point as
the Clerk's reply to the Host. The satire in the Tale of
the Nun's Priest on Geoffroi de Vinsauf confirms the
suspicion that in all these passages Chaucer implies
specific criticism of the *poetriæ*

For the language of the Franklin's prologue, in spite
of his disclaimer, is literary. Chaucer knew as well as
Shakspere that he who announces "a plain, unvarnished
tale" may command a better art than the rhetoric that
he disclaims. It is worth while to explore, therefore,
the mention of rhetoric in connection with story-telling,
the conjunction of Cicero and Parnassus. As *Sir Thopas*
parodies not only the conventional motives of romance,
but also particular faults in its conventional technic, so
Chaucer's references to "colours of rethoryk," instead
of being taken as general disparagement of grandiloquence, may well be sounded for their particular significance. In any age, indeed, the man of letters con-
templating the rules of his art laid down by pedagogues
is moved to sarcasm; but Chaucer's sarcasms may suggest specifically wherein the pedagogues that he knew
went wide of the narrative art that he came to comprehend as artist and as critic. His reference in the *Hous
of Fame* merely glances at "prolixitee." The passages
in the four Canterbury tales, ampler and more specific,
together suggest that the application of "colours of
rethoryk" to narrative is a perversion, that Cicero is
out of place on Parnassus.

The notion that the citing of "Pernaso" and "Cithero"
in the same breath is meant to exhibit the Franklin as
"a burel man" is dispelled by literary history. Cicero
as a master of style had long been invoked to teach poetry.

*Poetria*, as conceived by the medieval manuals, is essentially elaboration of style.[35]   That it is a distinct mode of composition is never even hinted.   Focused on diction and devoted to elaboration, it draws upon the ancient *colores* until poetic is indistinguishable from rhetoric. Either, then, Chaucer is merely accepting this merger, without particular intention in his "Pernaso" and "Cithero," or he is hinting that the very conception hinders straightforward  narrative.

In the fourteenth and fifteenth centuries the English word *rhetoric* denoted style generally, whether in prose or in verse.  So *rhetor* or *rhetorien* meant master of style, and was freely applied to poets.  The familiar reference to Petrarch, therefore, is usually taken as general praise.

> Fraunceys Petrark, the laureat poete,
> Highte this clerk, whos rethoryke swete
> Enlumined al Itaillè of poetrye.   *Clerk's Prologue*, E. 31.

Nor should we pause over the conjunction of "rethoryke" and "poetrye," were it not identical with that of "Cithero" and "Pernaso."   Even if this pairing, like that, merely reflects medieval habit without reflecting on it, the Clerk's prologue as a whole is sufficiently definite.   Repeating the Host's term "heigh style," it goes on to consider Petrarch in this aspect.   The Host had been quite precise.

> Your termes, your colours, and your figures,
> Kepe hem in stoor til so be ye endyte
> Heigh style, as whan that men to kinges write.
> *Clerk's Prologue*, E. 16.

Whether or not "heigh style" is a misappropriation of a phrase of Petrarch's, its implication here is both

---

[35] See above, Chapter VII. B.

definite and significant.  "As whan that men to kinges
write" makes "endyte" refer unmistakably to *dictamen*.[36]
The Host deprecates the perversion of this to the telling
of a tale.  His sarcasm is directed not vaguely at grandiloquence, but specifically at the application of *dictamen*
to story-telling.  To measure its significance, one must read
the doctrine pervading *poetria* and *dictamen* alike.  That
doctrine is rhetoric; it is nothing more and nothing else.

The Clerk, taking up "heigh style," admits that it is
a hindrance in Petrarch's descriptive opening.

> I seye that first with heigh style he endyteth,[37]
> Er he the body of his tale wryteth,
> A proheme, in the which discryveth he
> Pemond and of Saluces the contree,
> And speketh of Apennyn, the hilles hye
> That been the boundes of West Lumbardye,
> And of Mount Vesulus in special,
> Where as the Poo, out of a welle smal,
> Taketh his firste springing and his sours,
> That estward ay encreseth in his cours
> To Emelward, to Ferrare, and Venyse,
> The whiche a long thing were to devyse.
> And trewely, as to my Iugement,
> Me thinketh it a thing impertinent.
>
> *Clerk's Prologue*, E. 41–54.

[36] The "heigh style" in the Squire's joke may have the same reference.
> Accordant to his wordes was his chere,
> As techeth art of speche hem that it lere.
> Albeit that I can nat soune his style,
> Ne can nat climben over so heigh a style,
> Yet seye I this, as to commune entente,
> Thus muche amounteth al that ever he mente.
>
> F. 103–108.

For *dictamen* see above, Chapter VIII.

[37] If *endyteth* here also refers to *dictamen*, Chaucer is underlining
Petrarch's rhetoric.  But the word is not necessarily technical.

What the Clerk is made to challenge here in the application of "heigh style" to a tale is the separable description. No device for dilation was more magnified in the
*poetriæ*. More than apostrophe, contrast, and other
"colours," it was inculcated to give poetry what Chaucer's eagle calls

> gret prolixitee
> Of termes of philosophye,
> Of figures of poetrye,
> Or colours of rethoryke. *Hous of Fame*, 856–859.

Chaucer's *bête noire* of "prolixitee" among these
pedagogues was Geoffroi de Vinsauf; and that brings us
to the familiar sarcasms of the Nun's Priest.[38] They
pursue not merely an ass, but still more a perverted
poetic. Chaucer pillories Geoffrey not merely because
the *Nova poetria* is an Ovidian nightmare, but because
its constant object, alike in the rules and in the manufactured examples, is to inculcate the stalling of composition by "colours." [39]

The separable description challenged by the Clerk is
challenged also by the Squire, and in terms that confirm
the significance of the Franklin's.

[38] B. 4537, seq.

[39] The reference to romance which follows the Nun's Priest's sarcastic
dilation of truisms suggests that here too, as well as in the direct reference
to Geoffrey, Chaucer was glancing at rhetorication of narrative.

> God woot that worldly joye is sone ago;
> And if a rethor coude faire endyte,
> He in a cronique saufly mighte it wryte,
> As for a sovereyn notabilitee.
> Now every wys man lat him herkne me.
> This storie is also trewe, I undertake,
> As is the book of Launcelot de Lake. B. 4396–4402.

Perhaps also he was thinking of Geoffrey's dilation on the instability of
"worldly joye" (277–291, *Quid gaudia tanta*).

A doghter hadde this worthy king also,
That yongest was, and highte Canacee.
But for to telle yow al hir beautee,
It lyth nat in my tonge, n'in my conning.
I dar nat undertake so heigh a thing.
Myn English eek is insufficient.
It moste been a rethor excellent
That coude his colours longing for that art,
If he sholde hir discryven every part. F. 32–40.

The Squire's later sarcasm is more open and more constructive. It may well sum up Chaucer's criticism of the deviation of poetic by rhetoric.

The knotte, why that every tale is told,
If it be taried til that lust be cold
Of hem that han it after herkned yore,
The savour passeth ever lenger the more
For fulsomnesse of his prolixitee.
And by the same reson thinketh me
I sholde to the knotte condescende,
And maken of hir walking sone an ende. F. 401–408.

A rhetoricated poetic, though in other mouths than Geoffrey's it has often had a fairer sound, is always a perversion. The confusion of poetic with rhetoric has always tended to obscure the imaginative value to narrative of onward movement. The medieval pedagogues who reduced the greatness of Vergil to mastery of all "three styles" of rhetoric would doubtless have recommended embellishing the eloquences of *Aucassin et Nicolete* at the expense of the story, dilating the *Tombeor de Notre Dame*, and making the *Chastelaine de Vergi* static. Their conception of narrative has no room for such composition as makes the Pardoner's Tale a fatal sequence.

Even Chaucer is too responsive to the taste of his time to abandon the accepted means of dilation. Some of his own apostrophes differ from Geoffrey's to Friday [40] only in eloquence, not in method. But as early as the House of Fame he was critically aware of the "pro- lixitee" inherent in "colours of rethoryk." The inter- polated description, which he had elaborated to make the Knight's Tale magnificent,[41] he parodied in *Sir Thopas* and challenged through the Clerk and the Squire. In these passages he reminds us that his achievement of narrative composition had taught him to distrust rhet- oric as a means of enhancing when the tale, Pardoner's, Squire's, or Franklin's, was really the thing. Further he implies general denunciation of the staleness and ineptitude of medieval rhetoric as poetic method.

## 4. The Poetic of the *Canterbury Tales*

Within the Canterbury frame narrative composition is widely various. The early tale of the Man of Law follows the pattern of a saint's legend; the Clerk's is rather iterative than progressive. In such cases Chaucer has not recomposed; he has limited his art to style. What distinction he could achieve even so is most con- spicuous in the exquisite tale of the Prioress. Without

[40] "O Veneris lacrimosa dies!" 375. Chaucer's reference is at B 4531. The Pardoner's apostrophes (C 512, 534, 551, 895) are subtly tinged, as everything else that he says, with demagogy. Those of the Nun's Priest (B 4416, 4529), of course, are played flat. But in other places (E 2056, 2242, G 1076) Chaucer's use of this "colour" seems conventional.

[41] The rehearsal of all the conventionally appropriate *loci* of description at the funeral of Arcite (A 2919–2966) sounds to modern ears impatient, if not sarcastic. But, after all, the whole long passage is the "colour" *occupatio* (præteritio). The shorter *occupatio* in the Squire's Tale (F 63– 75) suggests sarcasm less by itself than in its connection with lines 32–40 and 401–408 quoted above.

crisis, without even salience of moment, with no more re-shaping than the shift of focus from the horror of ancient superstition to the beauty of childlike devotion, he wrought by adjustment of tone and cadence a marvel of simplicity. The Merchant infuses into his *fableau* realistic suggestions of senile sexuality; but the *fableaux* generally, Miller's, Reeve's, etc., are told in their typical form for their typical values. Beast epic in the mouth of the Nun's Priest, never livelier and seldom so rich in suggestion, is little reshaped as a story. Even the Wife of Bath tells her fairy mistress tale without origi-nality of composition.

The artistic interest of the narrative couplet in the Knight's Tale has been heightened by Dryden. Be-neath the superficial differences which mark each verse with its time is a difference of conception. Chaucer's time gave him easier variations; but he himself bent them narratively. The larger movement of the Knight's Tale conveys the magnificence of princely chivalry less in action than in pageantry. Romance as story was not for Chaucer, one might say but for the tale of the Frank-lin. Here he shapes a plot complementary to that of *Troilus and Criseyde* in briefer compass, but with equal onwardness. The issue again is convincing because it is reached by distinct stages. The fourth, for instance, culminates upon the squire's desperate triumph.

> Doth as yow list; have your biheste in minde;
> For quik or deed, right ther ye shul me finde.
> In yow lyth al, to do me live or deye;
> But wel I woot the rokkes been aweye. F. 1335–1338.

And the next begins:

> He taketh his leve; and she astonied stood.
> In al hir face nas a drope of blood. F. 1339–1340.

The crisis upon Dorigen's taking all to her husband, thus fulfilling her character while she flies in the face of the code of secrecy, is rendered in dialogue of sharp interaction.

> "Is ther oght elles, Dorigen, but this?"
> "Nay, nay", quod she, "God help me so, as wis;
> This is to muche, and it were Goddes wille."
> "Ye, wyf", quod he, "lat slepen that is stille.
> It may be wel, paraventure, yet to-day.
> Ye shul your trouthe holden, by my fay!
> For God so wisly have mercy on me,
> I hadde wel lever ystiked for to be,
> For verray love which that I to yow have,
> But if ye sholde your trouthe kepe and save.
> Trouth is the hyeste thing that man may kepe."
> But with that word he brast anon to wepe.   F. 1469–1480.

No less eloquent is her reply to the squire at their meeting.

> [He] asked of hir whiderward she wente.
> And she answerde, half as she were mad,
> "Unto the gardin, as myn housbond bad,
> My trouthe for to holde, allas! allas!"   F. 1510–1513.

Such passages, as in *Troilus and Criseyde*, are narrative leads.   The last leads directly to the squire's fine renunciation; for the tale of generosity has been embodied in individuals working out its issue.   Even the illusion of the rocks is lifted above magic because they were first an obsession of the anxious wife.   An *exemplum* and a tale of marvel have been reconceived and recomposed in a moving story.

No triumph of Chaucer's is more evident than the art of narrative swiftness in the tale of the Pardoner. Verse narrative has nothing more seizing, more breathless, more fatal.   Yet even this is no greater than the

art that reveals the Pardoner himself. The tale is no
more triumphant than the interlude and the prologue.
Rather they belong together. So the ordinary romance
told by the Wife of Bath is heard amid the echoes of her
brutal realism. The familiar story of the cock and the
fox takes both color and shape from the Nun's Priest.
Readers opening their *Canterbury Tales* for the second time,
or the third or the tenth, are as likely to turn to an interlude as to a tale. Even an adequate account of the poetic
of every tale would fall short of the total artistic value.
For the interludes play a part in a scheme more ambi-
tious than any other medieval "framework". Gower's
plan in the *Confessio Amantis* is no more than a classified series. The preface to the *Decameron* proposes
"a hundred tales . . . told in ten days by a noble company of seven ladies and three youths in the time of the
late pestilence . . . in the which tales appear pleasant
or rude chances of love and other incidents of fortune
happening as well in modern times as in ancient." After
describing the plague in Florence, the "noble company",
and the fair country house to which they withdrew for
safety, Boccaccio makes each of his ten persons tell a
tale each day on the same general theme. Thus he arranges ten groups of ten tales each, with charming interludes of conversation, song, and description. But only
the charm of style saves the connective from monotony.
The narrators are merely mouthpieces; the interludes
are not used, as by Chaucer, to bring about contrast
and interchange; the setting, though more attractive
than the allegorical fiction of the *Confessio Amantis*, is
merely repeated with variations. The ancient plan of
*The Seven Sages* remains inflexible through all the versions. The king, stayed by the tale of the first sage,

finds the queen in tears, and is won back by her counter-tale to reaffirm his sentence on the prince. With mere variation of the dialogue this scene is repeated six times. Instead of being always different, as in the *Canterbury Tales*, the interlude is always substantially the same. Not only are the tales generally alike in form, being all by the necessity of the plan *exempla*, but the plan itself is little more than a vehicle.

The scheme of the *Canterbury Tales* is at once more flexible and larger in scope. The fiction of a traveling company offers more opportunity than that of a confession, a trial, or even a house-party. But further the interludes, instead of being pauses, whether pleasant as Boccaccio's or tedious as Gower's, act upon the tales. They add an individualized teller in action and interaction. The parody romance of *Sir Thopas* gains in point by the rude interruption of the host. Revenge for this may be meant as excuse for the dulness of the following prose morality. At any rate, the host's rueful comparison between the wife of Melibeus and his own, and the domestic comedy of Chantecler and Pertelote, suggest cues for the marvelous prologue of the Wife of Bath; and her tale opens the way for other *maistrye* of women in marriage.[42] Though the grouping remains conjectural because the scheme remained incomplete and the manuscripts do not agree in the order, there is no doubt that Chaucer projected a larger technic of dramatic setting. The general prologue describes each teller by summary indications of make-up, costume, and

---

[42] See W. W. Lawrence in *Modern Philology*, 11: no. 2 (October, 1913), with his references to Kittredge and Tatlock; and for a summary of considerations of the order of the tales, R. K. Root, *The poetry of Chaucer*, 153–159.

personal style, not in order to review medieval social classes, but to prepare for the various interaction of the interludes. Far from exemplifying Chaucer's descriptive habit, it is specifically adjusted to a list of *dramatis personæ*.

Medieval verse narrative was recited or read aloud. Chaucer had learned early that setting need not interrupt its oral course. Making description run instead in that course, he had learned further that inanimate background is both less tractable orally and less significant narratively than the environment of men and women. Dialogue, the most oral means of liveliness, he pointed by gesture, and from mood and emotion advanced it to interaction. Finally he staged his tales by characterizing the tellers and suggesting their interplay with an audience. Though this is not often carried out so dramatically as with the Pardoner, it is evident as a narrative scheme. For the "framework" of the *Canterbury Tales* is human.

# SYNOPTIC INDEX

[For further references see the alphabetical index following.]

## MEDIEVAL RHETORIC

### A. SOURCES

I. Inheritance of *declamatio,* as typically through Sidonius, 77–87

II. Authorities
1. *De inventione (rhetorica prima),* 89, 152, 175
2. *Rhetorica ad Herennium (rhetorica secunda),* 90, 181
3. *Ars poetica,* 86, 88, 129, 159
4. (secondary) Martianus Capella, 92–95, 179, 193
5. (occasional) Cicero, *De oratore,* 143; Quintilian, 169, 175

### B. FIELDS

[Of the three ancient fields, deliberative, forensic, and occasional, the characteristically medieval use was of the third.]

I. *Dictamen,* 206–227

II. *Preaching,* 51–73, 228–257

### C. COMPONENTS

I. Investigation (*inventio*) largely transferred to *dialectica* (which see, and also *judicium, status, topica*), 172, 182, 192
1. *inventio* perverted, 187, 191

II. Order (*dispositio*) little taught, 171, 180, 196; perverted, 179
1. conventional items for encomium, 30–32, 187
2. natural order and artistic, 180
3. traditional parts
   a. exordium (in *dictamen*), 215, 221
   b. statement (*narratio,* in *dictamen*), 215, 222
      (1) *narratio* perverted to narrative, 193
      (2) *fabula, historia, argumentum,* 161, 175

303

(a) *figuræ verborum*

30. *permissio* (*concessio*), yielding
31. *dubitatio*, feigned hesitation
32. *expeditio*, logical exclusion
33. *dissolutio*, asyndeton
34. *præcisio* (*aposiopesis*), unfinished sentence
35. *conclusio*, syllogistic summary

[the ten *tropi*]

36. *nominatio*, onomatopœia

37. *pronominatio*, title or epithet for name
38. *denominatio*, metonymy
39. *circuitio*, periphrasis
40. *transgressio*, hyperbaton
41. *superlatio*, hyperbole
42. *intellectio*, synecdoche
43. *abusio*, catachresis
44. *translatio*, metaphor
45. *permutatio*, allegorical or ironical allusion

### (b) *figuræ sententiarum*

1. *distributio*, itemizing
2. *licentia*, boldness
3. *diminutio*, disparagement
4. *descriptio*, descriptive detail
5. *divisio*, dilemma
6. *frequentatio*, cumulation
7. *expolitio*, iteration
8. *sermocinatio*, direct discourse
9. *commoratio*, iteration
10. *contentio*, antithesis

11. *similitudo*, simile
12. *exemplum*, instance
13. *imago*, comparison
14. *effictio*, portrait
15. *notatio*, ethopœia
16. *conformatio*, prosopopœia
17. *significatio*, suggestion, insinuation
18. *brevitas*, rapid narration
19. *demonstratio*, ecphrasis

2. sentence movement (*compositio*), 83, 216
    a. *prosaicum* (*epistolare*), *metricum, rhythmicum,* 220
    b. *stilus Aurelianensis, Hilarianus, Isidorianus, Romanus, Tullianus,* 194, 217
    c. *distinctiones*
        (1) *dependens* (*cæsum*), 218
        (2) *constans* (*membrum*), 218
        (3) *periodus* (*circuitus*), 219
    d. euphony, 83, 218, 221
    e. balance, 42–48, 80, 145, 252
        (1) prose rime, 252, 253
        (2) refrain, 254–257
    f. cadence, 69, 70, 250
        (1) *cursus: planus, tardus, velox,* 223–227

IV. Delivery (237) and V. Memory (163) little discussed

# GENERAL INDEX

## A

Abbo of Fleury, 130, 144

Abelard, 138, 167

*Abjiciamus*, 236

Abrahams, P., 141

*abusio*, 305

accentual verse, 107–123, 133, 141, 148, 184, 189, 190, 191, 194, 195, 197–205, 220, 226, 281

*accentus*, 219

Achard of St. Victor, 252

Adam of St. Victor, 201–204

*Adesto, Christe, vocibus*, 133

*adjunctio*, 304

*Adnue, Christe, sæculorum Domine*, 136

*Adoro te devote*, 205

Advent antiphons, 203, 273

Æsop, 23, 190

*Agnus et leo, mitis et terribilis*, 136

Alain de Lille (Alanus de Insulis), 79, 104, 172–174, 175, 189, 190, 238, 239, 241, 254, 284

Alberic of Monte Cassino, 214, 219, 223

Alcuin, 127, 128, 130, 136, 140, 142

*Ales diei nuntius*, 117

Alexandre de Villedieu, 184–186, 190, 198, 219

Alexandrianism, 19, 20

allegory, 92, 104, 130, 172, 173, 174, 185, 237, 240, 273

*Alleluia, dulce carmen*, 135

Allen, P., 184

alliteration, 44, 47, 105, 144, 145, 148

allusion, 40, 77, 79–82, 86

Alphorabius, 175

Ambrose, St., 56, 71, 102, 107, 108, 116, 123, 125, 137, 250

Ambrosian hymns, 111, 112, 116, 117

Ameringer, T. E., 1, 17

Ammianus, 22

*amour courtois*, 267, 281, 282, 286

*anagoge*, 237, 240

Anderson, R. B., 259

*Angularis fundamentum*, 134

*annominatio*, 43, 304

Anselm, St., 151, 152, 229, 254

Anthony, St., of Padua, 234, 249

*Anticlaudianus* (Alain de Lille), 79, 104, 172–174, 189, 190

antithesis, 6, 43, 47, 80, 81, 237, 252, 294, 304, 305

*apangelticon*, 131

Aphthonius, 23, 31

*Apollonii, Gesta*, 141

apostrophe, 42, 188, 239, 296

*Apotheosis* (Prudentius), 105

*Apparebit repentina*, 111, 119

appropriateness to type, 33, 35, 78, 83, 159, 187, 191, 194, 215, 220, 235, 261, 268, 274, 281, 284

aptness, 54, 62, 64, 78, 159, 162, 187, 191, 194, 214, 215, 216, 219, 220

Aquila Romanus, 95

Aquinas, St. Thomas, 202, 204, 205, 229

Arabic versions, 153, 175

archaism, 40, 65, 86, 100, 110, 227, 250